BRITANNIA

BRITANNIA

THE ROMAN CONQUEST
AND OCCUPATION
OF BRITAIN

By GEORGE PATRICK WELCH

WESLEYAN UNIVERSITY PRESS: MIDDLETOWN, CONNECTICUT

Library of Congress Catalog Card Number: 63-16204
Manufactured in the United States of America
First Edition

For Jinky and Wiley Reynolds, Jr.

CONTENTS

LIST OF ILLUSTRATIONS

INTRODUCTION

THE STORY OF THE ROMAN PROVINCE OF Britain is a sparsely trod bypath of history. A frontier province throughout its existence as part of the Roman Empire, it remained remote both in distance and in interests from the teeming center of the Mediterranean world.

Ancient authors, generally centripetal in their points of view, mention it but in passing, or when the island province's problems and dangers brought emperors to its rescue. An exception is Tacitus' *Agricola.*

So there are sizable gaps in our knowledge of the nearly half-millennium during which Britain, or at least its southern part, was included in the ecumene of Rome. Some of these gaps have been filled by modern archeology. Through the devoted work of British scholars over the last fifty years, much that was lost has been found, much that was vague made clear. One result has been to render obsolete the mixture of fact, fancy, and cavalier disinterest with which the period was treated by earlier historians of Britain. But there is much to be learned, and the work goes on. One justification for this book, intended for the general reader, is that much of our newly acquired archeological knowledge remains relatively inaccessible to the public in technical and academic journals.

The story of the Province is derived more from archeology than from contemporary authors. However, a further limitation on this study lies in the fact that many of the remains of Roman Britain still in existence are military in origin, leading to what may appear an overemphasis on military matters. Nevertheless many studies now in progress are steadily giving both depth and perspective to our understanding of the social organization, economy, life, arts, and religion of the Province's civil population.

In writing this tale the obtruding fact that the life of the Province, for all its remoteness, was inextricably involved in events occurring at the center of Empire has made it necessary to include reference to those occurrences in the Empire as a whole which influenced, directly or indirectly, the fortunes of the island province.

The fact that Britain was Roman before it was English is not unimportant to us in America today, for this long period—comparable to the time there have been people of European antecedents on the two continents of North and South America—constitutes a link, vague perhaps, certainly for many centuries nearly forgotten, yet still a link in the continuity of Western civilization.

To understand why this is so, it is necessary to appreciate that Rome, at the time of the conquest of Britain and thereafter to its fall, was never a nation in the modern restricted sense. It was a world state with a population of perhaps one hundred million, composed of diverse peoples, bound together not by a common racial or geographical origin but by a culture, a civilization, a common official language, a law, and a sense of order in society which, of itself, was deeply rooted in the oldest traditions of republican Rome.

Therefore men did not cease to be Britons when they became Roman, any more than others ceased to be Gauls, Africans, Greeks, or Syrians. As prosperity rose with the imposition of order, with observance of a unified law, the peoples of the Roman world, while remembering their antecedents, took pride in being members of a polity which represented civilization itself.

Thus, after the Empire fell in the west, Britons who held themselves Romans in the heritage of a civilization common to the great world of the Mediterranean continued to survive, to intermingle with the savage invaders from North Europe, and in the age-old pattern of human affairs to marry, interbreed, and raise descendants of mingled parentage. This mixed strain, partly of Romanized Britons, partly of Saxons, Jutes, Angles, Danes, with undoubtedly some of its remote issue joining in later centuries with the conquering Normans, became in its way a sort of melting pot out of which has arisen the modern, relatively homogeneous population of the British Isles.

Hence it follows that both racial memory and tradition in England derive much from Rome, arising in part from the long period of association within the Empire and in part from the later advent of the Church.

It is not therefore unreasonable to assume that much of what we in America have inherited from the dynamic island people—our customs, our law, our concepts of government, above all, the intangible values for which our generations have again and again proved themselves ready to die—can be traced through Britain to Rome and through Rome to the classical Hellas whose art and culture, ethos and philosophy Rome, perhaps without ever fully understanding and certainly without ever wholly approving, absorbed, then protected and disseminated to the West.

It remains to be acknowledged, with admiration and gratitude, that in putting together this tale from slim classical sources and modern archeology, I have drawn heavily on the British scholars who have specialized in this period. Additionally, in order to clothe with some flesh the bare bones of fact left us by Tacitus, Dion Cassius, and a few other ancient writers, I have found it necessary to go to the mass of available knowledge on Roman customs, imperial administration, military tactics and doctrine. In so doing, I have tried to follow the rule of inherent probability, as cited by J. F. C. Fuller.

For these interpretations, as well as for inevitable errors, I alone am responsible.

—G. P. W.

BRITANNIA

I

EARLY BRITAIN

Besides, the question as to what race, whether indigenous or immigrants, originally inhabited Britain, has
never, as one might expect from barbarians, received
attention.

—TACITUS, *Agricola*, 11

1

E KNOW MORE ABOUT THESE MATTERS
nowadays than was available to Tacitus. We know
that long before the last Ice Age * there were men
in Britain. There might not have been many, but
those that lived there knew and used fire. They
were capable of making crude stone tools and
weapons. They possessed, in their continuing generations, the hardihood and adaptability to meet the many challenges to survival imposed by violent if long-drawn-out changes in climate.

About the time when the famous Piltdown man (known as
Eoanthropus Dawsoni) was exposed as a rather grisly hoax, in 1935,
A. T. Marston, an enthusiastic amateur anthropologist, dug into a
gravel bank at Swanscombe, some twenty miles southwest of London. He was luckier than many of his colleagues, amateur or professional. For the fragment of skull he found, surrounded by many
stone implements, was later proved to date from the Acheulean period.
The pitiful remnant, preserved and discovered against all probability,
had been part of a man who lived and hunted, perhaps loved, some
200,000 to 300,000 years ago.

The Swanscombe man, in his day, had relatives ranging across

* The "Second Intermediate Ice Age" ended perhaps 50,000 years ago.

southern Europe and Africa to India. He belonged to the type slowly evolving into *Homo sapiens,* escaping the fate of his competitor the Neanderthal man, who, physically far more apelike, was to die out, perhaps through failure to adapt to cruelly altered conditions of life.

But for generations these two distinct types lived and died in Britain while time was measured in millennia. Neither seems to have possessed any larger social organization than the family. Limited in their hunting by the crudeness of their weapons, they probably lived largely on roots and berries, such small animals as they could attack and kill, and rarely, some bigger game.

Slowly, by degrees imperceptible to the living, the warm climate of the Second Intermediate Ice Age, in which the Swanscombe man had lived and died, gave way to the last Ice Age. Far to the north of Britain, the area of Arctic ice that remained unmelted in summer spread over more and more territory. Slowly the icecap crept down over Europe, over the whole Northern Hemisphere. In Britain it spread down as far as the line joining the Wash to the Bristol Channel.

Britain during the last Ice Age must have been a grim storm-swept habitat offering little attraction and less hope for prehistoric peoples clinging grimly to survival. We do not know if the descendants of the Swanscombe man stayed in Britain, or were forced south to join their brethren in the caves of southern France and Spain whence, long generations later, they returned.

For at long last, perhaps fifty thousand years ago, the great climatic cycle reversed itself. The Northern Hemisphere grew warmer. The hostile world the tribes knew from racial memory was changing for the better. After ten thousand generations when it was enough simply to exist, Man perhaps dared again to hope.

Each year for thousands of years the icecap retreated farther north. Each year on the average, the summer sun grew warmer. Each year the hunting grounds of Europe extended farther north, adding strange new lands, lands perhaps ice-covered in the memory of older men.

The forests advanced behind the retreating ice. Lichens and hardy conifers, first to appear, gave way in time to oak and beech, to other deciduous trees dependent on less harsh conditions for growth and survival. Great areas of grasslands reached northward too, providing pasture for the multiplying herds of wild animals, a fauna far different from those which had flourished before the ice killed them. Wild cattle and bison, reindeer and shaggy ponies spread across the savannahs. The hunters followed.

Food, that essential preoccupation of men in every age, was to be had in increasing plenty. The tribes multiplied. Some among them had time to think. The Old Stone Age, with its primitive implements and weapons, with its primarily nomadic way of life, gave ground by imperceptible degrees to the improvements of the Middle Stone Age.

The hunting tribes that moved across western Europe, some going north while others headed west over the land bridge to Britain, could not have been expected to understand that the disappearing ice must necessarily turn up somewhere as water; or that the inexorable result of its melting must be a rise in the ocean level.

The hunters on the broad, richly forested alluvial plain that then connected the eastern littoral of Britain with the continent, a plain watered by the mighty river system of the Rhine to which the eastward-flowing Thames was tributary, could have had no sense of sudden catastrophe. They may have noted, because they were forced to retreat, that year by year the roaring ocean surf hurled itself farther inland. Now and then strips of forest would be undermined, the trees crashing down in groves to become forever part of the advancing North Sea bottom. The intervals of grasslands between the forests, cropped by herds upon which the life of the tribes depended, were slowly inundated by the advancing waters.

So the herds and the hunters drew slowly back, moving to higher ground both east and west. Some animals, perhaps some hunters, were surely isolated on the plateau now forming the Dogger Bank, there to die as the North Sea continued its inexorable rise. Every so often, from the sea bottom of the Dogger, trawlers bring up lumps of black wood called "moorlog," remnants of the trees that once spread their branches to the life-giving sun. Occasionally will be found imbedded in these "moorlogs" harpoons or spearheads, identifiable as of the Middle Stone Age, belonging to the Great Bog culture of the Baltic shores.

Eventually the once vast plain was water-covered, the mouths of the Rhine forced back to what are now the Low Countries, the Thames, no longer tributary, emptying its own flow directly into the North Sea.

The plain gone, the still rising waters started to tear at the chalk barrier joining the high ground of Dover-Folkstone to Cape Gris-Nez in what is now France.

Somewhere about 9000 B.C., perhaps a few millennia later, this barrier gave way as well, letting the North Sea join the Channel and the Atlantic. Thus it came to pass that about the time other men were gathering in cities along the lower Tigris and Euphrates in Mesopotamia, and along the deep-breathing Nile in Egypt, there devising laws and customs by which men, if they would, could live together in amity, the Stone Age inhabitants of Britain found themselves living on an island, moat-protected, separated from continental Europe, yet a part. The fact and its consequences were again and again to play a major, and often decisive, role in human affairs.

2

PROBABLY by the time Britain became an island the Neanderthal stock once there had succumbed to competition and disappeared, leaving in control the medium-sized, long-headed type called Alpine. The fact that they now lived and hunted on an island appears to have had no immediate effect. Yet, they would develop characteristics which, compounded over generations, would differentiate them from their cousins on the continent, characteristics peculiarly indigenous to an island people.

It is hard to reconstruct the lives of these primitive folk, scarcely to be distinguished from their modern descendants in physical appearance or basic intelligence. The problem of eating, even with infrequency, was then, as it remains in much of the world today, an ever-present urgency. Perhaps there was some diminution in the herds of wild animals for there is evidence, in huge piles of shells left near the river mouths, of winters when life was preserved only by the supply of shellfish. In the summers the families seem to have migrated into the hills, hunting the still available red deer, otherwise subsisting on roots and berries.

Some of the caves then inhabited have been found in Devon, in the rugged valleys of Derbyshire, in Yorkshire, and in Scotland. Where caves did not exist—or were perhaps pre-empted—families built bough shelters against the wind and left them behind with the mute evidence of half-circles of long-dead fires on the leeward side and the characteristic flints of their primitive culture, to mark their passing.

So with little change in modes of existence, using the flint tools of their forefathers, hunting game in summer, subsisting on shellfish in the brutal winters, perhaps two hundred generations of early Britons succeeded each other for some six millennia.

It was surely a hard struggle for survival. Over the years, echoing down through time, could be heard the wailing of infants ripped from the wombs of mothers all too often destined to die in the process, victims of ubiquitous filth. The young in their turn begat others before their surely short and always hazardous lives ended under the flint axe of an enemy, more often perhaps from the stresses imposed by hostile, unrelenting nature. But life went on somehow, in caves, in barrows, in wind-riven huts, unchanged, unchanging—two hundred generations knowing hardship and malnutrition as normal; accident and injury, along with the vicissitudes of tribal warfare, as hazards stoically to be endured; sickness, disease, and chronic ill health as the unalterable lot of man. But after two hundred generations, somewhere around 3000 to 2500 B.C. in our chronology, a major change was in the making.

3

FAR FROM the whirling mists of Britain, the simple agricultural settlements of Mesopotamia and of Egypt had developed great civilizations. In the fertile, productive soils men could sow and reap, expending in the maintenance of life less than the sum total of their human energies. From the surplus of time so gained, from the increase in populations so engendered, the need for order among men stimulated the growth of law on an ever increasing scale. Cities were built, where men congregated together, to trade, to gain the protection of numbers, to worship in diverse forms the still unknown and therefore mysterious powers of nature. The cities combined, sometimes by agreement, more often by conquest, into kingdoms, encompassing their agricultural hinterlands. The kingdoms came into contact, wars ensued, and the victors formed often mighty, sometimes beneficent empires. In these areas, around the Fertile Crescent of the eastern Mediterranean, civilization, for weal or woe, often enough for both, was on the march. Writing was invented, the thoughts and hopes of men could be set down for posterity to read, and history began.

In the harbor cities of the coast, but perhaps predominantly in Crete, men made another discovery. They found that things of utility and of ornament could be made, and if carried by sea to markets, could there be exchanged for food and other necessities. So sea-borne commerce arose. From the wealth so brought to their rocky island the daring sailors and shrewd traders of Crete built a thalassocracy that at its zenith nearly monopolized the trade of the Mediterranean. Since cargoes excited avarice and so attracted pirates, the rulers of Crete devised warships and from rude experience developed the first concepts of the role of sea power in human affairs. From their work and initiative developed the great Minoan and Mycenaean civilizations.

The effects, perhaps even the knowledge, of these transcendent developments were slow in reaching island Britain. Perhaps they might have been even longer delayed save for other mighty developments of a different kind.

Far north of the centers of Mediterranean civilization vast populations were on the move, generally to the west. These migrations arose from little-understood pressures originating in the limitless steppes of Asia. Over many generations, centering perhaps around 2500 B.C., these pressures displaced tribes and peoples ahead of them. Some of these, greatly daring or merely desperate, were driven to the Channel and crossed, under what difficulties we may imagine, to Britain.

Other movements, perhaps smaller but of a similar nature, originating in southern France and Spain, dared the dangers of the Atlantic to cross to Cornwall, to Ireland, to west Scotland, and even into the Orkneys.

Most of these space-seeking or life-preserving adventurers were racial kindred to the Britons they found on arrival. Native and intruder alike were long-headed Alpine folk, already the admixture of perhaps a quarter-million years.

For the most part, and to greater or less degree, these newcomers acted as have invaders before and since. If resistance were offered, or even without it, a certain amount of indiscriminate slaughter, accompanied by pillage, fire, and rape, was a customary precursor to settlement. Thereafter ensued a live-and-let-live adjustment which might in its early stages involve for the weaker side a status indistinguishable from slavery. Later, as always in human affairs, the groups would interbreed and intermarry, producing in a few generations a reasonably homogeneous population ready in its turn to be pillaged, raped, and murdered prior to assimilation in successive waves of immigrants.

More positive and vital to the development of Britain was the fact that these invaders possessed a culture so advanced over the Middle Stone Age level of the indigenous inhabitants as to bring about a nearly complete break with the past. In their movement across Europe the newcomers had come sufficiently into contact with the already rich civilizations of the eastern Mediterranean to acquire some ideas concerning the regular raising and nurture of crops; the domestication and care of cattle; the division of labor; and importantly, the entrusting of tribal order to chieftains forming, in all major respects, a governing class.

The immigrants brought with them their shaggy shorthorn cattle, their swine, and their sheep. They brought seeds of a rough kind of wheat, which when dried and stored could sustain life through the winters, even through occasional droughts. They brought a rude kind of plow that for all its elemental weaknesses was superior to the scratching of the soil with pointed sticks. They brought a knowledge of weaving, novel to the fur- and hide-clad indigenous population. They knew how to make pottery and had a crude ability at metal working. Above all they knew how to make, of flint and other hard stone, tools and weapons infinitely superior to what they found being used on their arrival.

The New Stone Age, already in its progress foreshadowing the Age of Bronze, had reached Britain from the continent.

It could not be expected that the spread of the New Stone Age culture throughout the island would be uniform. Some of the tribes, or merely families, clung with modern pertinacity to old habits, older customs. This refusal to be improved appears to have been particularly in evidence on the east coast, where the old stock, with some admixture of even more primitive immigrants from Scandinavia, eschewing agriculture, clung to their hunting and fishing for a sparse livelihood. One imagines them looking askance on the newcomers as dangerous radicals.

Nevertheless, by slow degrees, the augmented population appears to have been largely absorbed in the higher culture brought from abroad.

Flint was a material in universal demand. Some genius originated, or perhaps merely applied in Britain, the idea of putting men to work close to the flint mines to make the tools, the axes, the cutting edges, the flint knives which then by a process of barter found their way all over Britain and even back to the continent. In these humble necessities began the export trade of Britain.

The accident of drifting sand dunes has preserved intact for modern discovery and assessment a New Stone Age community at Skara Brae, in the Orkney Islands.

Here was found a group of stone houses, each consisting of a large room with recesses in the walls for closets and beds. Equipment was all of flagstone, including shelves, a dresser of sorts, and benches. A central hearth burned peat cut from the local bogs. The several houses were connected by roofed passages affording communal protection against the winter gales. What seems to have been a communal workshop provided a safe, if not warm place for work in the unseasonable periods when going outdoors was a major risk of life and limb.

This tiny community, apparently some forty or fifty souls, had no metal, and lived on its herds, from which it derived clothing, meat, and milk.

Surprisingly they had built under their houses a water-flushed sewage system, contemporary perhaps with more elaborate but not necessarily more efficacious installations in the palaces of Crete.

Less surprisingly, in propitiation of unknown gods, they had sacrificed and buried beneath the houses, before construction, two old women.

For the generations of its existence, it appears to have been as self-contained, as self-supporting a community as one can imagine. Nevertheless mute evidence of some dependence on outside skills was found in the shape of axe and adze heads of stone, quarried and smoothed on the mainland of Scotland, brought to this outlying village by some unknown, but surely intricate, process of barter and transport.

These New Stone Age people of Britain, like men everywhere before and since, sought contact with the mysteries of life and death through religious customs traceable to early Mediterranean concepts of the great Earth Mother. These customs—perhaps beliefs—found expression in their care for the dead, and in rituals connected with the inevitable mortality of man, as well as with the ever-recurring fertility miracle of his rebirth.

At a heavy cost in time and labor they reared long barrows of stone for communal burial places. Where stone was not readily available, as in southern and eastern England, earth barrows, supported originally by wood, served the same reverent purpose.

The stone barrows, earth-covered and often quite large, of varying architectural systems are found all the way up the west coast of Britain from Cornwall to the Orkneys, and in Ireland where the huge round cairn of New Grange remains an outstanding example. The earth barrows of the chalk hills of southern and eastern England, in Lincolnshire and Yorkshire, remain today, after the passing of nearly four thousand years, conspicuous features of the landscape.

The New Stone Age seems to have held sway in Britain over perhaps some seven hundred years, approximately from 2500 to 1800 B.C. During this time agriculture and animal husbandry took firm root. Homesteads and small communities intended for permanent residence appeared, changing for the better the face of Britain, lending some credence to the thought that this once wild and forbidding island was in the process of being tamed, being wrought by human hands into a fair abode of man.

But even as this perhaps not unduly harsh but surely humble life went on, in lands far distant the Age of Bronze was born.

Living out their pastoral lives, the swarthy folk of Britain could have known little, save from the incredible tales of occasional itinerant traders, of the far-off eastern Mediterranean, where the mighty civilization of Egypt was approaching its zenith; where the rich valley of the Two Rivers echoed the rise and fall of populous cities, the turbulent lives of people already well advanced in law, in science, in the arts of writing and counting, in the raising and marching of predatory armies.

Nor could they have known of the discovery that copper, mixed with tin in the proportion of approximately nine to one produced an alloy called bronze; that bronze was capable of being hammered to hardness and of taking a suitable cutting edge; that by heating and immersion in cold water, in a reaction opposite to that of the later-discovered properties of iron, it could be restored to softness for reworking when desired. Here was a metallurgical discovery quite revolutionary in its results, not only to the civilized world but to agricultural and pastoral Britain, humbly unaware of the great deposits of both copper and tin untouched beneath its fields and hills.

Hidden too from the folk of Britain was a resurgence of the population movements from east to west, movements the result of which they were shortly to feel themselves in new invasions. What they could not have known, or knowing have appreciated, was the existence of certain tribal groups along the northern shores of the Black Sea, preparing to move into the rocky mountainous peninsula of Hellas, into both sides of the Aegean basin, there to overwhelm the once mighty Minoans and Mycenaeans and, after a time, to explode in intellectual and artistic glory.

These majestic, far-reaching changes were unknown in Britain. The island was cold and damp, its people poor, its approaches unhospitable.

Nevertheless, about 1800 B.C., coming in successive waves across southern Germany and the Low Countries, a new species of immigrant, surely driven remorselessly from pressures to the east of them, swept over Britain.

4

THESE NEWCOMERS were taller, stronger than the Britons they overwhelmed. Their hair was if not predominantly blond, at least lighter in color than that of the Alpine folk they found on arrival. They spoke an Indo-European language perhaps ancestor to the Gaelic dialects still to be heard in Wales, along the west coast of Ireland, and in the Scottish Highlands. They appear to have been the first arrivals in Britain of that heterogeneous racial group called Celts.

They were great archers and pastoral nomads, disdaining agriculture as fit only for serfs. They were mighty builders in stone, not of houses, but of places for worship, for obeisance to a vaguely held religion dominated by a male sky god, a concept wholly at variance with the Earth Mother beliefs and practices of the indigenous population. They were vaingloriously fond of lavish personal ornament and considered flamboyant jewelry of solid gold none too good for themselves. And, if they were not hard drinkers, it is difficult to imagine to what other use they put the copious drinking pots left behind them in such numbers as to establish their name in prehistory—the Beaker Folk.

They came with burial customs different from those they found on arrival, and stuck to their own. Perhaps as an expression of their exuberant individuality, they buried their dead singly, curled up in fetal position, in round barrows. In some of these have been found long-headed skulls typical of the earlier population, indicating the normal development of intermarriage with the older indigenous stock. Later they cremated their dead, depositing the ashes and charred bones in cinerary urns of pottery deriving design and ornamentation from their everyday food bowls.

They seem to have arrived still wedded to the use of stone arrowheads and beautifully polished stone battle axes. But they knew of metal, and soon made a market for the bronze weapons already being manufactured from Mendip copper and Cornwall tin. Following their penchant for lavish ornament, they also patronized the native craftsmen of Ireland, working on gold from the Wicklow hills. Perhaps through kinsmen still on the continent, they passed this knowledge and demand through western Europe, from Denmark to southern France, spreading an extravagant polish of rich personal ornamentation over Bronze Age Europe.

These precious commodities—gold, tin, and copper, in that order —inevitably attracted traders to Britain. The long-established overland trade routes, dating back to the New Stone Age, that crisscrossed Europe added another market, through cross-channel communication, to their network of barter.

There was also the sea route, connecting by various stages island Britain with the world of the Mediterranean. It seems likely that the traders of Tartessus on the Atlantic coast of Spain near the mouth of the Guadalquivir, by some means, either direct or through unknown intermediaries, early learned of the tin supplies available in Cornwall, so much in demand in the tin-poor Mediterranean.

At all events, and by unknown hand-to-hand passing, metal ingots of oxhide shape, originating in Crete and serving as a rude medium of exchange, found their way to Falmouth in Cornwall. It is perhaps no coincidence that the Celtic name for the British Isles—the Cassiterides, or "Most Distant Isles"—turns up in Greek as *kassiteros*, meaning "tin."

The role of the Beaker Folk in bringing Britain into the swirl of continental and Mediterranean trade and commerce is perhaps the most lasting of their contributions. But they are chiefly remembered for their building in stone. The megalithic circles of Stonehenge and Avebury, of Gorsey Bigbury, of Stennis in the Orkneys, of Maumbury Rings and other lesser religious structures throughout the island attest not alone the propitiatory sense of the Beaker Folk toward the dimly perceived supernatural, but also their pragmatic skill and indomitable persistence as builders.

The awesome stone circle of Stonehenge, on Salisbury Plain, has been, like the Pyramids, the subject of much esoteric and mystical nonsense. The fact of its being is enough. The Beaker Folk might have been congenital alcoholics, but they were men; men with the strength of character and technical knowledge adequate to devise means to quarry the huge "bluestones" in Pembrokeshire in Wales and to transport them some two hundred miles to the site of Stonehenge, there to be assembled in a monument to man's eternal aspirations.

There is little remaining of their living places. Like the Greeks who came later in time, they spent their wealth and their energy, their labor and their architectural skill, their dreams and their engineering know-how on temples to the gods rather than on dwellings for themselves. We can imagine them richly rewarded when in their solstice ceremonies the sun's reassuring glory burst its chains below the horizon to be greeted by a long-drawn sigh of relief, a paean of gratitude, a temporary release from atavistic fears as old as Man.

5

THE BEAKER FOLK were scarcely established in dominance over Britain, and proceeding with the inevitable process of assimilation, when, about 1700 B.C., new waves of invaders appeared, itinerants in the vast stream of Celtic migrations originating centuries before in the steppes of central Asia.

Landing in the southwest of England they brought with them improved techniques in bronze metallurgy and up-to-date acquaintance with trading opportunities rapidly developing across Europe.

Amber from the Baltic, with or without imprisoned Oligocene flies and other insects, was about this time first offered for sale in Britain. Under the name of *elektron,* and endowed with magical qualities, it was in high demand throughout the Mediterranean.

Further evidence of British involvement in continental commerce rests in the discovery of beads of blue Egyptian faïence work which ended their long journey from the hands of an Egyptian craftsman of about 1400 B.C. in a grave in Wiltshire. What persistence of the profit motive, what changes of ownership, what perils of transport and commercial handling, what middleman profits or losses were engendered in the process, we can only surmise.

These Celts, latest in the long stream of invasion, and themselves most probably composed of many different groups arriving in Britain at many different places over long periods of time, brought with them more than a hope of safety from enemies behind them, more than desire for plunder ahead.

Their contact with the widening flow of European commerce gradually carried its own vitality and broadened outlook to the mixed population they found already resident. Their knowledge and example gave to British life over the following half-millennium a stimulus and sense of common purpose the result of which still remains, a deep and powerful current flowing through island affairs.

The improved processes of agriculture and animal husbandry they brought with them resulted in an expansion of the food supply which in turn permitted an increase in the total population. Unneeded in agriculture, the surplus individuals found occupation in artisanship. To shelter these artisans, to facilitate the exchange of goods and products, communities arose, homes of specialists in mining, in smelting, in metal work, in jewelry, in pottery, and in weapons manufacture.

For participation in the trade of Europe, the newcomers established ports, first tiny hamlets in tidal estuaries, later larger and more protected harbors. Although we do not hear of London until Roman times, the advantages of the site, where the navigable River Thames narrows into a bucolic idyll, giving access to both sea and hinterland, may have attracted traders of the time. If so, men of commerce have been there ever since.

There came a day, or a year, or a decade, when the long-established trade routes through Tartessus in Spain or overland from the mouth of the Garonne to the mouth of the Rhone, both finding their ultimate distributors in Crete—the routes through which the gewgaws of civilization were exchanged for good solid ingots of Cornwall tin—died away. The Britons could not know that the day of the proud Cretan seafarers had passed, that the palaces of Cnossus and of Hagia Triada, white and shining in the Aegean sun, had been shaken apart by earthquake and destroyed by fire, so that invading Dorians found but the massive ruins of a two-thousand-year-old civilization.

But after a time came other ships, manned by dark, hook-nosed, black-haired men, sharp to a bargain but faithful to their contracts and their word. Somehow these Phoenician sea merchants, operating first out of Sidon and Tyre, later out of Carthage, had managed to overcome the Atlantic dominance of Tartessus in so ruthless and permanent a fashion as to make the site of that ancient mart uncertain even today. In its place they established their own trading post of Gades which has had a continued if not unharried existence up to the present time.

The Phoenicians seem early to have established a monopoly of the tin trade initiating in Britain. Their staunch galleys, wind-driven where a following or at least quartering wind permitted, carried three banks of oars to insure progress in the doldrums and steerage way entering or leaving port. Their owners and captains traded in haste, assayed their purchases, paid out their worth in goods and money, then with cargoes loaded hastily departed, striving to make yet another voyage before the end of the sailing season made hardihood foolhardy.

In the meantime, and over many generations, the life of Britain developed within the general culture of the Bronze Age, yet never reaching the levels of the eastern Mediterranean. Time and again new Celtic immigrations landed on the island, following the normal process of struggle, land seizure, fighting, and assimilation. Something called the Urn culture developed, largely a reflection, save perhaps for the impress of a persistent insular psychology, of the general cultural level of the Celtic tribes living north of the Mediterranean basin.

Like their predecessors the Beaker Folk, these new arrivals brought more to Britain than they took, in spite of their first innovation, a novel and deadly weapon, a short sword, of bronze hammered to hardness, nicely balanced and lethal at close quarters. Of this weapon it could be said that, like Napoleon's artillery, God traveled in its shelter.

They also brought new improvements in agriculture and manufacturing. Their artisans learned to work bronze into sheets and to rivet the sheets firmly together. Surviving shields and swords from this period are marvels of painstaking, conscientious craftsmanship.

But in their mastery of bronze for both use and ornament, these now British Celts were nearly the last of their kind. Far away in Asia Minor, many centuries earlier, the warrior Hittites had discovered or stolen the early processes for smelting and forging iron. The new weapons made of this material were far superior to bronze, more durable, stronger, and capable of taking a sharper, more lasting edge. The Hittite Empire was built on the fighting superiority so engendered, and although many diverse factors were involved in its eventual collapse, the loss of the secret to its enemies contributed.

Naturally, it took centuries for knowledge of this technical kind to reach and be absorbed by the Celtic tribes relentlessly moving, or being pushed, across central Europe. However, by perhaps 450 B.C. the Celtic tribes moving across the Channel and into Britain brought with them all the knowledge then acquired on the preparation and uses of iron. With the discovery of ample and easily worked sources of iron ore in Britain, the manufacture of iron weapons and tools destroyed the business of the bronzesmiths in these items. However, since they were able to maintain their monopoly of bronze ornaments and luxury items, even being stirred to improve both quality and artistry in the process, the island economy seems not to have been unduly disturbed by this technical revolution, known today as the Hallstatt culture.

Following close on the heels of the Hallstatt Celts came a new and even richer accretion to Britain. Perhaps around 400 B.C.—about the time when the Golden Age of Athens disappeared in the destruction, defeat, and humiliation of the Peloponnesian War—a branch of the Gallic tribe Parisii, from the territory of the middle Seine, packed up and moved to the Low Countries, thence by ship in successive waves to Yorkshire. Quickly they overran what is now Yorkshire and part of Lincolnshire, established themselves as masters, and founded a small tribal capital far up the estuary of the Humber. With them they brought, full-blown and exciting, the high artistic standards, the meticulous workmanship, and the delight in intricate design motifs that together define the culture known as La Tène.

The La Tène culture, both on the continent and in Britain, super-imposed on the older Hallstatt a sense of the spirit and subtlety of Greek artistic values. The development had already reached a high state in eastern France when the Parisii, under unknown compulsion, decided to emigrate. Once in the hands of the Celtic workmen of Britain it gained new delicacy, new vigor, new assurance, new bold-ness in execution. In the roughly three centuries of its development in Britain and Ireland, it produced articles of lasting beauty—weap-ons, ornaments, jewelry, horse harness, and luxury items like the famous Desborough Mirror—which together form a striking artistic tradition.

The Parisii brought more with them than a mastery of decorative art. They appear to have introduced into Britain the horse chariot, both as a means of transport and as a vehicle of war. In the then current stage of warfare, it possessed mobility and shock effect com-parable in tactical impact against the unwary to that of a modern tank. Its ruthless use against the briefly resisting earlier residents of the Yorkshire and Lincolnshire wolds easily established the Parisii as overlords.

6

ONE DAY in the later years of the fourth century B.C. (possibly but not certainly in 325 B.C.) a staunch, seagoing vessel, captained by one Pytheas of Massilia, a geographer and scholar as well as seaman, appeared off Cornwall. Uniquely in his time, he had come not to trade but to explore.

The voyage he made, reported in detail in his book *On the Ocean* and possibly in another, *The Periplous,* was one of the most ex-traordinary voyages of the ancient world, comparable to the circumnavigation of Africa by Carthaginians in the employ of the Egyptian Pharaoh Necho about 600 B.C., or to the voyage of about 500 B.C. when Hanno the Carthaginian went down the coast of Africa probably as far as the mouth of the Congo.

Both books of Pytheas are lost to us, and known only as they are quoted or referred to, frequently with distrust or outright disbelief, by Polybius, Strabo, and other ancient writers. Yet he is hard to dismiss, and has been the subject of much scholarly discussion in modern times. According to our classical sources, Pytheas reported that he had circumnavigated Britain in forty days of sailing, interspersed with visits ashore; that he investigated and reported faithfully on the tidal phenomena of the Atlantic coast, so strange and frightening to sailors nurtured in the tideless Mediterranean; that he had sailed north of Britain and found an island he naturally identified as "Ultima Thule" (which might have been Iceland or the Scandinavian coast), where the days and nights were each six months long.

Pytheas reported on the sub-Arctic seas, likening them to mollusks in being neither earth, sea, nor air, but a mixture of all three. To anyone who has traveled in the deep fog and oily sea of northern waters, laden with the apprehension of nearby ice, the description seems not far off the mark.

Our interest in Pytheas rests in the fact that his work is the first in classical literature to establish Britain definitely as an island, and is also the foundation of all later classical knowledge of the island. From his time on, Britain belonged to the ancient world, distant yet a part, little knowing that events in the turbulent civilization of the Mediterranean basin were inexorably moving to encompass the island and its people within its grasp and heritage.

7

IF IN FACT Pytheas' ship arrived off Britain in 325 B.C., thus symbolizing the coming impact of a vastly superior civilization on the island people, it is a good year to take stock. In a thousand ways, for long centuries before, the Mediterranean world had been impinging on the life and ideas, the markets and the needs, the unfulfilled dreams of transalpine Europe. But the world of civilization was itself at this time in a process of rapid change.

Ancient magnificent Egypt, after twenty-five hundred years of recorded history and vicissitude had fallen to the energy and organizing ability of the Persian Empire founded by Cyrus the Great. The Mesopotamian Valley, cradle of civilization with its successive empires of Sumer, Ur, Assyria, and Babylon, had again been brought forcibly to order and to a whilom peace by vigorous conquerors.

Hellas, after gloriously turning back the Persians at Marathon and Salamis, after establishing the foundation of modern values in every field and phase of human activity and thought, wore itself out in that fratricidal Peloponnesian War so lugubriously reported by Thucydides.

To Greece and to Persia, an outsider, barbarian Macedon brought an order and a polity they themselves had not been able to establish. Philip, King of Macedon, the cool strategist, the able tactician, the wily politician, first subdued proud but hopelessly disunited Greece. His flaming son, Alexander, one of the most fantastic biological sports in history, subdued Persia and pressed on into the distant East, afire with a vision beyond his time, a dream of a world of many peoples, united in peace, sharing a common civilization, a common loyalty to mankind.

By force of arms and courage he unified the world from the Danube to the second cataract of the Nile, from the islands of the Adriatic to the shores of the Indus. In 325 B.C. he defeated the Indian potentate Porus and under pressure from a semi-mutinous army was forced to give up his eastern progress and return, by way of the Persian Gulf littoral, to Babylon.

There, in 323 B.C., from an ill-advised plunge in the Euphrates he contracted an illness which swiftly brought death at the age of thirty-three. We cannot guess how history might have been changed had he lived the Biblical span of threescore years and ten. But then, even today, no Western visitor would dare swim in the Euphrates without the same lethal expectation.

The world empire he made he had not time to consolidate. It was quickly broken up and parceled out among his generals who soon, in fighting each other, lost all memory of the Alexandrian dream which had raised them out of the ruck of tawdry Macedonian villages to power among men.

In the west, in 325 B.C., the commercial city of Carthage—named by its settlers of 800 B.C. as Kart-Hadasht, or "Newtown"—was at the height of its glory and prosperity. It controlled the North African coast from the Greek city of Cyrene to the Pillars of Hercules, or Gibraltar, where its war galleys, patrolling the narrow straits, denied access to the Atlantic to all non-Carthaginian shipping.

Carthage traded throughout the civilized world and beyond. It established colonies in the Canary Islands to grow vegetable dyestuffs. These introduced a wholesome competition into the textile markets where for centuries the far-famed Tyrian purple, derived from the shellfish *Murex,* had held a monopoly.

Carthage traded north to the Bay of Biscay, to Ireland and Cornwall, and south along the African coast to within perhaps twelve degrees of the equator. Its ship captains seem to have known the Azores, as evidenced by the eighteenth-century discovery on the island of Corvo of a pot containing Carthaginian coins dating from 330 to 320 B.C.

A navy of some five hundred war galleys patrolled the western Mediterranean, established the reality of Carthaginian sea power, and protected, none too gently, both its commercial bottoms from piracy and its professional market secrets from discovery.

Carthage itself, in 325 B.C. was the most magnificent city in civilization. A citadel, the Byrsa, crowned by the great temple to Eshmun supported on its slopes the villas of the wealthy merchant governing class. The lower town boasted a pillared *agora,* or market place, and a double harbor, one part a naval dockyard, the rest for commerce. The whole was surrounded on the land side by a triple wall, into which were built barracks for twenty thousand soldiers and stables for four thousand horses and three hundred elephants.

The annual revenue of the city at this time has been estimated at 12,000 talents—the equivalent of $43,000,000 in gold, surely far more in purchasing power.

It was a proud city, proud of its wealth, proud of its commercial enterprise, the majority of its citizens too proud to fight; a city that preferred to entrust its wars, and therefore its existence, to mercenaries. It had less than two hundred years to live.

Across the Inland Sea, far enough up the Tiber to be safe from sudden seaborne raids, a small Italian city state—less a republic than an aristocracy, in the same sense that Carthage was less an Aristotle-admired democracy than a ruthless plutocracy—was in 325 B.C. engaged in a punitive expedition into the neighboring countryside known in its later histories as the Second Samnite War. A mere sixty-five years earlier, this city state, inhabited by a stern and on the whole rather humorless people who called themselves Romans, had been sacked by a marauding wave of Gauls, part of the Celtic stream moving restlessly across Europe.

Rome was poor, Rome was hardy, and Rome was tough. Its governing aristocracy then nurtured a rock-ribbed integrity, a streak of stubbornness easily convertible into indomitability in adversity, a political turn of mind, and a genius for organization. Rome in its development lost some battles but won its wars.

But in 325 B.C. Rome was of no importance, save perhaps to the chastened Samnites who in that naïve age had not yet learned to identify the imposition of order with aggression and colonialism. In the teeming world of the fourth century before our era the graces of civilization were of Hellas, the glory Alexander's, and the money Carthage's. Who cared about Rome?

8

FOR BRITAIN the ensuing 250 years (during which the city Rome was advancing with swift, often incredible strides to mastery of the Mediterranean world) were largely a repetition or continuation of the preceding millennium.

New arrivals of Celtic tribal units, scarcely to be called invasions, continued. Hardly had the Parisii been settled in Yorkshire, than other Celts arrived in the southwest. These too possessed in greater or less degree the La Tène culture. They might perhaps have been kinsmen of the Veneti, the stout sailors of the southern coast of the Brittany Peninsula. Their purpose was conquest and exploitation. The booty they sought was control of the still-rich mining and metals industry of Cornwall and the southwest.

Recognizing the resentments engendered by their deeds, they took measures to defend their own security in the form of an interlocking series of round forts across the conquered and subdued countryside. Other forts, perhaps penultimate retreats in the event of defeat, they created by building strong earthworks across the land side of strategically located promontories, retaining access to the sea.

So the tribal life of Britain went on, with frequent fighting, some destruction of primitive villages, probably much intertribal raiding for cattle and women, but probably not too much actual misery. Each decade saw some accretion in pasture and farm land, wrenched from the forests. As generation succeeded generation, some progress in homogeneity of culture ensued.

Generally about the time each of the incoming tribal groups had been in residence long enough to deem itself entitled to resent new immigration, another congeries of Celts would land from the continent, armed with the price of real estate—a stealthy night attack, a shower of arrows, and close-in lethal work with the flashing Celtic straight sword.

Among the more persistent of these later arrivals were successive groups known in Latinized form as Belgae, who entered Britain from northwestern France. Although exposed to the La Tène culture and speaking a Celtic dialect, they shared also the more primitive tribal notions and ruder culture of their Teutonic neighbors just across the Rhine.

These truculent gentry spread across Britain on both sides of the Thames, reaching into Wiltshire in the west and on the north through Buckinghamshire, Oxfordshire, Hertfordshire, and Essex. One tribal group among them, the Catevellauni, coupling an instinct for leadership with harsh measures, slowly established a loose suzerainty over the tribes of Southeast Britain.

One gift the Belgae brought to Britain was the heavy-wheeled plow, equipped with sod-cutter and moldboard, which actually turned the earth instead of merely scratching it. Its effects on agriculture, and therefore on the food supply, were marked. New arable land in unheard-of extent was cleared from the forest. New farming communities grew up in the rich lands thus made available for planting.

Around 58 B.C., small groups of new arrivals with a different cause for flight from the continent began to recite their woes to fascinated British listeners. They were once Gallic chieftains seeking not conquest but refuge. They told, perhaps with Celtic grandiloquence, of the northward movement of invincible armies from Italy. The armies were Roman, led by a demon, a certain Julius Caesar, already middle-aged and balding, perhaps slightly mad for every so often he suffered from epileptic fits, but who could not be beaten in battle.

There was no room anywhere in Gaul, they reported, for him who would not submit to the arms of Rome. These chieftains, with their families and some portable wealth if they were lucky, alone and penniless if less fortunate, but still alive, arrived in Britain seeking first succor and then revenge.

Naturally enough, they were an unsettling influence. The intrigues they set in motion, the ambitions they aroused, were not too far away in time to bring to Britain the very fate from which they had fled.

If they warned of a mighty aggressive power on the march, the listening Britons seem to have been no more impressed by a still distant menace than has been, to its misfortune, many a modern nation. The tribes remained divided, hostile, incapable of union even had the danger been apparent.

Over the centuries a distinctive island culture had spread through Britain, save for the remote areas of Wales and Scotland.

Agriculture and stock-raising provided sustenance for the tribal populations, while mining and manufacture of a few industrial items combined with hides and wool as exports to be traded for foreign merchandise. The artistic genius of the island Celts had made its impress on the adornment of the person, and while not influencing living quarters, at least had provided some worthwhile objects of utility. A drinking cup of Irish gold, delicately and intricately worked in chased designs of complex interlocking spirals, could excite in the goldsmiths' stalls of blasé Rome the surprised delight and appreciation of connoisseurs long familiar with the best artistic creations of Hellas and the Near East.

But there was no sense of island order, of a common destiny to be jointly defended. Like the tribes of Gaul already falling one by one before Caesar, loose tribal organizations covered the countryside, obsessed by jealousies, raids, and frequent forays one against the other. Internally, the tribal organizations were oligarchic in form, ruled through councils by chieftains who could command, through fear and terror more than through love and loyalty, the allegiance of lesser folk. Within each tribe there was always both room and occasion for dynastic squabbles watched with greedy interest by neighbors. Order and law within the tribes were always in precarious balance. Order among the tribes was nonexistent.

For all the fundamental homogeneity of culture, wide surface differences contributed to the interminable clashing of neighboring tribes.

These differences were especially marked in Southeast Britain where contact with the advancing Mediterranean civilization had introduced new customs and expensive tastes. Here were the Catevellauni, north of the Thames; the Trinovantes in Essex and Suffolk; the Cantii, who have left their name in the County of Kent; and the Regnenses of Surrey and Sussex. All succumbed in greater or less degree to the temptations which could be imported from Rome at a price.

An aping of the more flamboyant aspects of Mediterranean civilization revealed itself in riches of dress and ornament among the ruling oligarchies; in the use of Latin titles of distinction; and in the issuance of currency, of which the coins of the Catevellauni carrying the sculptured reverse of the corn ear and those of the Regnenses, sporting the vine emblem, are superior examples. An appreciation of Italian wine and household furniture nurtured demand for these luxury items of trade. In general, it may be said that the cultural and economic standards of these tribes approximated those of the southern Gauls, long exposed to Roman influence.

Beyond this southeast circle, life became simpler. In Dorset and Devonshire the Durotriges, builders of great fortresses like the extant Maiden Castle, exhibited less of continental influence, more of sturdy persistence in their old Celtic ways. The same appears to have been true of the mining Dumnonii of West Devon and Cornwall, of the Dobuni in Somerset and Gloucestershire, of the Coritani of Leicestershire and Lincoln, of the loose-knit confederation of the Brigantes of the Midlands, and of the powerful Iceni of Norfolk.

Beyond these tribes lived others in the outer perimeter, hardy mountain and forest people, displaying then as now uniquely resistant attitudes toward change. Wales was the territory of the Silures of the southern counties, the fiercely intractable Ordovices of the northern; beyond these, other tribes held vague territorial sway over the land until farther north, lost in the rising mists of the Highlands, were the Caledonii and their kinsmen, tribes fierce in legend and myth, the terror of the settled Border folk, stubborn recalcitrants whose life today, save for the sparse introduction of some technical luxuries, is not markedly different from that lived in Caesar's time.

So, after long millennia of simple survival; after centuries of invasion, assimilation, and turmoil; after decades of increasing contact with the continent; came mid-year of 55 B.C. Britain, in tribal anarchy, carried on the rude but by no means barbarous culture it had inherited and perhaps improved from its early Celtic accretions.

But on the mainland, near Calais, then known as Itius Portus, three thousand years of Mediterranean civilization, culture, and political experience waited to impinge on the mist-hidden island across the narrow sea.

II

CAESAR'S FORAYS INTO BRITAIN
55-54 B.C.

> . . . it would have been a great advantage could I
> have visited the island to see what kind of people
> lived there, and to learn something of the country,
> its harbors and feasible landing places. But of all this
> the Gauls knew nothing.
> —CAESAR, *De Bello Gallico*

1

NOT ONLY TO THE GAULS AND TO CAESAR, but to Rome, Britain was *terra incognita*. For most of the educated people of the Mediterranean the remote, fogbound island was beyond the limits of the *ecumene,* the concept of that portion of the earth's surface fit for human habitation for which the world was indebted to the Hellenes. In Rome itself, in a city grown wealthy beyond avarice from the plunder of a dozen ancient centers of civilization, the pleasures and amusements of an incipient decadence presented greater fascination than the curiosities of geography. Even among the best informed, among the most intellectually inquisitive of Rome's governing class, the voyages of Pytheas, not yet denigrated by Strabo, had been forgotten. Yet an adventurous streak in the national character had applauded Caesar's advance into northern Gaul, and could be counted upon to applaud with vicarious delight the Roman courage which would send him, for Roman glory, into the feared, because unknown, northern seas.

The reasons which caused Caesar to embark for Britain must

have been more complex than the simple motives he himself left for posterity. Although condign punishment of those who aided and encouraged resistance to Rome was a fundamental military policy of the Republic and the later Empire, it scarcely justified undertaking so perilous a task so late, as Caesar himself notes, in the campaigning season.

Nevertheless, to a fiercely ambitious and shrewdly calculating politician, wholly aware that among his countrymen a long-standing martial tradition made military prestige the shortest path to power, the conquest of the island offered some definite advantages. Among them was the knowledge that so dramatic an undertaking, if successful —and in the absence of any journalist reporting the outcome other than Caesar himself, who would say it was not a success?—would go far to raise him to a military stature comparable to that of his much more famous colleague Pompeius Magnus. He could have known as historical fact that before him no Roman general, not even Pompey himself, had ventured into the superstition-filled Atlantic. He could know that the Roman people, particularly the impressionable, turbulent plebs with whom he was already a favorite, would accept with vociferous acclaim the news that their darling had dared to lead his legions across storm-tossed waters to an island so perilously close to the rim of the world.

Once informed of the feat—and Caesar, master of the concise, studiously modest narrative, would make sure they were informed—the plebs would certainly insist to the skeptical Senate that an additional triumph be awarded him. At that stage in his fortunes a triumph would go far to reduce to silence such enemies as Cato the Younger and such vacillating weaklings as the golden-tongued Cicero, and would change Pompey's amused condescension to perhaps troubled respect.

On balance, the risk must have appeared worth while. But only the event was to show how great the risk was in truth.

On reading between the lines of Caesar's own narrative, it seems clear that he expected little resistance and conceived of his invasion as largely prepared for by political infiltration ahead of time. There was no attempt at secrecy, for he speaks himself of "traders having revealed our plans to the Britons." He goes on to say that as a result some British tribes sent envoys offering submission in ad-

vance. When he sent them back, presumably reassured of his helpful
intentions, he sent with them one Commius, a Gaul, a chief of the
Atrebates who had kinsmen of the same tribe already settled in England, with instructions "to visit all the tribes he could, emphasizing
the value of Roman protection and announcing his own imminent
arrival." Surely here was the value of surprise not only lost but
thrown away. It is difficult to avoid the conclusion of overconfidence
on Caesar's part, resting perhaps on a nearly complete ignorance of
the country and its inhabitants.

Yet he took the precaution of sending in preliminary reconnaissance one of his officers, Caius Volusenus. This gentleman went off
in a swift *navis longa,* or warship, and without landing reported
back in five days. We do not know what his report had to offer. Assuming reasonable military competence, it should surely have located
a port or roads where the fleet of eighty transports, already assembled
and ready to load the two legions of the landing force, could find
shelter and safe anchor.

It seems to have done nothing of the sort. In any event, Caesar,
after coasting past the high chalk cliffs east of Dover, watching the
Britons following his progress, attempted to beach his ships on an
open and exposed strand—probably Walmer, near Deal. One wonders how Volusenus, in his five-day reconnaissance, could have failed
to discover, only a few miles farther north, the protected roadstead
behind the Isle of Thanet.

In any case the heavy-loaded transports grounded in waist-deep
water while the Britons poured down onto the strand with obvious
bellicose intent far removed from the acceptance Caesar seems to
have presumed. For a while the situation was critical, and solved only
by the famous incident of the standard-bearer—the *aquilifer*—of the
Tenth Legion, wading ashore through deep water, the brazen eagle
held high, and shouting encouragement to his fellows. The legionaries
followed, and after a furious melee, managed to establish through discipline and training the long fighting line of Roman infantry against
which no army or mob then known could long stand.

Even so it was a near thing. Caesar's own unvarnished account
makes clear that the landing and slow establishment of a beachhead
was a maneuver so fraught with peril, so uncertain of success, so
founded on faulty intelligence and erroneous political assumptions,

that one must conclude Caesar's generalship, at least at this stage of his career, combined a strong streak of recklessness with astounding luck.

Nevertheless, the courage and discipline of the legions forced the enemy back. But pursuit was impossible, for by another mischance which few generals of our day would be able satisfactorily to explain, the ships carrying the cavalry had lost their way and never did arrive to help.

In any event the enemy was driven off and a fortified camp set up around the beach perimeter. The Britons, perhaps wholly unnerved by the steadiness and indomitability of the legionaries, perhaps more willing to achieve the departure of this impertinent and too self-assured Roman by Celtic guile than by the doubtful issue of armed attack, made overtures for peace, even to the point of delivering unharmed Caesar's ambassador Commius, whom they had arrested and thrown into jail on arrival.

While these doubtless wordy negotiations were proceeding, the failure of Volusenus to find a protected harbor exacted its payment. One of the sudden North Sea storms, accompanied by an extra-high tide, swept in on the exposed beach, throwing the Roman transports into disorder, allowing them to buffet each other, while some, dragging anchors, careened about, spreading both damage and confusion. It must have been a wild night, and the beach the following morning a scene of chaos not at all lost on the negotiating Britons who saw in this disaster their opportunity. At any rate, in Caesar's laconic prose, "after renewed protestations of mutual trust and loyalty, they slipped away, one by one, and secretly reassembled their forces."

The qualities which in spite of obvious defects made Caesar one of the truly great generals of antiquity showed themselves never so well as when their possessor faced imminent disaster. Far from giving way to panic or despair, Caesar with furious energy reorganized his camp, set the technicians among his troops to cannibalizing the hopelessly wrecked vessels for materials to repair the others, detailed other units to go into the fields outside the camp and harvest the still-standing grain. In the course of one of these forays, a detachment of the Seventh Legion was set upon by harassing Britons. Caesar himself seems to have led out the rescue party, an action which is wholly consistent with his personal bravery and sense of leadership. The details of the Seventh were brought safely back into camp, the work of rehabilitating the ships went on, and the enemy, seeing the unlikelihood of easy victory, renewed negotiations.

Caesar was stern, upbraiding them for their perfidy and demanding twice the number of hostages previously discussed; but wholly if secretly aware that in this exposed situation time was his real enemy, he agreed that the hostages should be sent later over to Gaul. Packing his troops into the reduced fleet—twelve out of the original eighty vessels had been broken up—he sailed back to Gaul, landing most of the contingent safely enough. One convoy of three hundred men—perhaps two ships—lost the way, landed down the coast, was set upon by the Gauls, and was rescued; and in retribution for the attack, the territories of the guilty tribe were devastated.

We may believe that Caesar's dispatch to the Senate differed little in essence from the account later included in his *Gallic Wars*. Under the circumstances we may wonder for what "achievements" the Senate, as he says, "decreed twenty days' public thanksgiving."

2

CAESAR, perhaps with unbroken faith in his star, seems to have ignored his narrow escape from an ignominious death at the hands of the British, and the taking into slavery of his legions, a fate that only two years later was to engulf his colleague and bankroll Crassus, at Carrhae, while leading another Roman army against Parthia. In any event, even before he left for Cisalpine Gaul for the winter, he ordered the building of additional vessels, carefully describing their dimensions and shape, together with additional orders for a new invasion of Britain the next summer (54 B.C.).

He seems to have learned that his hopes of intimidating the Britons into peaceful surrender were without foundation. At least, the next expedition was planned to include five full legions, plus heavy cavalry and auxiliary support, a force which later experience was to show was adequate to conquer and subdue most of the island. But of the necessity to find shelter for his ships against the fearsome tides and storms of Britain's southeast coast he appears to have learned nothing.

Conscious at least of his too late start the previous year, he ordered the loaded fleet to sea early in July—perhaps the sixth—just before sunset. The incoming tide and feeble southwest wind carried the flotilla nearly due north, for he says that at dawn "the coast of Britain was seen receding on our port quarter." Setting the ships' crews to the oars, he changed course to the northwest and about noon reached the shelving beaches south of Deal.

Perhaps intimidated by the immense size of the fleet—over eight hundred ships of all kinds—or so fraught with intertribal dissension that no decision could be reached, the Britons presented no opposition to the landing. The five legions and two thousand cavalry were quickly ashore, the campsite selected and fortified, a camp guard of approximately one legion and a squadron of cavalry designated, and the balance of the army started on its march inland, all by midnight. Here one sees at its best Caesar's furious driving energy, his sense of the importance of striking quickly, of keeping the enemy off balance. At the same time his unawareness of what changing weather could do to his anchored fleet is summed up in the bland sentence: "No concern was felt for the ships, as they lay at anchor on a pleasant open shore."

Some twelve miles inland and shortly after the early dawn of that season and latitude, probably at a crossing of the River Stour, the Britons, from a fortified hill, attacked the column. Driven off, they retreated to their fortification which the Seventh Legion proceeded to storm. The Britons fled in disorder into the woods. Caesar ordered no pursuit, apparently because the day was well gone and the necessity of building his camp for the night restrained his normal impetuosity. Early the following morning, however, three columns were sent out after the Britons and the rest of the army was preparing to follow when couriers from the base camp brought word of disaster. During the night a great tempest had wrecked the fleet, casting many ships ashore; anchors and cables had parted, sailors and pilots had been helpless and heavy damage had resulted from pilotless ships swinging into collision.

Aside from the repetition of the previous year's disaster in almost identical terms, it is curious that Caesar, only about twelve miles inland, gives no hint that he was aware of so furious a storm until the couriers arrived. Perhaps, in fact, there was none great enough to alarm him, and the damage to the fleet was done by an extremely high tide, some wind, and the often demonstrated ineptitude of the Romans when it came to the simplest matters of seamanship.

In any case, the damage was real enough. The pursuing columns were recalled; the whole army returned to the shore camp; the damage, which included some forty ships totally wrecked and useless, surveyed; and steps taken to repair the others. After ten days of hard work the diminished fleet was beached for safety and the fortifications extended to enclose the area, and Caesar was ready to resume his advance.

In the meantime, under what exhortations and general sense of peril we cannot know, the tribes of the area accepted the unified command of one Cassivellaunus, King of the Catevellauni. After one attempt at a full-scale engagement, in which the Britons were badly defeated, this wily chieftain resorted to harassing tactics, keeping watch on the legions as they moved, cutting off small foraging parties and patrols. But it was evident, not to Caesar alone but also to the Britons, that the Roman army could move anywhere in Britain that its commander wished.

So Caesar advanced cautiously west and north through Kent and into Surrey. Reaching the Thames, and following its narrowing banks, he found a ford, probably at Brentford, now a western suburb of London.

Even while engaged in military operations, Caesar the politician kept his eye on political actions which could affect the course of affairs. In one case, Mandubracius, son of a king of the Trinovantes of Essex whom Cassivellaunus had killed, applied to Caesar for protection. This, Caesar was pleased to give. The assurance to the Trinovantes of freedom from Roman attack weakened the alliance headed by Cassivellaunus, perhaps even more than did the assault and capture of the latter's own chief settlement near present-day St. Albans.

Seeing the approaching breakup of his coalition, Cassivellaunus made one last attempt to reach behind Caesar and destroy his base camp and ships. When his surprise attack failed, with heavy losses inflicted by the camp garrison, Cassivellaunus came to terms.

In spite of the fact that the summer was nearly gone and return to the continent before the equinoctial storms was imperative, Caesar remained his self-confident and stern self. The terms required freedom from later molestation for Mandubracius and his Trinovantes, hostages for good behavior, and an annual tribute to Rome.*

With victory and tacit submission by the Britons thus assured, Caesar, whose affairs in Gaul and back in Rome were imperiously demanding attention, perhaps considered that he had done enough to impress the Roman plebs and to earn his triumph. It may well be that he was glad enough to draw off his men and ships without serious loss, and under a quiet starlit night, over a limpid sea, cross back to Gaul and destiny.

3

WHATEVER influence the announced submission of Britain to his arms may have had on Caesar's political fortunes in Rome, his two expeditions were in fact merely armed reconnaissance, by themselves of no lasting significance in the affairs of either Rome or Britain. Yet through them contact had been established between a mighty and highly organized civilization and the loose tribal polity of the island. Nearly a century was to pass before the two cultures again clashed, in prelude to the absorption of Britain into the civilization and hegemony of Rome.

In the interim Rome itself in a series of bloody internecine struggles underwent metamorphosis from turbulent Republic to stable, if at the top despotic, Empire. Since we have seen, in the preceding pages, something of the growth and development of Britain, it is perhaps now desirable to outline the characteristics of the Romans and the organization of the Roman world state as it functioned when once again Roman armies sailed for the island.

* The exacted tribute seems never to have been paid.

III

THE CONQUERORS

Remember, Romans, your mission is to crown peace
with law, to spare the conquered, and in war to tame
the arrogant.

—VIRGIL, *The Aeneid*

1

FROM THE INFLUENCES OF GEOGRAPHY, ORIgins, and traditions, nations seem to develop an intangible something called "national character." It is a term which generally defies precise definition and is invariably plagued with a myriad of individual exceptions. Nevertheless, in spite of anthropological evidence of a common origin, most of us know what we mean, though we may not be able to explain it, when we speak of what makes an American different from an Englishman, from a Frenchman, from a German or a Russian.

This national character in a people the Romans called *genius*—literally, the collective attitude of the tribe toward life.

Roman thinkers and philosophers, along with perhaps a great many lesser folk, never doubted, from earliest times to the end, that they knew and understood the correlated group of abstract values which together constituted the Roman genius. So immortal are the great intangibles, so much of public conscience do we derive from Rome, that the Latin terms for these values have descended, little changed, into our own language.

Pre-eminent was *pietas,* a sense of subordination to divine forces at work in the world, an earnest desire to play an honest and worthwhile role in life toward the gods, the nation, one's family, tribe, and friends.

Gravitas was a serious-minded approach to affairs large and small; a sense of responsibility, heightened by *constantia,* strength of purpose, and *firmitas,* a refusal to be moved from the right and proper course of conduct.

To be serious without being priggish, *comitas* brought a sense of proportion, of modesty anointed with humor, and a tolerance of the views of others.

Disciplina was for the Romans primarily training in character—and it might be well were it so with us. *Virtus* literally "manliness," was courage, magnanimity, greatheartedness, indomitability in adversity. *Frugalitas* was not penny-pinching, but a reasonable austerity in life and conduct.

Like the ideals of other nations before and since, these noble concepts throughout Roman history were "more honoured in the breach than the observance." They could not always control a strong streak of cruelty, a low estimate of the value of human life, and a reckless ambition, coupled with greed, which ran like malign threads through the warp and woof of Roman history. Nevertheless, they remained strong influences, never wholly silenced, criteria of greatness in man or woman throughout the thousand and more years of Rome's march from river village to mistress of the world.

Unlike the Greeks, who carried overpraised individualism to ruinous excess, the Romans possessed a strong sense of corporate unity, originating and nourished in the basic unit of Roman life, the *familia,* or family.

A sense of continuity, of participation in a deep-flowing irresistible life stream, was inculcated by the reverence shown to ancestors. The death masks of those gone ahead, carried reverently in funeral procession when a member of the family died, were constantly obtruding reminders that the *Di Manes,* the Kindly Shades, were ever watching protectively over the living, were gravely concerned that the growing child should become a Roman they could claim with pride as their descendant.

The many festivals extending through the year—some, like the Lemuria in May or the Feralia in February, gloomy propitiations of the dead; others, like the Floralia of April, the Lupercalia of February, and pre-eminently the Saturnalia of December, joyous, unrestrained, often quite uninhibited expressions of gratitude for the many-sided joys of pulsing life—these public festivals all emphasized in gregarious observance the community of Rome and Nature.

The state honors bestowed on public benefactors; the majestic progress of newly elected public officials to sacrificial ceremonies before the temple of Jupiter before taking up their civic duties; the glittering triumphal processions awarded by vote of the Senate to victorious generals—all combined with a thousand lesser influences in daily life to develop the abiding conviction that to be a Roman was to be favored of the gods; and that because of that awesome nepotism, great deeds and the ready assumption of duty in the uttermost fulfillment of pietas would be demanded.

For centuries of the Republic, military service by every able-bodied Roman male was taken for granted. Ten years' military service had long been an essential prerequisite to standing for elective office. The Romans, perhaps less sure than we of the political genius inherent in every citizen, seem to have considered this lengthy submission to the iron discipline of the Army a necessary precursor to the exercise of responsibility in public affairs.

The Romans so bred never made of Rome a Utopia. There was always faction and, with a lusty population, both turbulence and physical violence. Patricians, equites, and plebs, the three main classes of Roman citizenry, distrusted each other and fought for power among themselves. They could temporarily unite on external conquest or at times of extreme national danger, but never for long.

Through the years of expanding conquest, the slave population grew so fast as to destroy the free labor market, creating in the city an always troublesome and frequently dangerous proletariat. The once incorruptible aristocracy of the Senate accepted venality as the price of wealth. Bribery tempered justice. In the name of Roman glory, leaders descended to demagoguery to engage the loyalty of the fickle plebs and to maintain the authority of the polluted Senate. The forensically defeated took to arms in retaliation. Victory remembered with murder votes adversely cast.

It was not all corruption, not all decadence. There were senators who stooped to accept bribes; others pursued in simple integrity their duties to family and to Rome. Although many provincial governors greedily exploited and robbed the people of their provinces, not a few set high examples of incorruptible and enlightened public administration. Although many equites pursued profits undeterred by ethics or law, others were content with honest, constructive, and mutually advantageous commerce and trade.

Although brutalized mobs cheered the shedding of blood in the gladiatorial shows—exhibitions which regularly drew audiences comparable in numbers to those of our own heavyweight championship matches—thousands of loyal, disciplined Romans of the legions fought with self-sacrificial if grumbling ardor in distant lands, while all through Italy and the provinces small farmers tilled the soil, harvested their crops, tended their vines, and gave thanks in pious reverence for the gods who had made life so ample.

We are much misled by the historians of Rome who found newsworthiness in crime, corruption, treachery, and malfeasance while ignoring the placid, uneventful existence of the great majority who, in private or public, by hard work and honest dealing, created and sustained the life of Rome. This phenomenon of misplaced emphasis is not wholly unfamiliar to us in America, where the deeply decent currents of our national life attract little publicity and, often enough, less praise.

On balance, for all the turbulence and chaos of the last days of the Republic, evidence primarily that the simple order of government which had served a city-state had broken down under the burdens of world dominion, the idealized Roman genius, buttressed by custom, the *mos maiorum,* seems to have provided a substructure sturdy enough to have established, after many a vicissitude and internal struggle, a peace based on order under enforceable law throughout the civilized world.

The process was not easy. Three brutal and destructive civil wars, encompassing roughly the first two-thirds of the last century before the Christian era, enlivened the struggle. Marius and Sulla, Caesar and Pompey, Antony and Octavianus in turn debated with the sword the mastery of the Roman world. When Octavianus, Caesar's nephew and heir, emerged victorious, the Republic died, and the Empire was born.

Yet the old and honored, the traditional forms, were slow to change. The Roman genius for organization could change the substance when necessary without altering the form. It had become necessary, if Rome were not to commit suicide, that irresponsible faction be eliminated from the summit of affairs. In carrying out this requirement Octavianus, under his conferred title of Augustus, proved himself clearly aware of the potency of the Roman genius and a shrewd practitioner in its application.

By his public modesty, his careful deference to the Senate, his watchfulness over the welfare of the plebs, his encouragement and employment on public affairs of businessmen, his studied reverence for the gods, his punctilious observance of traditional forms, Augustus managed to convince a majority that he had acted merely to restore to its ancient integrity, firmness, and glory the aristocratic and oligarchic democracy so simply styled *Senatus Populusque Romanus* —the Senate and People of Rome.

So it might have seemed to men. But in substance Augustus had gathered into his own hands command of the Army, control of the Treasury, personal mastery of the outlying provinces, and the unfettered right to select executives responsible to himself alone.

In these powers we may recognize an approximation of those of the President of the United States. But to them he added legislative and judicial functions held jealously separate in our Constitution.

As *Princeps Senatus,* or first member of the Senate, he was what we might call the majority floor-leader, with the difference that he was seldom challenged and almost never opposed in the passage of legislation he introduced or mildly recommended. And by natural evolution from his fundamental position of untrammeled power, he became the court of final appeal, filling, by review of the judicial decisions of the praetors and provincial governors, the role assigned to our Supreme Court.

If order within the body politic and absence of contention were more to be desired than irresponsible demagoguery masquerading as democratic freedom, these despotic powers, considering the problems he faced, were doubtless necessary. There was always, of course, the question as to whether or not they would be exercised by himself and his successors with wisdom and restraint.

Probably Augustus himself realized the absurdity of any such hope in view of the corruptibility of uncontrolled power. However, he himself exercised his great powers, on the whole, with magnanimity and reserve reflecting the idealized qualities of the Roman genius. Facing stubborn fact rather than theory, he met his problems with a pragmatic eye fixed on results rather than principle.

During his forty-five years of unchallenged power, ending with his death in 14 A.D., Augustus consolidated the far-flung provinces into an empire; established a large degree of local self-government, as that much abused term was then understood; revitalized the economy; stabilized the Treasury; created a widespread and a theretofore unmatched prosperity; reduced, disciplined, and tamed the Army; arranged for his successor while signally failing to establish an acceptable system for later selections; and in the correlated process introduced to history the comparative felicity of the Pax Romana—order, peace, and obedience to law within the long-battered world of Mediterranean civilization.

His achievements, so monumental in character, so lasting in history, rested on his understanding and practical use of two Roman creations long antecedent to his reign, both of which he developed and fashioned to serve his farsighted purpose: the Law and the Army.

2

SOME FOUR HUNDRED YEARS prior to the assumption of sole power by Augustus, the legal traditions of the then weak and struggling Roman Republic were codified in the "Twelve Tablets." This simple code governed the relations of Roman citizens to each other, and to the State. They became the foundation of the *ius civile,* the "civil law."

In time, changing conditions required interpretation of the Tablets. Other laws were passed, *leges* by the Comitia Centuriata, on the proposal of a magistrate of senatorial rank, and *plebiscita* by the Comitia Tributa, on a proposal of a tribune of the plebs. Judgments between contending parties became necessary, and to meet this need an official, the *praetor,* was annually elected to hear cases and disputes, and to decide them within the law as he interpreted it. As the volume of praetorial decision grew, the law became still more complex, giving rise to specialists, *advocati,* who presented a case for a client or friend, and *iuris consulti,* "consultants on the law."

Soon it became necessary for each newly elected praetor to publish, before assuming office, the principles he would follow in interpreting the Twelve Tablets and supplementary laws. These published statements of legal policy were called *edicta,* "edicts," and came themselves to have the force of precedent. Such edicts, carried forward over many successive praetorships, became *ius honorarium* or "law of the offices."

As Rome expanded through conquest and alliance, the personal affairs of citizens spread beyond the city. More and more cases arose involving foreigners, people whose customs and ideas of justice differed from those expressed in the civil law.

To the rather fair-minded and reasonable Romans some adjustment was clearly required. So in 242 B.C. another praetorial office was created, that of the *praetor peregrinus* to deal with cases involving non-citizens. The original praetor then became the *praetor urbanus,* wholly concerned with cases involving Roman citizens only. From the judgment seat of the new praetor rose the *ius gentium,* which in making allowance for non-Roman legal tradition and custom was to grow with Rome into the law of nations.

The two praetorial courts in Rome and the provincial governors, who held praetorian powers under their *imperium,* or authority to rule, adjudicated new laws and reinterpreted old ones in new conditions. Thus the Roman legal system developed, meeting change without revolution. Naturally, instances occurred where the new laws conflicted with long-accepted principle or where a praetor or governor rendered judgment reversing a predecessor. These contretemps occur even today, and are less usurpations of power than exemplifications of the dynamism required if law is to grow with changing social, economic, and political custom.

The realities of human nature could not imply, nor history confirm, that Roman law was invariably administered with integrity and wisdom. Particularly in the death throes of the Republic, juries were notoriously purchaseable and judges not above suspicion.* The confused state into which the body of the law had fallen, due to centuries-old accumulations of conflicting edicta, contributed to abuse and gave birth to a demand that the law be again codified so that a reasonable man might have a chance of knowing where he stood.

As early as the beginnings of the first century B.C. the Scaevolas, father and son, sought to bring order and consistency to the law. Cicero clothed learned discussions on the philosophy of the law in

* As Cicero observed (*Ad Quintum,* iii, 2), "Trials are now so corrupt that nobody will be found guilty of anything, save murder."

his inimitable Latin style. Caesar had on his mind the clarification of the law as an urgently needed reform when assassination ended his preoccupation with the public good. The assumption by Augustus of final decision in all important cases had at least the advantage of applying the consistency of one lucid mind to the problems.

Nevertheless, the need for orderly codification and reform was not met until the Emperor Hadrian in the early years of the second century A.D. gathered together a commission of distinguished jurists under the chairmanship of Salvus Julianus with instructions to codify in a Perpetual Edict, all the *iura honoraria* still in effect. When completed, the Perpetual Edict could be altered only by the Emperor himself.

In time alterations and interpretations became necessary. These were known as *constitutiones principum,* consisting of: *edicta* issued by the Emperor in exercise of his supreme judicial authority; *decreta,* decrees issued by him sitting in judgment on a particular case; *rescripta,* opinions annotating a legal question submitted in writing; and (in the growing field of administrative law) *mandata,* instructions on legal questions to his officers throughout the Empire.

Supplementing the development of official law were the *responsa* of distinguished, or at least licensed legal practitioners, the *iuris consulti* and the *iuris prudentes.* The most famous of the scholars of the law, men like Julianus of Hadrian's time, later Gaius, and in the third century A.D. brilliant jurists like Paulus, Ulpian, and Papinian, developed the great body of Roman law into the majestic, all-pervading edifice which, set down in the still later Institutes, Digests, and Code of Justinian, became the indispensable foundation of all later legal development in the West.

As the Western world derives its concepts of individual liberty from the Greeks, so it finds its concepts of the governance of man in society in Roman law. The problem of civilization as we understand it, as true now as in ancient time, is the reconciliation in justice of these two divergent if not necessarily conflicting requirements: the preservation of the maximum degree of personal freedom with the necessary limitations on the conduct of men living together in a complex society. That the nations of the West still struggle to achieve its solution, rather than surrender to tyrannies as old as Man's recurrent failure to govern himself, we owe in large measure to Roman concepts of order and justice coupled with our heritage from Greece.

3

WHILE ROME GREW, as its conquests spread over Italy and the world of the Mediterranean, the means of conquest, the Army, became in far places the means by which Roman law was introduced and enforced. Side by side with the growth of the law, in part dependent upon it, the Roman sense of order and organization addressed itself to the myriad problems involved in building an army.

Polybius, the Greek philosopher-historian and friend of Scipio Africanus the Younger, writing about the time of the third Punic War (149–146 B.C.) told how the legions were at that time enrolled from among the eligible males of the city Rome; how they were trained and exercised until habit and discipline drove out fear and stifled caution; how the legions were led by the consuls, how they marched, how they set up each night a fortified camp, and how the watch was kept.

The legions described by Polybius were made up of unpaid citizens, serving in time of war as a matter of unquestioned civic duty. About one hundred years later changes were introduced by Marius which in effect turned the Army into a professional, long-service organization. Enlistment was for twenty years, with opportunity to advance through the many grades of *optio* and *centurio* to the rank of *primipilus,* literally "first spear," the senior centurion of the first cohort of the legion. Military tribunes, at first drawn from young aristocrats gaining military experience before embarking on political careers, were later opened to all ranks.

With the reduction and reorganization of the Army under Augustus, the legion was fixed in a form which endured without major change for nearly three hundred years. It was the basic unit of the Army possessing both tactical and logistical capabilities. It was organized into ten cohorts of 555 men each, with the strength of the first cohort nearly doubled, probably to provide for administrative and specialist personnel. At full strength it numbered 6,100 men, but as with our army it is unlikely that any legion ever achieved this happy state for more than short periods of time.

It carried with it a *quaestor,* who combined the functions of quartermaster and finance officer; a surgeon with assistants and medical attendants; an engineer officer who could draw on trained specialists within the fighting cohorts to throw up a bridge, survey a camp, lay out roads, and supervise all the heavy construction tasks inseparable from war as waged by the Roman Army.

A baggage train of ox wagons, more often of pack animals, carried the legion's *impedimenta;* tents of leather, picks and shovels, tent poles, palisade stakes, extra weapons, forges, spear shafts and arrows, reserve supplies of food, spare boots, and the thousand other prosaic items of the soldiers' trade.

The legion was supported by an artillery train. The weapons were constructed of heavy wood beams, could be disassembled for transport, and drew their power from twisted strands of horsehair—therefore known collectively as *tormenta*—from *torqueo,* "to twist." The *scorpio* was a sort of oversize crossbow for shooting long, heavy arrows; *catapultae* were of several shapes and sizes serving the same general purpose; *ballistae,* of different design, hurled heavy stones. Repetitive practice made their crews proficient in sustained and reasonably accurate fire up to about four hundred yards.

Providing the symbolism all nations in all times have found necessary to encourage combativeness, to restrain the human urge to run from battle, was the *aquila,* the eagle of the legion. In its half-opened wings and vicious beak poised ready to rend, this image of gilded bronze surmounting a pole was the personification of the legion's *numen,* its protecting spirit, or collective soul.

It went into battle carried by a senior centurion, the *aquilifer,* protected by a guard from the First Cohort. In camp it stood on an altar before the commander's tent, attended by morning and evening ceremonies serving the same inspirational purpose as do those which are paid to our national colors flying over distant camps and army posts, over our ships at sea. The loss of the eagle in battle was a major disgrace, its repossession at no matter what cost in bloodshed an imperative on officers and men alike.

The arms of the legionary were the Spanish short sword, the fearsome *gladius;* the heavy throwing spear, the *pilum;* and the curved, rectangular shield, *scutum,* of wood covered with leather, bound in iron and mounted in the center with a heavy iron boss—the last not without authority when slammed into the face or ribs of an enemy attacking from the left while the soldier was engaged with another on his right.

Daily exercise for long periods, using practice weapons heavier than the combat models, conditioned the legionaries in strength of arm and accuracy. The pilum hurled at a range of about fifty feet might penetrate both shield and armor of an adversary. It was about six feet long, four feet of polished wooden shaft, the balance a two-foot iron head.

Hurled in unison and with devastating accuracy by the charging Roman line, it was a formidable weapon in its own right, but its primary function was to throw the front ranks of the enemy into confusion and disorder, thus opening the way for close-in assault with the gladius.

The gladius itself, about two feet long, tapering to a razor-sharp point, was the weapon of decision. Although it was suitable for both thrusting and slashing, the legionaries were assiduously trained to rely on its thrusting use for victory. They learned to avoid getting the blade stuck in an enemy's breastbone or rib cage, and to concentrate on sharp thrusts into the abdominal cavity. Only when virtually surrounded would the Roman soldier revert to slashing strokes, and then simply to clear fighting space around himself.

The legionary's head was protected by a helmet of iron, close-fitting and provided with a slot on top into which, for parade or ceremonial purposes, a tuft of colored horsehair could be inserted. His leather tunic, close-fitting over a woolen or linen undergarment, was reinforced with strips of iron on the shoulders and around the waist. An apron of iron strips, to lessen the understandable fear of emasculation, hung from the front of his waist. His feet, in cold climates enclosed in woolen socks with separated big toe, were shod in heavy leather marching boots, *caligae*. An Emperor, raised as a small boy in his father's camps, was to take his nickname from the diminutive form of the word—Caligula. Caesar added a low heel to the caligae, vastly increasing the marching comfort and endurance of the legionaries.

The soldier carried a large cloak of rough wool, serving both as garment and blanket, along with about forty pounds of individual equipment. His pay in Caesar's time was 240 *denarii* per annum. It was increased by Domitian, again by Hadrian, later by Severus.

Roughly keeping pace with inflation, it seems to have been generally comparable to what a skilled workman could earn in a year in Rome. The military career did not therefore suffer from the competition of greater reward in civil life.

Out of his pay the soldier was charged for his initial issue of clothing and equipment and for his food—four *modii*—about a bushel —of wheat per month, together with tart Italian wine, and occasional issues of leeks and garlic. The all-conquering legionaries of Rome were by habit and preference vegetarians who protested if breakdowns in the grain supply kept them too long on a meat diet. Additional charges were made against the legionaries' pay for membership dues in burial societies, for camp banquets, and other extras.

The backbone of the Army was its corps of long-service professional non-commissioned officers, the centurions. There were two in each maniple, six in each cohort, sixty in a legion. Seniority in rank ran from the junior of all, the second centurion of the last maniple in the tenth cohort—*centurio decimus hastatus posterior*—to the senior centurion of the first cohort, the *primipilus*. This austere and unapproachable warrior was the last word on the state of the men's health, their morale, and their combat effectiveness. He knew who were the recalcitrants, the troublemakers, the buck-passers, the malingerers. He held the confidence of the legion commander or lost his job. He participated in all staff planning and all councils of war.

Although promotions within the several grades of centurion were normally made one step at a time, the Roman system encouraged and rewarded outstanding ability or conspicuous leadership in battle by jumping a man over several grades at one step. One example, far from unique, occurred in Caesar's army while it was besieging Pompey at Dyrrachium during the Civil War.

> . . . when the shield of the centurion Scaeva was brought to Caesar, one hundred and twenty holes were found in it. For his services to himself and to the Republic, Caesar, having presented Scaeva with 200,000 sesterces and eulogized him, announced that he had transferred Scaeva from the eighth cohort to the post of primipilus—for it was clear the redoubt had been in large measure preserved by Scaeva's exertions.

Under the Empire even higher posts were open to centurions who had reached the level of primipilus. Most frequent among these was that of *praefectus castra,* or as we would put it, post commander.

This officer was responsible for the housekeeping of a legionary fortress but did not command the legion itself.

There were other opportunities open to an enterprising primipilus, such as command of a *vexillatio* or detachment, often of several cohorts, sent on an independent mission. Command of a unit of auxiliary cavalry, *praefectus alae,* also often went to legionary centurions of proved ability. In later years of the Empire, centurions often enough rose to command legions and armies, while there is at least one example of a former centurion becoming Emperor.

The Republican custom of assigning amateurs from the aristocracy to command of the legions had been stopped by Caesar because of its inefficiency. In place of these high-born youths he appointed older, more experienced officers in whose ability he (sometimes mistakenly) had confidence. These officers were called *legati* lieutenants, or deputies.

The Army reforms of Augustus firmly established this practice. Beginning with his time and continuing for centuries, legion commanders were carefully selected Romans who had reached praetorial rank in progress through a succession of civil and military assignments, and who were eligible for further advancement in the mixed civil-military career pattern of imperial servants, through the consulship to posts as provincial governors.

Under Augustus and his successors, for at least two centuries, the governors of the imperial provinces—outlying provinces requiring a garrison of one or more legions—were almost always experienced civil and military administrators known as *legati Augusti pro praetore,* or deputies of the Emperor with praetorian powers.

The Army was backed up by an intricate supply and communications system, in which the roads throughout the Empire, built in the first instance by the legions, played an essential role.

From early times, to each Roman legion were attached units of allies and provincial drafts of non-citizens. In time these became regularly organized units of *auxilia,* commanded by a Roman officer, the praefectus, and possessing a cadre of Roman centurions and specialists. The auxilia, both cavalry and infantry, and including such special-purpose troops as Cretan archers and Balearic slingers, were paid by their provinces of origin, or by allies who sent them in discharge of their obligations to Rome. Up to the time of Caracalla, who in 212 A.D. granted full citizenship to all free-born males within the

Empire, the great incentive to enlistment and service in the auxiliaries was the gift of Roman citizenship at the expiration of the individual's term.

This was the legion, mainstay of the Roman Army. Wherever Rome went, the legions went first. In addition to fighting, they administered the conquered area, built roads and fortresses, then cities. With them, *pari passu,* went Roman Law, administered first by the legion officers, later by a procurator assisted by trained law officers.

With the legions went also the Latin language, some of the arts, the engineering, and the architecture of Rome. The legions were the great civilizing agents of newly conquered territory, the means by which Roman order was established throughout the expanding Empire.

In time, each legion established its own traditions, cherished its decorations for victories long past, relived in memory defeats suffered, the endless miles of roads marched, the myriad camps built and fortified, the days of rain and snow and torrid heat, the nights of calm beauty which could so easily conceal the stealthy onrush of barbarian enemies.

These traditions became the folklore and bible of the legion, told and retold to each recruit until he too had absorbed its ideals, learned to revere its eagle and to wear in quiet pride, blasphemously discounted in speech, the uniform, insignia, and decorations of his army home, the stern, demanding, eternal legion.

4

WHEN AUGUSTUS planned the stabilization of the Empire he seems originally to have intended to make its northern boundary in Europe the Elbe River. Through the lands between that river and the Rhine, his generals, Drusus and later Tiberius, brought about the sullen submission of the surly forest tribes. With the pacification apparently complete, Tiberius was called from Germany to put down a revolt in Pannonia (the western part of what is now Hungary). He turned over his command to Quintilius Varus, who had been transferred for no one knows what indiscretion from the highest office in the gift of the Emperor, the governorship of Syria.

When in 9 A.D. that incompetent sybarite allowed his army of three legions to be ambushed and totally destroyed in the trackless wastes of the Teutoburg Forest, the appalled Augustus summarily gave up hopes of further expansion and set the Rhine and the Danube on the north, and the Channel on the west, as the Empire frontiers, earnestly recommending to his successors that they go no farther afield.

Although he was surely acquainted with Caesar's reports on his two expeditions into Britain, and well aware that the tribute imposed by Caesar was not being paid, Augustus may have contemplated, but never initiated, measures to invade Britain. Nor did his successor Tiberius.

During the reigns of these two Emperors, the internal condition of the Empire steadily improved. The Gallic provinces in particular, reaching to the Rhine, speedily embraced the standards of Roman civilization, and participated fully in its economic life. Tranquillity and order, peaceful trade and commerce, replaced the quarreling anarchy the Gallic peoples had known before Caesar. In three generations, with only occasional flare-ups, the concept of being part of a civilized world community had taken root and flourished. The resulting prosperity was not without effect across the Channel in Britain.

Rome was willing enough to trade beyond its borders, and so long as things went peacefully, to live and let live. Roman men of business had moved quickly into Gaul after its pacification, establishing agencies for the purchase and sale of goods of all kinds then available within the Roman economy. Those who reached the towns of the Channel coast scanned with eager curiosity the trade which had been conducted for centuries between the Channel ports of Gaul and the fogbound island lying within sight of the Itius promontory.

There was a ready market within the Empire for some of the surplus products of Britain. Although British copper was not in demand because of the volume production of the Spanish copper mines, and tin from Cornwall had largely lost its market in bronze manufacture, iron, lead, and silver were still eagerly sought. These metals Britain had for sale or exchange.

In addition, hides and wool, sturdy Celtic slaves picked up by the more aggressive British tribes on foraging expeditions among their unwary brethren, and giant hunting dogs, ancestors of the Irish wolfhounds and Scottish deerhounds of our day, which commanded immense prices in Rome, all passed in more or less regular shipments through Roman customs houses in Condivincum (Nantes) on the Loire, in Burdigala (Bordeaux) on the Garonne, in Gesoriacum (Boulogne), and in Itius Portus (Calais).

Going back, the merchant galleys catered to the taste for Roman luxuries, for choice pottery, silver table services, silks from the island of Cos, jewelry of all kinds and values which had percolated from the southeast through the chieftain classes of the more remote tribes. Nearly always among outgoing cargoes were shipments of Italian wines to allay aristocratic thirsts to which the local potent mead and barley beer were now fit only for the loutish lower classes.

Trade and commerce are prolific generators of friction. Contracts and agreements not spelled out are subject to misinterpretation. Where a law common to buyer and seller exists and is enforceable, commercial controversy can be safely channeled into litigation, with a chance for satisfactory settlement.

But there was no law common to Rome and to the British tribes. Cargoes were long in being prepared, longer in delivery. There was always ample opportunity for errors to occur, for goods delivered in Britain to be not those ordered or expected. The merchant involved, who could well have been acting in the best of faith, was often put to substantial loss.

By the same process British goods shipped to Gaul sometimes brought prices less than those expected. There was no reasonable prospect that the British exporter who had consigned the goods for sale, and often enough had ordered against a predicted price, could understand the economic hazards of which he was the victim. To these honest difficulties were added the cheating and chicanery of the marginal larcenists who then as now infested the markets.

The irritations and the compensating satisfactions of a growing commerce with Britain were but one factor in the increasing interest with which Roman officials looked across the Channel. Since time began, raiding one's neighbor had been an honored means of livelihood in Britain; as indeed, before Caesar, it had been in Gaul; and, before the respectability of conquest sanctified new rules, in Rome itself. But in Britain it remained a way of life, subject certainly to possible retribution, but not to moral condemnation.

As the prosperity of the Gallic countryside and towns facing the

Approximate distribution of Celtic tribes in Britain,
first century A.D.

Stonehenge: The Awesome Structure of the Beaker Folk at Salisbury Plain

La Tene Art: The Aylesford Bucket

La Tene Art: The Desborough Mirror

Romans Against Barbarians: From a Sarcophagus at Rome

Channel waxed under Roman-imposed order, cupidity and temptation on the opposite side conquered any risks involved in an overnight crossing. But the Roman officials on the spot, responsible to the
distant but omnipotent figure of the Emperor in Rome for the peace
and security of their respective territories, could not be expected to
look with equanimity on a night's looting of an unsuspecting seacoast
town, on the resulting damage and slaughter, and on provincials
kidnaped from under Roman protection to appear later in the slave
markets of Britain.

An added factor rested in the irreconcilable fury of the Druid
priesthood, large numbers of whom, driven from Gaul not because
of their religion but because they opposed the imposition of Roman
custom and law, had fled to Britain and there constantly harangued
their faithful on the crimes of Roman tyranny.

All in all, as Gaul became Roman in thought, language, and custom, in the eyes of many peaceful provincials, as well as in those of
the responsible officials, Britain was slowly becoming a nuisance.

There were tribes in Britain, chiefly the Regnenses and Cantii of
the southeast, which were already civilized enough to welcome Roman
suzerainty. But they were in the minority. The powerful Catevellauni
and Trinovantes in Buckingham, Hertford, and Essex, and the Atrebates and Belgae on both sides of the Thames rested content and
bellicose in their liberty to harass their neighbors.

This liberty, with the possession of the superior power, proved
irresistible to the ambitions of Cunobelinus, king of the Catevellauni,
a gentleman who has come down in literature, with some poetic
license, as Shakespeare's *Cymbeline*.

His ancestor, Cassivellaunus, had learned at first hand from
Caesar the lesson of Roman invincibility. But both Caesar and
Cassivellaunus were long dead. No imperious Roman had ever come
to inquire why the solemnly pledged tribute had not been paid. Surely
the Romans were fully occupied elsewhere. It may well have occurred
to Cunobelinus, as to other dictators before and since, that a swift,
judicious conquest, propagandized beforehand as self-defense, then
presented to the world as a *fait accompli,* would excite little moral
indignation and no retaliation in Rome.

So, in the early years of our era, Cunobelinus unleashed his war
chariots and swept over the fertile lands of the Trinovantes. Deep in
their territory, about 10 A.D., he established his capital, Camulodunum

—the Fort of Camulos, war god of the Catevellauni—near the site of modern Colchester, in Essex. It was less a town than a huge dike-enclosed area, some twelve square miles in extent, with access to the North Sea via the then navigable River Colne, but probably only sparsely populated.

After some years, during which this conquest was consolidated, the appetite of Cunobelinus for further territory at the expense of his neighbors seems to have been whetted rather than assuaged—a recurrent phenomenon in history. Looking around him, he fastened on the Romanophile kingdom of the Regnenses, then headed by a King Verica, as offering the largest profit with the least risk.

But temporarily at least, domestic difficulties intervened. Cunobelinus seems to have had three sons whose names have come down through the intervening centuries. So patriarchal were the customs of Celtic royalty there is little reason to believe them born of the same mother. Of the three, Adminius, exhibiting a typically Celtic intractibility, quarreled violently with his royal father and was banished, fleeing to the continent. His example, coupled with signs of advancing age in the King, seems to have induced in the other two, Togodumnus and Caractacus, a salutary, if expectant patience.

The exile of Adminius occurred in 40 A.D. Tiberius, successor to Augustus, had died, with some rumored assistance, at Capri in 37 A.D. He was followed in the Principate by young Gaius Caesar, a sadistic schizophrenic once affectionately dubbed "Caligula" ("Little Boots") by the soldiers serving under his admired father, the general Germanicus. At this time he was with the Rhine border garrison in Gaul preparing again to invade Germany in emulation of his father's achievements. It was his one and only attempt to impress the people of Rome with his military genius.

To him, seeking succor, came Adminius accompanied by a small escort, probably cronies who had also incurred his father's wrath. In the process of making submission to Caligula he may have overstated his importance and influence in Britain. Here was obviously a malcontent of a type even then familiar and today a nuisance.

But according to Suetonius, who loved gossip more than history, Caligula interpreted the personal submission and probable request for aid from Adminius as carrying with it the submission of the entire island. In letters reflecting his somewhat clouded majesty, he informed the Senate and consuls of his latest conquest. Then abruptly ceasing his pseudo-military clowning on the Rhine, he marched what troops were on hand to the Channel, in the meantime ordering ships to be made ready, as if to embark on his imagined conquest.

For one reason or another, lost in the misting of his unbalanced brain, and unreported by contemporary historians, the expedition was called off at the Channel shore. Perhaps some of his generals, horrified at the total absence of preparation, and justifiably distrusting his leadership, by what might have been diplomacy but more probably approached psychiatric dissuasion, managed to get the venture dropped. In retrospect, it was just as well for Rome's military reputation.

Nevertheless, Caligula's boasting letters with their references to the submission of Adminius were read in Rome. Perhaps after considerable discount, they were filed along with the growing mass of information available on Britain to the hard-headed secretariat who under good Emperors and bad decided imperial policy in Rome. To these men, Britain presented a problem.

Augustus had considered the Channel littoral of Gaul a frontier that required no defense. The Britons, in their impulsive greed for other people's property and their mischievous capacity for intrigue, were proving it otherwise.

In the view of the secretariat there were two methods of defending the Channel coast of Gaul, extending from the Brittany peninsula to the Rhine Delta. One was by establishing garrisons and interlocking sea patrols over a distance of some 350 miles, along a coast indented with river mouths and countless coves suitable for stealthy landings from Britain. A fleet would be required to support the garrisons and maintain the patrols. The cost would be extremely heavy, involving at least four legions in addition to the fleet. And there would be no compensating increase in revenue, no augmentation of manpower fit for military service.

The sole alternative apparent to the Roman policy-makers was to conquer the island, thus eliminating the cause of trouble. Conquest would involve, in the first instance, no more troops than would be absorbed in coastal garrisons. After the island was taken and order established, Roman traders and men of business would be protected and their contracts enforced. Thus trade between the island and the Empire would increase with its wholly beneficent effect upon the imperial revenues. Normal provincial taxes would meet the expenses of occupation and probably provide a surplus to Rome. And not the least of all the good to be expected would be the wholesale availability of young and virile British males for the activation of new auxiliary cohorts which, deployed on the Rhine and Danube frontiers, would simultaneously ease that imperial burden and lessen the chances of revolt within the island itself.

Given the spirit of the times, the argument for conquest was nearly unanswerable. But another potent policy consideration made the matter conclusive.

Ever in the minds of the planners in Rome was the delicate balance of military power among the several provincial governors responsible for defending the long imperial frontier. Augustus, aware from personal experience that loyalty to a general, rather than to Rome, was the major motivation of the legions, had laid down a policy that the forces entrusted to the several provincial governors, while necessarily varying in size with their military responsibilities, would in no single case be so predominant as to make a particular governor on the death of an Emperor, a nearly unchallengeable candidate for the succession.

Therefore, it was clear that four more legions, not to mention a fleet, added to the forces of the Rhine army would give a dangerous power to the governor should he be disposed to debate the succession. Four legions, on the other hand, safely on the island of Britain with plenty of fighting to occupy their time, and under command of another general directly responsible to the Emperor, would leave undisturbed, if it did not enhance, the delicate balance of power among the frontier commanders.

In the interim the hardy Cunobelinus had died, leaving his kingdom and conquests to his two faithful sons, Togodumnus and Caractacus. Ignoring any claims of their exiled brother, and with a singular lack of foresight, the two divided the kingdom; Togodumnus taking the eastern half, Caractacus the western portion reaching up the Thames Valley.

Caractacus, both at this time and later, appears to have possessed more initiative and energy than judgment. With or without brotherly encouragement he soon put in train his father's projected expedition against the Regnenses. The king, Verica, fled to the continent and appealed to Rome for help.

There, in 41 A.D., Caligula had died, killed by a tribune of the

Praetorian Guard in exasperated protest against the Emperor's obscenities. Contemplating the deed, the tribune and his supporters in the conspiracy must have realized that their sole hope of safety lay in selecting the next incumbent. Chancing on a grandson of Augustus, Tiberius Claudius Drusus Germanicus, who theretofore had shown a passion only for books and for anonymity, they convinced him that his duty to Rome required not only his ascent to the Principate but the payment to them of a liberal donative for supporting his candidacy. Once Claudius agreed—and it is difficult to see how he could have refused and lived—the consent of the Senate and the approval of the people followed as a formality.

The new emperor was a mild and scholarly man, without military experience and therefore lacking the aura of soldierly glory expected of a Roman Emperor. Perhaps he would be amenable to the suggestion that a new conquest—nominally under his command but with an experienced general on hand to see that he did not get into trouble—to be followed by a glittering triumph and the honorific "Britannicus" bestowed by vote of the Senate, would raise him on a par with his doughty ancestors.

The majesty of the Pax Romana, with its orderly life, its arts and civilization, its law and language, was about to be introduced to Britain. To make sure of its welcome, and to guarantee its acceptance, the legions would go first. After a period of possibly strained adjustment, with some rough lessons, if necessary, in the folly of contumacy, the people of Britain would have cause to be grateful to Rome. Who would live in tribal anarchy and economic chaos when Rome offered peace and tranquillity?

The foreign policy of Rome did not require that the Empire be liked, or loved, but merely that it be respected. Respect, its officials and generals knew how to earn. If at first, through barbarian ignorance, respect were absent, for the short period before its creation a healthy fear of vengeance would be an adequate substitute.

Britain had become a nuisance. Something had to be done. The Roman policy-makers were engaged not in aggression but in extending order. In the process they would confer on the Britons the priceless boon of civilization. So it had always been, since the founding of the City. So it would be, the gods of Rome willing, *per omnia saecula saeculorum.*

IV

INVASION AND CONQUEST
43-60 A.D.

Where power compels, moderation and righteousness
are qualities self-ascribed to the stronger.
—TACITUS, *Germania*

1

ONCE CLAUDIUS DECIDED TO IGNORE THE long-standing advice of Augustus and to embark on a course of imperial expansion, preparations for the assault on Britain were soon in train.

Amphibious operations against a hostile shore were as hazardous in Roman times as in ours. Weapons and resources change with advancing technology; men, weather, and the moods of the sea combine to keep the difficulty constant. The peculiar problems of an operation across the Fretum Gallicum—the Strait of Dover—were well understood in Rome. There were on record not only the frank admissions of Caesar that both his expeditions had been imperiled by sudden and furious storms but also much data compiled from the reports of merchants and traders, along with possibly biased accounts of political conditions derived from the animadversions of Adminius, the refugee King Verica, and perhaps others.

There was probably little disposition to underrate the difficulties. On the other hand, for Claudius the Emperor, success would be proportionately more the handmaiden of glory.

The selection of a commander-in-chief for the expedition was a matter of first priority. The officer had to be one whose loyalty to the Emperor was beyond question, one who could be trusted not to run away with the conquest in self-glorification. He had also to be of proved competence in generalship, for failure in the invasion itself could not be countenanced. He had also to be available, capable of being spared from his present duty, whatever it might be. That meant, in practice, that he would have to be taken from one of the more quiescent imperial provinces.

There were not too many of these experienced senior officers; or so it would appear from a letter to the Senate written by Tiberius some ten years earlier, complaining that outstanding personnel, capable of commanding armies, were refusing appointments, and that he had been reduced from proffering an honor to entreating acceptance of responsibility. There may have been some tongue-in-cheek whining in this complaint, as Tacitus implies. Nevertheless, it is likely enough that able citizens with acceptable military records, after living through the vagaries of Caligula, were hesitant to attract imperial notice.

One promising general who might have been named to the post was a certain Suetonius Paulinus, but he had already been committed for a projected expedition into Mauretania. Whatever the process of selection, the choice finally settled on Aulus Plautius Silvanus, *Legatus Augusti pro praetore* in Pannonia.

This province, comprising parts of eastern Austria, western Hungary, and northern Jugoslavia, had been conquered for Augustus by Drusus and Tiberius in 14 B.C., as part of the Emperor's plan to base the northeastern frontier of the Empire on the Danube. Two settlements had been founded on the river, which were to persist and grow in history to our own day: Vindobona, now Vienna; and Aquincum, now the city of Budapest.

Pannonia had revolted in 6 A.D., raised an army of insurgents, massacred all Roman citizens in the area, and for a while posed a threat to Italy. Augustus recalled the energetic Tiberius from Germany and sent him against the rebels with an army which soon taught the recalcitrants the wholly unprofitable and generally fatal nature of rebellion against Rome. So great had been the slaughter, and so rigorous the methods of pacification that in 43 A.D. the province was quiet, the remaining population cowed into docility, and the garrison idle. There were not yet, as were to come later, warlike tribes like the Marcomanni pressing on the frontier. The provincial governor and one legion of the garrison could be spared for the British venture.

History has not preserved the reaction of Aulus Plautius when the imperial courier reached him with orders outlining his new command and responsibility. Whether welcome or not, we do know that he discharged it with vigor, competence, and loyalty. His conduct of the campaign as a whole reflects the qualities of the Roman genius maintained generation after generation in the ancient families.*

The *gens Plautia,* of plebeian origin, early gained recognition with the election in 358 B.C. of Caius Plautius Proculus as consul. Thereafter, with consistency, the gens kept supplying leaders and some gifted individuals to Rome, including around 250 B.C., a certain Plautius Novus—undoubtedly a freedman of the family—an artist of considerable merit in ornamental ironwork, *caelatura.*

One member of the family, Plautia Urganilla, had been the first wife of Emperor Claudius. Since he had divorced her for various infidelities and general misconduct some years before, his selection of even a possibly distant relative for this important command speaks well for his magnanimity.

Taking with him Legio IX, Hispana, and some cohorts of Thracian auxiliaries from the Pannonian garrison, Aulus Plautius left with dispatch for the Channel coast of Gaul. Ahead of him, or more probably direct from Rome, carried by the highly organized courier system, surely went orders to the commander of the Rhine frontier to provide him with the three additional legions deemed necessary. Among these was Legio II, Augusta, under command of a rude Sabine plebeian turned soldier, a man more careful and parsimonious with the public funds than with his own, one Titus Flavius Vespasianus, the future emperor, then about thirty-four years of age. The Second was then stationed at Argentoratum, now Strasbourg, on the upper Rhine. Legio XIV, Gemina, at Mogontiacum, now Mainz, on the middle Rhine; and the cocky Legio XX, Valeria, in barracks at Neuss, across the Rhine from Düsseldorf, completed the draft on the Rhine garrison, with what protests from the frontier commander we can only imagine.

The assembly point for the gathering army appears to have been near Gesoriacum, the site of modern Boulogne-sur-Mer, where the

* Aulus Plautius appears as a benign character in Sienkiewicz' *Quo Vadis.*

Channel narrows to the Dover straits. Fancy will recreate the excitement, wonder, perhaps consternation tempered by the prospect of huge purchases for goods and services, with which the coastal population awaited the convergence of the legions and auxiliary supporting units on the port town. Nor is it hard to imagine word of the assembly swiftly carried to Britain, to alert Togodumnus in his chief town of Camulodunum, and Caractacus farther west, along with other tribal chieftains of southern England.

We do not know where in the vicinity of Gesoriacum the army engineers, sent out in advance of the main body, decided to build the embarkation camp. Plautius may have dispersed his legions into separate camps, led by considerations of sanitation, water supply, and adequate training areas. However, this seems unlikely. Three of the legions were new to his command. A prudent general would keep them close at hand under his disciplining eye. He would also need to be in daily contact with his four legion commanders, not only to plan the campaign, but to settle details of the complex operation involved in embarkation and landing. Also, the large amount of physical labor the legionaries would have to perform as the shiploading got under way would dictate their concentration. It is probable the army was lodged in a single camp, close to the waiting ships.

Long-established doctrine dictated the shape and arrangement of such a camp. Gently sloping land for good drainage was essential. The dimensions were determined by the number to be accommodated. The shape would be rectangular, one and one-half times as long as it was wide. Plautius commanded 4 legions, or 40 cohorts, and an indeterminate number of auxiliary units both infantry and cavalry, which for the sake of round numbers we may assume to be 24. With these 64 units, the Roman engineering formula for the width of the camp—200 times the square root of the number of cohorts—would give a width of 1,600 Roman feet and a length of 2,400, enclosing an area somewhat short of 90 acres.

Around the perimeter of the camp a ditch, *fossa,* would be dug and a wall of stakes erected, with a gate on each of the four sides. The main gate, the *Porta Praetoria,* was at one end, and the rear gate, the *Porta Decumana,* at the other. The gates on the long sides, the *Porta Principalis Dextra,* on the right facing the *Porta Praetoria,* and the *Porta Principalis Sinistra,* on the left, were connected by a broad crossroad, the *Via Principalis.* Another road ran from the *Porta*

Praetoria meeting the *Via Principalis* at right angles at the location of the commander's headquarters, the *Praetorium*. Behind the commander's offices another main building, the *Quaestorium,* or supply and finance center, faced a minor crossroad without exit gates, the *Via Quintana*. Perhaps because along the crossroad were located such camp recreational facilities as were available, the name has come down to us in the ubiquitous "canteen."

Each unit had its own demarcated area, the legions near the wall, the auxiliaries farther in, perhaps to guard against their sometimes erratic behavior.

The essential features of such a camp would be erected in a day—fossa dug, wall stakes emplaced, tentage installed, roads laid out and smoothed, picket lines set up, latrines dug and guarded against abuse, baggage stored in orderly rows, the watch of three reliefs set, and the business of the camp begun.

It was simple, it was straightforward, it was quick, and it was effective. Because every soldier knew what was expected of him, once the engineers had staked out the ground the work went ahead swiftly, surely, with a minimum of orders and questions and nothing forgotten. This was the Roman way to build a camp. For centuries it had been so and for centuries it was to remain. Wherever Roman armies went, their camps, many surviving in foundation to this day, were laid out on this basic plan.

We know almost nothing of the fleet that was assembled. Reference to what is known of Roman maritime practice at this epoch would indicate that to move his army of some forty thousand men and five thousand horses across the Channel, Plautius would require about four hundred transports, or *naves onerariae*. Although these broad and cumbersome sailing vessels, with a beam one-fourth of the length, were not too seaworthy if overloaded, each of them could on a short voyage accommodate two hundred men, or fifty horses and fifty men, over and above the crew of sailors and rowers. In addition, he required a fleet of naval vessels both to protect the convoy en route and to assist if the landing were opposed. The *naves longae,* or fighting ships, were probably sleek destroyer types of the time, called Liburnians, about 150 feet long and 18 feet wide, slender and swift, propelled by two banks of oars. They were mounted with various *tormenta* for throwing projectiles; and in addition to master, crew, and rowers, they carried a deck force of marines trained in archery and boarding tactics. Perhaps fifty of these slim fighting craft would serve to guide and protect the transports and guard the flanks of the landings.

2

IF NOT already known to the troops, their destination soon became apparent from the training in loading ships, in boarding and assault landing techniques to which they were subjected. The novelty of an assault across "Ocean" water could not fail to impress with its dangers the landbound Romans of the legions as well as the more ignorant and perhaps more superstitious auxiliary units. For both, Ocean was a world-surrounding river, and somewhere had an edge over which the water flowed from the flat earth-surface in a mighty stream, never ending. The very audacity of embarking upon it was an appalling, because new, thought.

There were of course officers and centurions, even many literates among the men, who knew of Caesar's forays into Britain nearly a century earlier. They knew therefore and could tell others that the venture upon which they were now engaged had twice been safely performed. In addition, conversations with local traders and seamen would assure them that the Channel crossing, for all the existing superstition about the Ocean, was by no means unduly hazardous.

That there was some fear of the unknown, and consequent perhaps widespread grumbling, seems in retrospect reasonable enough. But it seems inadequate to explain the curious story told by Dion Cassius of a mutiny which required the Emperor to send his freedman and secretary, the notorious Narcissus, to quell it.

Mutiny, en masse, ever had short shrift in the Roman Army. The powers of commanders to deal with such a lamentable lapse of duty were unlimited. The grim punishment of *decimatio* where one in ten of the mutineers, drawn by lot, were put to death in front of the remainder; the crucifixion and lingering death of convicted ringleaders handled in all its grisly details by their erstwhile fellows; and for lesser insubordination, carrying the burden of shame and ridicule, the punishment of being put on sparse rations of barley instead of wheat combined to establish the crime in its various degrees as beyond serious thought. At the same time, positive influences constantly at work—pride in Rome the Invincible, hope of promotion, expectation of generous retirement benefits, above all pride in the legion—operated together generally to prevent the thought from ever arising.

As a matter of record, mutinies among the legionaries were extremely rare. Insurrections led by commanders who carried their troops with them, often in contest for the imperial throne were, as the Empire grew older, another matter.

In addition, it is inconceivable that Aulus Plautius would have appealed to Claudius for help in putting down a mutiny, or that, having done so, he would have not been immediately cashiered. That he was not, we know.

Yet that there was trouble with the troops seems clear, since it appears that the embarkation was delayed some two months from the scheduled date of early spring. The cause may have rested in more mundane considerations.

Since Augustus had established the Rhine and Danube frontiers the legions assigned to their protection had been moved very little. Their permanent quarters were comfortable stone barracks, with mess halls, wine rooms, common rooms, canteens, and other amenities. Normally they had been drawn away from these pleasant and stable living arrangements at most a few months' summer campaigning each year; in general just enough to relieve boredom at the start, to make return a delight at the end.

In the course of this garrison life men had fulfilled their terms of service, been discharged, received their *honoraria* upon retirement, and settled down in the nearby *colonia* † where free land was made available to veterans. There they had legally married, often legitimizing a prior relationship. Their children had been born, the sons to enter the legion in their turn, the girls to expect marriage with the discharged "twenty-year" men still in the prime of life. Thus the roots of the legion in its garrison town were deep and strong, embellished naturally by the illicit but recognized relationships the soldiers, forbidden to marry, would in the course of an exuberant and straining manhood form with girls of the village.

† A settlement in the form of a community of retired veterans, often close to the frontier where its members constituted a ready reserve—*"subsidium adversis rebellis"* (Tacitus, *Annales* XII, xxxii). Organized under both the Republic and the Empire, many coloniae afterward became famous cities: Cologne, Trier, Augst, in Europe; Beirut in Lebanon; and in Britain, as we shall see, Lincoln, Colchester, Gloucester, and York.

From this pleasant existence the men of the legions had been suddenly called, put into combat gear, and moved off under orders to the western shore of the continent from where on clear days they could see in the misty distance a green and menacing island, a destination of no return.

It could be no surprise to Plautius or his commanders, understanding these sundered ties, that the murmuring, fed by indignation and self-pity, grew apace. But that it ever reached mutiny seems highly improbable. It is much more likely that Dion Cassius, writing perhaps 150 years after the event, embroidered what might have been a routine inspection by Narcissus of the progress of the invasion into a more dramatic story. Dion Cassius reports that Narcissus, a freedman, was sent to the camp by Claudius to recall the mutinous men to their duty; that he addressed them, Roman citizens all; that they listened, then jeered him with the cry: *"Io Saturnalia!"* reminding him that only during the Feast of the Saturnalia were ex-slaves allowed impertinence.

Another possibility is that Aulus Plautius, seeing inevitable delays building from logistic problems, devised the whole episode as a cover plan to deceive the expectant Britons, in the process grossly exaggerating the unrest among the troops, and letting the expected visit of Narcissus be turned into a despairing plea for imperial assistance, all the time making sure that the most lurid tales of the matter reached the ears of the British chieftains.

In any case, preparations were at last completed. The troops loaded the transports and marched aboard, with no recorded hesitation. There came at last an evening in late June when all was ready, and the fleet sailed.

Even today, the sight of a fleet of four hundred or more ships, setting forth on an errand of high emprise, would stir the blood of those committed and those who watched. Undoubtedly it was so then.

3

THE DELAY, which perhaps lulled the British kings into a false sense of security, gave Plautius opportunity not only to perfect in daily practice the assault training of his army, but also to marshal the heterogeneous data of political, terrain, and weather intelligence so vital to the success of his mission.

Political intelligence made him sure his major resistance, even if tardily assembled, would come from the sons of Cunobelinus. His plan of operation, therefore, addressed itself to a swift challenge and destruction of their power. At the same time, he knew from other sources that he could count on the friendship and assistance of Cogidumnus, successor to Verica as king of the Regnenses, and on the neutrality of other tribes whose relations with the Catevellauni were less than friendly.

Terrain studies, based on merchants' reports and surely supported by preliminary reconnaissance parties, had determined landing areas possessing both protection from sudden storms and shelving beaches on which his troops could quickly disembark and deploy, even in the face of opposition. Three such semi-harbors, all apparently in commercial use, were designated for landing. The westernmost was Portus Lemanis (Lympne), thirty-six miles northwest of Gesoriacum; the second, Portus Dubrae (Dover) also thirty-six miles distant, northwest by north; and the third, Rutupiae (Richborough, near Sandwich), around the South Foreland, sheltered by the Isle of Thanet, forty miles distant, a shade west of north.

We do not know exactly how Plautius divided his forces among the three landing areas. Since Vespasian's Second Legion later appeared on the left flank of the consolidated beachhead, it is a reasonable assumption that to it was entrusted the Lympne landing. Plautius himself seems to have taken the Rutupiae sector, and would probably have had with him his own trusted Ninth Legion. Since the Twentieth had a reputation of working best untrammeled by the presence of a higher headquarters, it is possible that to it was entrusted the landing at Dover. Under these assumptions the Fourteenth would have joined the Ninth under Plautius, forming a strengthened right flank of the over-all operation. In the absence of definite evidence, all we know is that the several landings took place without serious opposition about daylight after a crossing marked, according to Dion Cassius, first by contrary winds then by reassuring portents.

There are times in war when nothing but furious driving energies in commanders, alert to waste no second of priceless time, will serve. Such a time is the interval between landing an amphibious force and consolidating a beachhead broad and deep enough to provide a secure lodgment. This Plautius and his separate commanders proceeded to do. Fanning up and out of the harbors, across the moors, the left flank and center forces moved north as Plautius drove west along the valley of the Stour. By nightfall the three forces were in contact and the main line of advance west to the Medway River reconnoitered.

Togodumnus and Caractacus could not have been wholly surprised by the landings, since they were able during the day to get a force of infantry and war chariots to the Medway by nightfall. Counting on the river for defense, they halted.

The Medway rises in Sussex and flows generally northeast to the neighborhood of Maidstone where it turns north and in a westerly curve flows into an arm of the Thames estuary at Rochester. Somewhere along its route, probably not far north of Maidstone, the Roman Army, less detachments left behind to guard the beachheads, arrived the next day to find the western bank crowded with armed Britons and a multitude of two-horse war chariots.

But Togodumnus and Caractacus seem to have trusted to the protection of the river barrier to an extent which proved them wholly ignorant of Roman tactical skill in forcing river crossings. As soon as Plautius, arriving, had time to assay the situation he threw across several cohorts of German auxiliaries, men adept at swimming while fully armed. Once across, under instruction, they merely defended themselves against the British warriors while putting all their offensive efforts into hamstringing the chariot horses.

The shrieks of horses in pain, the frightened plunging and falling as severed tendons failed to support, the resultant upsetting of the chariots combined with other clamor to confuse the Britons. Nevertheless, they fought bravely and well, if without the disciplined direction of the legion which followed the auxiliaries across the river. When night fell, although badly disorganized and hurt, the British forces were still on the field, while the Roman forces broke off action and retired to the riverbank where, if they followed custom, they strongly entrenched themselves for the night.

But if the committed forces rested, Plautius was awake and busy. During the night he detached the Second Legion with its auxiliaries under Vespasian with instructions to move south along the right bank and find a ford. The legion was then to cross the river and as early as possible after daylight attack the enemy's right flank.

West Kent was not then the exquisitely patterned country it is

now. Moving through forest and swampland, the scouts ahead of the
quietly shuffling legion found and reported back paths and tracks
through the thick woods, while every so often stopping to gauge the
depth of the running water. Sometime during the night the ford was
found. The legion column, nearly half a mile in length, might have
taken well over an hour to cross, with what muttered blasphemies,
instantly stifled by the centurions, we can reconstruct. Perhaps
Vespasian himself, entrusting the lead to his senior tribune, would
have stayed in the middle of the ford, waist deep in the water, whispering encouragement, watching every man, helping some, and by
his simple presence bringing new reassurance to every faint heart.
There is evidence to indicate he was that kind of commander.

The ford once crossed, the march north again along the west bank
could not have been without its trials, nor lacking in suspense. The
Britons may have been sufficiently inexperienced in meeting a first-
class army to have failed to foresee and guard against Vespasian's
move. But Vespasian himself was far too canny a commander to assume this. We may be sure then that the approach to the uneasily
resting enemy was conducted with the utmost caution and in the
greatest possible silence. With the paling of the eastern sky, the
legion would be deployed from column into line of battle, stretching
its deadly length westward from the riverbank.

Fully reported, analyzed, and studied battles like the Federal
defeat at Chancellorsville by Stonewall Jackson have given us stark
pictures of the panic produced by a sudden and unexpected flank
attack on troops set to fight in another direction. Where no enemy
were, suddenly the woods were full of them. Where did they come
from? How many are there? Why were we left here? Why didn't
somebody tell us? And finally, the logical query—isn't it time we were
getting out of here?

Bewilderment, surprise, uncontrollable fear of the unknown can
disarm men otherwise truly brave. So it must have been for the
Britons at Medway, braced to continue the battle of the day before,
confidently facing their foes along the riverbank, when they were
suddenly hit by a storm of pila from the right, startled by the brazen
notes of the legion trumpeters sounding the *incursus,* the charge, by
the hoarse shouts of exultation from the throats of the legionaries
advancing at a run with shields and short swords at the ready.

Far more disciplined troops than the unruly Britons had broken

A Roman Road: Watling Street at Stony Stratford

Invasion and consolidation, 43 – 47 A.D.

First phase:

(a) Cross-Channel invasion from Gesioracum (Boulogne), A, to landings at Rutupiae (Richborough), 1; Portus Dubrae (Dover), 2; and Portus Lemanis (Lympne), 3:

(b) Consolidation of beachhead on line from Rutupiae through Durovernum (Canterbury), 4, to Lemanis:

(c) Advance to the Medway, where Caractacus and Togodumnus are met in battle and defeated:

(d) Advance to the Thames crossing at the site of Londinium, 5, where Plautius awaits the coming of Claudius:

(e) Advance to Camulodunum, 6, designated the Roman capital after its capture.

Second phase:

(a) Northward advance of Legio IX, which establishes fortress at Lindum, 10:

(b) Advance of Legiones XIV and XX to the Severn and establishment of fortress at Viroconium, 11:

(c) Southwestward advance of Vespasian's II Augusta to the Isle of Wight, thence westward through Dorset; battles at Hod Hill, 7, and Maiden Castle, 8; northward movement to Glevum (Gloucester), 9, where fortress is established.

Third phase:

Provincial frontier established along the Severn-Avon-Trent line, patrolled by detachments from the legionary fortresses.

Note: The routes of march here shown are inferred from those followed by later Roman highways.

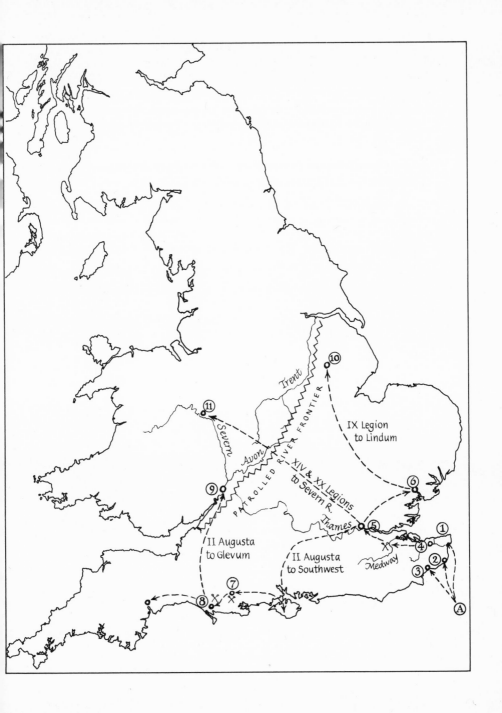

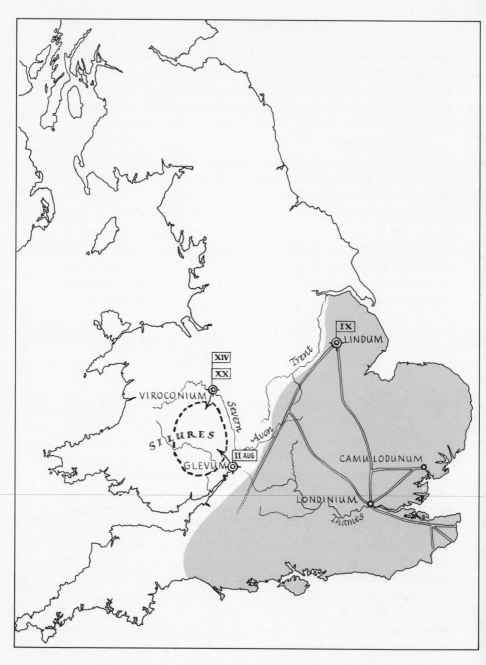

Scapula's campaigns against the Silures and Caractacus, 51 A.D.

under less surprise and pressure. The battle, a moment earlier swaying back and forth, melted into rout. The Britons, uncertain, fearful, started back, hesitantly at first, then faster, then in panic flight, throwing away arms and burdens that slowed their pace. Interspersed among them, the remaining chariots, dragged helter-skelter by pairs of furiously galloping horses, fought their way toward possible safety. Behind and on the right flank the legionaries pressed, shouting and cheering, but still under the control of their centurions, quickly and with murderous skill clearing the field of the living.

Togodumnus appears to have been killed in the battle. At least we hear of him no more. Caractacus, fleeing the field, hurried north and west, gathered his family, and disappeared for a while into the mountain fastnesses of Wales.

The battle of the Medway over, there was in the entire island no organized opposition capable of halting Plautius and his army.

4

IT IS a curious fact that there is almost no reference, in the classical writings on Roman campaigns which have survived, to the aftermath of battle, the burial of the dead, and the care of the wounded. Caesar seems to have assumed either that these matters were so well understood by his prospective readers that mention of them would be boring, or that wasting pages on such grubby details would detract from the political purpose for which he wrote. Even Vegetius, writing about 380 A.D. in a forlorn attempt to recall to the Emperor Valentinian II the doctrine and discipline of "ancient times," has nothing to say of the care and treatment of wounded, or burial of those of both sides killed in action.

Yet the surviving work of Celsus, written about 30 A.D. and therefore some thirteen years antecedent to the Medway victory of Plautius, exhibits a knowledge of quite advanced surgical operations and procedures, most of which we can believe were developed by army surgeons.

In addition, there are extant archeological evidences, like the remains of the Roman military hospital at Novaesium on the road to Colonia Agrippina (now Cologne, in Germany), which contained about forty wards connected by long corridors surrounding a huge central mess hall with appropriate administrative and staff housing buildings adjacent. So we can be confident that care of the sick and wounded was a major support function of the Roman Army, however little mentioned by classical writers, many of whom doubtless had never seen a battle.

Then too, the Roman preoccupation with public health and general sanitation precludes any notion that Plautius, pressing the pursuit of the defeated Britons, would have left behind him the shambles that any battlefield, ancient or modern, presents when the action is complete. Surely the dead were buried, with more or less haste. The Roman wounded were gathered up by the medical staffs of the several legions and, in hastily erected field hospitals, given some approximation of the medical and surgical care the writings of Celsus tell us was available. We can believe too that the British wounded received some care, if only to preserve for subsequent sale in the slave markets of Rome those whose injuries were slight.

None of these routine activities, however, including the temptation of individual soldiers to search for valuables among the abandoned properties of the Britons, could have interfered with the prompt reorganization of the army for further advance, beginning at daybreak of the day following.

Some thirty-five miles northwest, the Thames narrowed from navigable tidal estuary into graceful, meandering country stream. Here was the ford that Caesar had crossed. Here, where later Londinium was to grow, the British fugitives, or such among them as had been fortunate enough to avoid the cavalry pursuit, crossed and scattered, east and west. There seems also to have been a bridge, either already in existence or thrown up by the legions when they reached the south bank of the river. In any case, it appears that the fleeing Britons were still in such a state of panic and disorganization that no attempt was made to resist the advancing legions at this favorable defensive point.

Once across the river, with his access to the trans-Thames areas secured, Plautius called a halt. It was time to report back to the Emperor, to announce that the imperial orders had been carried out, and that the army awaited his arrival before moving to complete the campaign. Claudius came, bringing with him not only an escort of several cohorts of auxiliaries, but also, if Dion Cassius is to be believed, a troop of trained war elephants. This item may be discounted in view not only of the manifest difficulties involved in transporting these temperamental beasts over the long and difficult road and sea passage from Rome, but also because no later mention of their presence in Britain occurs.

Suetonius states that Claudius spent only a few days in Britain, and was absent from Rome only six months, receiving at the hands of the obsequious Senate the triumph so necessary to his vanity, and in fairness, perhaps to his prestige among the always irreverent city population.

An inscription now in the Barberini Palace in Rome gives him full credit for the invasion and its success:

> To Tiberius Claudius Caesar Augustus Germanicus, son of Drusus; Pontifex Maximus; in the eleventh year of his Tribunician Power; his fifth Consulate, and twenty-one times saluted Imperator; Father of his Country and of the People of Rome; who, without hindrance received the surrender of eleven conquered British Kings and for the first time reduced transoceanic barbarians under the power of the Roman people.

This is all we know of the Imperial arrival and short stay in Britain. Probably he joined the army at its camp near Londinium, assumed command with proper ceremony and sacrifices to the gods of Rome, led an unopposed advance eastward to Camulodunum, decreed that this settlement would be the site of the capital of the new province, made arrangements for the erection of a temple to "Rome and Augustus," the Augustus in this case being himself, confirmed Aulus Plautius as first Legate of the Imperial Province of Britannia, and departed, leaving that general, probably quite harried after the strain of the imperial visit, to get on with the conquest and pacification of the island.

Nobody, least of all Plautius, seems to have contested Claudius' role in the conquest. The legend remained and grew, until Paulus Orosius, writing in the fifth century A.D., could give him credit for having subdued not only the entire island but also the Orkney Islands lying off the northern tip of Scotland. But Orosius was a Spanish churchman, writing of the already dim past and more interested in propagating the Christian faith than in historical accuracy.

In getting on with his task, Plautius could be fairly sure that no organized opposition existed which would require the concentration of his whole army to subdue. He seems therefore to have decided to strike out in three directions, and by a show of strength in each, obtain the submission, by treaty of alliance if possible, by conquest if not, of the tribes met.

The Ninth Legion was detached and sent north, through the territories of the powerful Iceni, to Lincolnshire where, on a hill mass commanding the Lincolnshire plains and with a wide prospect west to the lands of the Brigantes, it established its fort, called then, possibly in Latinization of an earlier Celtic name, Lindum. Apparently there was no opposition and subsequently a treaty of alliance and friendship was entered into between Rome and the king of the Iceni, Prasutigas.

Plautius himself seems to have led the Fourteenth and Twentieth Legions northwest, again without recorded opposition, through Buckingham, Warwickshire, and Shropshire to where beyond the Severn River the brooding mountains of Wales lifted over the western horizon. Perhaps his camp was set up on the site which later became the thriving Roman city of Viroconium (Wroxeter) where today, in the midst of quiet fields, a row of truncated columns marking one side of the Forum, a large wall remnant of the *basilica,* or town hall, and a portion of the baths have been excavated to bear silent witness to long dead centuries of once bustling life.

There remained the southwest. This penetration Plautius assigned to Vespasian and his Legio II, Augusta, doubtless pointing out that the established friendliness of Cogidumnus, king of the Regnenses secured his rear. With the swift dispatch that characterized his leadership, Vespasian moved southeast, through Surrey and Hampshire along the border of the Regnenses' lands, and through the territory of the once virulent enemies of Rome, the Atrebates. Crossing the Solent, he subdued the Isle of Wight, known to the Romans as Vectis, returned to the mainland and headed west into Dorset, the land of the warlike Durotriges, a tribe that because of its location could have had much to do with the cross-Channel raids on peaceful Gaul which had played a part in bringing the Romans into Britain. Here he met heavy resistance, centering around the two hill forts of Maiden Castle, near Dorchester, and Hod Hill, near Blandford.

These immense earth forts were erected not against the Romans but as protection for the tribes and their cattle against the internecine warfare which had prevailed in Britain prior to the coming of the Romans.

Maiden Castle was, and is, particularly impressive. The inside area is about three thousand feet long by seventeen hundred at its widest point. It is surrounded by three immense ramparts separated by two ditches, wide and deep. The entrance ramps at either end were protected by huge outer earthworks.

Presumably on warning of enemy approach, it was possible for a large part of the tribe, together with its sheep and cattle, to enter this massive fort, there to find safety behind the ramparts until disappointment or hunger forced the withdrawal of the marauding foe. But the Second Legion was not an ordinary foe. The assault of fortified places was only one of many offensive operations in which it was fully trained.

Archeological investigation, conducted under Sir Mortimer Wheeler from 1934 to 1937, has thrown much light not only on the fortress itself but on the final stages of the Roman assault. Apparently the attack concentrated on the eastern gateway and was initiated by a storm of the heavy catapulted arrows of the Roman artillery train. Many were found on the site, and the skeleton of one defender, with the heavy arrowhead still sunk in his spinal column, is now one of the exhibits of the Dorchester Museum. Under the fierce barrage the Roman infantry cut its way from rampart to rampart, meeting desperate resistance when at last it reached the gateway proper, for here was found a hastily dug mass grave of young and old, male and female, casualties of the last despairing effort to bar the battle-mad legionaries from the enclosure. The broken arms and ribs, the deep cuts in skulls, seem to have been the work of the short Roman swords used in slashing strokes—a tactic seldom employed save when necessary to clear fighting space. In one skull was a small square hole that had let a murderously hurled pilum enter what was once a brain.

Some survivors there were, after resistance ceased and Vespasian, perhaps peremptorily, called a halt to indiscriminate slaughter. It is likely that others of the Durotriges, unable to assemble in the fort in time, submitted when they learned of its fall. Evidence indicates that the fort, its defenses dismantled, continued as a habitation for perhaps a generation, at least until the Romanized town built on the site of Dorchester was ready to receive the population.

The struggle at Hod Hill, near Blandford, was perhaps equally ferocious, its outcome equally determined by superior discipline, tactics, and equipment. Here Vespasian seems to have left behind, at least temporarily, a garrison to guarantee against a later renewal of resistance, for in one corner of the flat area inside the ramparts, surrounded by its own standard fortifications, has been found the outline of a Roman camp constructed in the age-old pattern, ample enough for a detachment from the legion reinforced with a cohort of auxiliary cavalry.

The discovery at Exeter (the Isca Dumnoniorum of the Romans) of many coins of the Claudian period may indicate that Vespasian moved at least that far west before turning northeast into the territories of the always belligerent Belgae, holding Wiltshire and Somerset, and extending his forces across the Cotswolds into the valley of the lower Severn in Gloucestershire.

Suetonius says, in his life of Vespasian, that he reduced to subjection two very powerful tribes—perhaps the Durotriges and the Belgae—and fought thirty battles, beside taking twenty great towns. This summary is possibly more reliable than much of what Suetonius has to offer, first because it is partly confirmed by archeological evidence, and second because there was probably a record in Rome—which Suetonius could have consulted or at least heard about—listing the achievements of Vespasian when on his return from Britain he was awarded the triumphal ornaments.

In any event, he seems to have subdued all the tribes he encountered in his progress to the Severn where, on the site of Gloucester, he erected his legionary camp as a permanent fortress for the area. Here with the river protecting him from the menace of the mysterious hills of Wales rising to the west, he could consolidate his conquest, establishing a line of posts along the lower Severn until he made contact with those established by the northwest thrust of the Fourteenth and Twentieth Legions.

The legionary fortress at Glevum (Gloucester), and its line of guard posts running north and east along the lower Severn and the Avon, seems to have been part of an over-all plan of Plautius' to establish across the island a defensible line behind which the consolidation of the Province could continue in safety. Such a line he found in the Severn-Avon system which at the watershed approached the headwaters of the Blythe, a tributary of the north-running Trent which emptied into the Humber estuary. Behind this line the guard posts rose from those of the Second in the southwest, through the central area, to those established along the line of the Trent by the Ninth Legion from its fortress in Lincoln. Soon a rough track connected these outposts to be later improved into a road which in a short time became the main Roman transverse road, now known as the Fosse Way. Extended southwest to Isca Dumnoniorum (Exeter) and continued by Ermine Street from Lincoln north to the Humber, it served in its early years to tie together the frontier of the Roman province. Parts of it, particularly the stretch from Ratae Coritanorum (Leicester) to Lindum Colonia (Lincoln) are in use today.

The area thus set off from the rest of the island represented, with some geographical license, a right triangle. Within this triangle was a major portion of the most fertile land, fewer forbidding mountain areas, the most civilized tribes, and closest contact with the continent.

There is reason to believe that the conquest and establishment of the defense line were completed before winter put an end to campaigning. For four years Aulus Plautius labored in the organization of the Province and the client kingdoms. The territories of tribes which had offered resistance and had been smashed in the process became the direct property and responsibility of Rome. The client kingdoms of the Regnenses and the Iceni maintained local authority subject to acquiescence in all higher Roman policy. For the Iceni this was later to prove too burdensome an invasion of their fancied independence. For the Regnenses and their foresighted king, Cogidumnus, no problem seems to have arisen; Tacitus, writing some fifty years later, says of him: ". . . he has remained continuously loyal down to our own times." A less onerous treaty with the Brigantian queen Cartimandua kept that loose and unruly confederation of Midland tribes from active opposition to Rome.

These four years saw the start of a flood of traders and merchants from the continent, all with connections reaching back to the mercantile and banking houses of Rome. Officialdom increased too, with the coming of a *procurator,* a Treasury official nominally under the Governor but answerable also directly to the *Fiscus* in Rome, who brought with him a staff of civil administrators and clerks to handle the civil side of provincial problems.

Rome was already experimenting with the division of authority between civil and military which has become a not always happy but unchallengeable principle of modern democratic government.

A road system was in all newly conquered provinces of first priority. Plautius' first task was to bind his ports of entry with the Thames crossing at Londinium; then Londinium with Camulodunum, the Roman headquarters; and finally with his border fortresses. Thus superbly engineered Roman roads cutting as straight as possible across country, through forests and across rivers, ignoring all but impossible grades, soon connected the ports of Lemanis, Dubrae and Rutupiae with Durovernum Cantiacorum, or Canterbury, which dates its continued existence and growth from the establishment of this military road junction.

A straight highway, Watling Street, connected Durovernum with Londinium, passed through Londinium to the northwest, and went on to Verulamium and to Viroconium on the Severn. It was later extended to Deva (Chester).

Another highway sped east from Londinium to Camulodunum in Essex, while Ermine Street, or the Great North Road, went from Londinium north to Lincoln and was soon extended to the Humber estuary opposite a tribal town of the Yorkshire Parisii, Petuaria.

Soon other highways, southwest and west to Glevum (Gloucester), and south to Noviomagus (Chichester), were in process of construction.

The geographical necessity of placing Londinium at the center of this radiating road system undoubtedly contributed much to the initial and continuous growth at that river town. From it as the years went on, other roads filled in the gaps, spread north, south, east, and west until, by the end of the second century of the Roman era, some six thousand miles of highway bound the island in a firm net across and up into Scotland.

These road projects and the building of a Romanized capital city at Camulodunum, centering on the great Temple to Rome and Augustus, were all initiated by Plautius. They could not of course be finished by him; requiring as they did many years of labor, drafted from the local population and put to work under engineers and surveyors, architects and stone masons, all drawn from the specialist technicians of the legions.

In 47 A.D., Aulus Plautius received his orders to report to Rome where at the hands of a silently grateful Claudius he received an ovation—a military honor second only to a triumph, now reserved for the Emperor himself. In the procession Claudius, as a signal mark of honor, marched on his legate's (provincial governor's) left hand. We do not know of his subsequent career or retirement, which properly should have been passed in the esteem and gratitude earned by hard-won honors in the public service. His wife, Pomponia Graccina, seems later to have been charged with unauthorized religious practices, which might mean she had become a Christian, as Sienkiewicz assumes for fictional purposes. There is a legend that Plautius was executed by the Emperor Nero, but this is possibly the result of confusion with a youth of the same or similar name who, of course, could have been his son.

He was succeeded in the governorship of Britannia by Ostorius Scapula, another able and energetic soldier-administrator. Tacitus calls him *belle egregius* ("distinguished in war")—surely no mean praise from an always skeptical author absorbed in praising to the skies a later general and governor of Britain, his own father-in-law, Agricola.

5

THE STILL-CHAFING Britons, both within and without the stabilized area of the island, had learned through hard experience not to annoy Aulus Plautius; it is understandable that in the relief of his going they might have been encouraged to test the firmness and ability of his successor.

The first to try the reaction quotient of the new governor were the Iceni, or at least that part of the tribe unimpressed with the lack of belligerency in their king, Prasutigas. Perhaps it was a strengthening of the guard detachments along the upper Trent, one of Scapula's first acts, which aroused their ire, and drove them to arms. Scapula, although temporarily without the nearby support of the legions, moved at once against them with what few auxiliaries he could gather. The restive Iceni were overwhelmed, disarmed, and dispersed to nurse their wounds and injured pride.

This disturbance appears to have occurred during the winter of 48–49 A.D. With the coming of spring, and no apparent trouble at his rear, Scapula prepared to move with his two reserve legions—the Fourteenth and the Twentieth—against the Deceangli of North

Wales who, from outside his defensive line, had been making a nuisance of themselves, probably in raids and cattle stealing from the Province.

This campaign had barely started, and certainly had produced no decisive effects, when various anti-Roman elements in the family of Queen Cartimandua of the Brigantes started some trouble (vaguely discussed by historians) which Scapula promptly recognized as a more immediate threat to the peace of the Province. Tacitus says laconically that "the Brigantian rising, it is true, subsided on the execution of a handful of men who were beginning hostilities and on the pardon of the rest." It seems likely that some male members of the royal line of Cartimandua, restive under her maternal control, got temporarily out of hand in the belief the Roman governor was elsewhere occupied. Those executed were probably the few ringleaders, so naïve as to suppose that when the Romans made a treaty of alliance, they would allow any others than themselves to break it.

Clearly this new governor was proving rather obdurate. The next to try his metal was the fugitive king of the conquered Catevellauni, Caractacus, who since his headlong flight from the battle at the Medway, had found refuge and a hearing among the Silures of South Wales.

Undoubtedly, from his haven during the intervening years this stubborn and courageous, but not very astute, Briton had been exhorting the primitive tribes of Wales to rise together and throw the Romans out of the island. He may well have pointed out that the establishment of a legionary fortress at Glevum, the presence of two more legions at Viroconium, and the setting up of a river frontier meant for Wales only a breathing spell before the insatiable Romans favored the area with brutal attention.

In this assumption he was probably quite right. Nevertheless, had it not been for his aggressive inspiration, which sent the Silures to a constant harrying of the Roman outposts and to ambushing the occasional forward patrols, it is possible that the Silures might have been left for a considerable number of years in unchallenged peace.

The territory involved, covering Herefordshire, Monmouthshire, and Glamorganshire, was difficult fighting country then, covered with heavy and often impenetrable forests and rough, semi-mountainous terrain. The Silures, with Caractacus to lead them and to furnish exhortation from his implacable enmity for the Romans, were no mean opponents. We do not know where Caractacus with his tribal warriors from the Silures and the Deceangli chose to challenge Roman leadership, discipline, and fighting skill. Tacitus described the formidable defensive nature of the terrain with an attention to detail only to be expected of one who had later studied the scene, although it is not certain that he ever visited Britain, even while his father-in-law was governor.

> . . . all things about the place chosen for the battle, entrances, approaches, and exits, were favorable to the defenders and rough on the attacking Romans; the hills were steep and wherever the slope eased, Caractacus constructed stone ramparts. In front of the position ran a river, barely fordable; squads of armed fighting men were in position in front of the defenses.

But even so formidable a position, maintained by desperate men courageously led, could not withstand the assault of the legions led by Scapula. Surmounting one obstacle after another, they drove in on the swarming, disorganized Britons, killing or disabling those their swords would reach, putting the balance to flight. Caractacus barely escaped, at the cost of leaving his brothers, wife, and daughters to be captured in the aftermath of the battle. Perhaps his reputation for personal bravery derived largely from his own oratorical praise of it. With a small group of followers, doubtless as anxious as he to put space between them and the terrible Romans, he fled to the Brigantes and sought the protection of the Queen Cartimandua. But this lady had already learned the sharp lesson that her own position vis-à-vis her unruly relatives depended on Roman support. Further, she had a right to suspect that they would take an exceedingly jaundiced view of an ally by treaty harboring a fugitive from their vengeance. With or without prior consultation with Scapula, she had Caractacus put in chains and turned over to the Roman detachment sent to expedite his delivery as a prisoner of state to Rome.

There, according to Tacitus, he delivered a stately and possibly apocryphal plea before Claudius who, either delighted with his insolence, as the story would indicate, or perhaps merely apathetic, spared him from execution, restored him his family, and arranged for them to live out their lives in permanent exile from Britain.

The victory and the subsequent capture of Caractacus were duly acknowledged by award of triumphal ornaments to Scapula.

6

IN THE meantime construction of the capital city of Camulodunum went forward.

Roman civilization, like that of the Greeks, was essentially urban. Its leaders planned that in every district of the Empire a town would be the center to which nearby farmers could bring their produce, meet and exchange news or gossip as inclination determined. This town would house the local government, maintain the district records, shelter merchants and small industry, possess one or more temples for the spiritual edification of the neighborhood and baths for cleanliness and conversation. Its planners established a water system, saw to the construction and maintenance of a road system, and always built a *mansio,* or guest house, with attached stables, for the shelter of visiting officials from the central government and the always urgent relays of the imperial courier system.

Similarly each province required a capital. Since Britain, before the coming of Rome, had none of these centers, or indeed any conception of urban living, it was necessary to provide a truly magnificent example in the provincial capital which could then be copied in the cantonal districts—on a smaller scale surely, but still in all essentials a Roman *urbs.*

There were many reasons, all excellent, which at the time blurred the superior geographical position of Londinium in settling on Camulodunum. The site was north of the Thames, therefore not separated by that river barrier from the larger portion of the island to the north and west. It was on a tidal and, for the ships of the time, navigable river, the Colne, in contact with the continental ports, from which it could be supplied or, *in extremis,* to which the Roman officialdom could be evacuated. It was far out on a peninsula which permitted successive lines of defense, the last the massive earthworks of the old British settlement. Finally, because of its former prestige as the city of Cunobelinus, it was assumed that Britons would see in it a sense of continuity and of power.

To provide both population and added security it would also be designated a colonia, where veterans of the legions, on retirement, would receive the plots of ground on which they could raise their families in quiet peace yet be available as already-trained reserves in the event of trouble.

So the Roman engineers laid out inside the old ramparts a rectangular area of 108 acres, with streets crossing each other at right angles. At the center of the town a spacious *forum* was designed, to be dominated by a stately temple, in the Graeco-Roman architectural manner, dedicated to Rome and Augustus.

This cult, identifying religion with patriotism, had been established, complete with an honorary priesthood, the *Augustales,* by Augustus when he was searching every medium to induce in his heterogeneous subjects the concept of a unified nation. Without shouldering aside the old gods of Rome, indeed permitting and encouraging their identification with local deities, he saw the imperative need to establish the numen, the everlasting spirit of *Roma Invicta,* in the minds of men.

The projected temple was therefore less a cathedral of divine worship in the medieval or modern sense than a shrine of exalted patriotism and national pride, comparable perhaps to the Lincoln Memorial in Washington.

Construction of the town and public buildings began about 50 A.D. As soon as the homesteads were laid out, veterans, honorably discharged from the legions, began moving in. The Colonia Victricensis Camulodoni (to give its official name) soon became a center of frenetic activity. Because the arts connected with the proposed construction were new to Britain, and a heavy strain on the specialist engineers and technicians of the legions, architects, masons, stone-carvers, plumbers (workers in lead), sculptors, and artisans expert in another dozen trades were imported from the continent. Many were to finish out their lives in this corner of a distant land.

It can scarcely be expected that all this activity was received with enthusiasm by the local Trinovantes. Many, wedded to their old customs and unbridled liberty, may have hoped that the Romans this time, as with Caesar, would eventually go away. The projects and work at Camulodunum clearly indicated that in their own opinion, at least, the Romans had come to stay.

As the city was laid out, on confiscated land, further, fertile stretches were more or less rudely taken from their native possessors and awarded to the legions. These dispossessions might have been borne, however resented. But the added indignity of requisitioned labor not only for the unskilled work of building the capital but for road construction shockingly violated British principles and beliefs on the nature of work. What little hard labor their former life had required, aside from agriculture, had been done by slaves. In the Roman requisitions of manpower they at last saw their servitude. The tribal resentment festered in ugly silence, awaiting opportunity for explosion.

While the building of Camulodunum proceeded apace, the Silures of South Wales had recovered from their defeat under Caractacus and resumed their predatory activities.

Tacitus tells of Roman cohorts surrounded and suddenly attacked, rescued only after heavy losses in officers and men; of ambushes cleverly laid against patrols; and of raids into the Province itself; which forced Scapula, already in poor health, to turn his attention again to the west.

The Governor had about come to the conclusion that total extermination of the Silures was a necessary preamble to peace in the area. The statement, somehow reaching the Silures' chieftains, served only to increase the fury and frequency of their attacks. The loss of two entire cohorts sent on a foraging expedition proved the last blow the gallant but weary Scapula could sustain. Overcome by directing that most frustrating of all kinds of war—the use of organized formations against hit-and-run guerrillas—he could no longer drive a mind and body worn out in the service of Rome. His death was a matter of rejoicing around the perimeter of the province, and may indeed have brought delight to many factions within.

Claudius in Rome acted as promptly as the news reached him to appoint and dispatch a successor.

7

AULUS DIDIUS GALLUS was already well along in years when he reached Britain to assume the governorship. Behind him was a long and honorable career. He had been *Curator Aquarum,* director of the water supply, in 40 A.D., during the reign of Caligula. In 50 A.D., about the same time that Ostorius Scapula was serving in Britain, Gallus, as governor of Moesia (that part of Bulgaria south of the lower reaches of the Danube) had conducted himself with great credit in a complex struggle involving Mithridates of Bosporus, a kingdom stretching along the north shore of the Black Sea and including the Crimea. In the course of his operations, his lieutenants moved to within three days' march of the Don River mouth, procured the submission to Caesar of one Zorzines (a prince of the Siraci, who appear to have lived in the windswept area between the Caspian and the Sea of Azov), and compelled Mithridates to surrender.

From what little we know of this campaign, reinforced by his conduct in Britain, we catch a glimpse of an emerging type of Roman officer, a cool, planning sort of general, seldom himself engaging in combat, but always directing his lieutenants and staff with the threads of the campaign controlled in his firm, objective mind.

He appears to have held his post in Britain for about five years. His maturity and judgment found expression in the steady, methodical consolidation of the provincial defenses along the river line, after he had acted energetically to restore discipline and order in the legions which apparently had become somewhat demoralized in the interval between the death of Scapula and the arrival of Gallus. We hear of one legion—probably the Fourteenth—under a Manlius Valens being roundly defeated by the Silures just prior to his coming. Even a minor reverse of a legion, depending for much of its aura of terror on its reputation for invincibility, was an event Gallus could not permit to pass unavenged. He quickly took measures which effectively stopped the marauding tactics of the Silures and made wholly secure the valley of the lower Severn.

Hardly was the frontier threat settled when new trouble broke out in the territory of the allied Brigantes. The ringleader was one Venutius, the banished husband of Cartimandua the queen. Apparently taking his dismissal from favor with bad sportsmanship if not ill grace, Venutius gathered some associated malcontents of the tribe and attacked Cartimandua's fortress village. Gallus intervened by sending some cohorts of the Twentieth Legion to rescue the Queen and to restore order. These Venutius had the hardihood to attack too. That gesture brought out the whole legion, under command of Caesius Nasica. The result was quick and inevitable. Venutius and his band were defeated and he himself captured. Brought before Gallus he had every right to expect death. But Gallus acted the part of statesman and peacemaker, arranged with Cartimandua to re-store Venutius to his half of the Brigantian throne, and contented himself with warning both that further family quarrels leading to breaches of the Roman Peace would be looked on with extreme dis-favor.

While these matters were occupying Gallus, back in Rome, in 54 A.D., the Emperor Claudius died at the age of sixty-four, accord-ing to Suetonius, from eating a dish of poisoned mushrooms served him by his turbulent and strong-minded wife, Agrippina. She was also his niece, which may have complicated the situation, but does not explain the poisoned mushrooms. Her son, by an earlier mar-riage, was first given the name Lucius Domitius Ahenobarbus, but after adoption by Claudius in 50 A.D., he changed it to Nero Claudius Caesar Drusus Germanicus, later taking lethal exception to anyone so rash as to recall his former name. He was seventeen years old when, by his mother's contrivance, he succeeded Claudius as Emperor.

Doubtless the affairs of Britain were of little consequence among so much sudden glory. In any event, Didius Gallus was graciously, or by default, permitted to retain his governorship for a time and to devote his declining years to the arduous task of advancing Roman civilization and power in the distant island.

Camulodunum was now a handsome Roman city of decent streets and wide main avenues. Inside scaffolding the stately columns, with their Corinthian capitals, were being put in place on enormous vaulted foundations of the temple to Rome and Augustus. The Forum and Basilica were nearly finished.

Other towns were growing into prominence. Thirty miles north of Londinium came into being Verulamium (St. Albans)—at first two strings of shops and hovels clustered along Watling Street. Londinium itself was growing rapidly, fed by the convergence of its access to the sea with the ever radiating roadnet. Each year more cargoes from the Channel ports were landed on its Thames foreshore, and more and more ships departed on the return voyage laden with the export items of Britain. Rutupiae, the original landing area of Aulus Plautius and his two legions, on the tidewater separating the Isle of Thanet from the mainland, was being developed into a major supply base and receiving station for military stores and personnel. Lindum and Glevum, originally legionary outposts, grew into towns and were later designated coloniae with the growing need for settle-

ment farms for retired legionaries of the Ninth and Second respectively. Both these coloniae were small in comparison to that established at Camulodunum. Each was forty acres in extent, and both
were laid out on the same identical plan. Probably the legionary engineers saw no reason to make two sets of plans where one would suf-
fice.

So time passed in Britain until in late 57 or early 58 A.D. an
imperial rescript arrived from Rome, issued in the name of Nero,
announcing the honorable relief of Didius Gallus and the imminent
arrival of his successor, Quintus Veranius Nepos.

8

THE HARD-WORKING ambitious Roman who took over from Didius
Gallus, bearing on his letter of appointment the resounding title of
Legatus Augusti pro praetore in Britannia Provincia, was the son of
that Quintus Veranius Nepos who, in 18 A.D. under Tiberius, organized for Rome the province of Cappadocia in Asia Minor. The father
was a friend and subordinate of Germanicus, commander-in-chief in
the East, and in 20 A.D. played a prominent part in the prosecution of
Calpurnius Piso on the charge of having poisoned Germanicus.

Veranius the son, the new governor of Britain, was born probably
about 12 A.D. and was therefore on entering his new province some
forty-six years of age. In view of the fact that the family was plebeian,
both his father's record and his own indicate the opportunities for
high distinction opening up to men of ability without the head start
of aristocratic birth so generally a requirement in the old days of
the Republic.

Veranius the Younger seems to have been early selected for advancement, holding as his first qualifying post that of *Triumvir
monetalis*—one of the three directors of the mint—and moving rapidly on to his first military duty as one of the tribunes on the staff of
the commander of Legio IV Scythica then stationed in Moesia.

In 37 A.D. he was named *quaestor* on the Emperor's personal
staff, and in 41 A.D. with the obvious support of Caligula stood for
and was elected one of the tribunes of the plebs—by this time a
wholly honorary office. The next year, 42 A.D., saw him elected

praetor for a term of one year which at its end made him eligible for his first command of a legion. After three years in command of a legion he was named governor of Lycia, a province of Asia Minor organized under Claudius in 43 A.D. In 49 A.D. he was advanced to the consulship in Rome, a necessary precursor to eligibility for the highest gubernatorial appointments within the gift of the Emperor.

Like his immediate predecessors and those who followed him shortly in the governorship of Britain, he seems to have been a serious, hard-working public servant, both administrator and soldier— *magna severitatis fama*—whose military prowess was sufficiently established so that Onosander, writing about the time of Veranius' consulship, dedicated his famous and extant work on tactics, *Strategikos Logos,* to him. Whatever friendship or politics went into such an honor, it could hardly have been taken seriously unless Veranius were widely acclaimed as one of the outstanding generals of his time.

The selection of this active soldier at the height of his powers suggests that perhaps in the minds of Nero and his advisors the time had come again to take the offensive in Britain and proceed by successive steps to the conquest of the entire island.

Once satisfied with the combat readiness of his legions, Veranius opened operations against the Silures in South Wales, thus initiating the work his successor was to carry on against the Deceangli and Ordovices of Flintshire and Denbighshire in North Wales. There are suggestions that he planned in the customary three years of his appointment to conquer, if not the entire island—of the whole extent of which he was probably unaware—at least that portion up to the narrow waist between the Firths of Clyde and Forth which had to wait for absorption into the Province for the later coming of Julius Agricola.

Whatever his hopes and plans, he died, as he had lived, in the harness of Rome after little more than a year in office. He does not seem to have been killed in battle but to have succumbed to sickness of one sort or another. Perhaps he was the victim of too long campaigning in softer climes, disarming an otherwise sturdy physique against the suffering, then as now, of a normal English winter.

Within the limits of the Province, the adjustment of the inhabitants to the customs and restraints of a civilized life was far from complete. Tribes whose excitements and luxuries had been derived in large part by raiding their neighbors looked with understandable resentment, if not plain disbelief, on the Roman requirement to stop fighting and stealing, obey the complex Ius Gentium, and stick under pain of punishment to the few ways open to them of earning taxes first and a living after.

Among the ruling groups of the various tribes the demands of the tribute, for the tribal collection of which they were held responsible in both money and in kind, strained notions of economy derived from simpler times. To meet the demands made upon them by the procurator and his agents they had recourse to eager financiers who flocked to Britain from Gaul and Italy willing to loan hard cash on the security of land. Since land tenure and ownership in Celtic tradition were wholly at variance with the legalisms of the Roman law of property, it is conceivable that many a mortgage on tribal lands was given by a chieftain hard pressed for cash without any clear idea of the engagement he was entering. Nero's teacher, Seneca, whose philosophic ideals and exemplary writings exceeded by a wide margin his conduct, invested through agents several million sesterces in British loans. Interest was high, seldom less than 12, in most cases nearer 20 per cent. The burden on the financially naïve Britons was real and onerous.

Nevertheless, or perhaps by connected causation, trade was increasing by steady steps. The over-all standard of living was rising in the modern sense that the luxury of yesterday became the necessity of tomorrow. People lived in greater security, free both from the marauding of their neighbors and from the temptation to engage in similar nocturnal amusements on their own account. Slowly a grasp of the benefits, if not of the responsibilities, of order under law was permeating the consciousness of rich and poor alike.

The acreage of tillable land was increased by methodical forest-clearing and in some areas extensively by the drainage work of Roman engineers performed in connection with road-building. Roman agricultural methods, measurably superior to those in use before their coming, increased the yields of field and pasture. A ready market existed, in the appetites of the legionaries, for the surplus grain so raised and reaped.

As the network of Roman roads grew and spread, people moved about to a degree never before known, with the result that tribal isolations were steadily broken down, allowing a widening social intercourse and dissemination of Roman ideas. Yet the Province was restive, restrained from active protest only by the demonstrated hopelessness of challenging the legions.

It was seventeen years since Plautius had landed, offering a new and better way of life on the point of his Spanish short sword. But along with what the Britons had learned, perforce, from Rome, the nostalgia remained for a lost freedom untouched by any sense of responsibility, a liberty all scorn for an order based on much work and no play. On the surface, in the bustling ports, in villages and towns bursting with new activity, on the wide-reaching roads carrying the rumble of market carts as well as the stamp of patrolling cohorts, the Province was at peace. But underneath, Celtic intractibility seethed like an animal just learning the restrictions of his cage.

And across the frontier, watching from thicket and mountain aerie the patrolling auxiliaries, listening to the morning and evening calls of *bucina* and *tuba* rising with the kitchen smoke from legionary fortresses, half-savage Celts, still unconquered, wholly unimpressed with Roman might, bided the time they knew would come.

V

THE GREAT REVOLT
61 A.D.

The Romans who have crossed the sea are but a
handful, if the Britons count their own numbers . . .
—TACITUS, *Agricola*

1

THE UNTIMELY DEATH OF VERANIUS DID
not alter the settled imperial policy to extend the conquest of Britain beyond the then existing frontier. The
problem before Nero's advisors was to find a general
with the necessary energy and aggressiveness. Their
choice, quickly made and approved by Nero, settled on
Caius Suetonius Paulinus, a soldier already distinguished by initiative, drive, and intense combat tenacity.

About the time when the first units of Claudius' troops were
landing in Britain, Paulinus became famous for having led a military expedition into Mauretania, crossed the Atlas Mountains, and
so pacified the country that Claudius was able to organize it into two
provinces—Mauretania Caesariensis and farther west, rounding down
the Atlantic coast, Mauretania Tingitana named after its capital city,
Tingis, the modern and stenchful Tangier. The efficiency and dispatch
with which Paulinus conducted this conquest marked him, its architect, for increased honors and responsibilities. By the time of his
appointment to Britain in 59 A.D. Paulinus' reputation for successful
generalship was second only to that of the fabulous Domitius Corbulo, the hero of victorious campaigns in Germany and Parthia, the
military darling of the Roman people.

Since gossip moves faster than man, Paulinus' reputation had preceded him to Britain. The legions, thoroughly disciplined and brought to combat pitch by Veranius, could surely expect a new call to action. The Celtic inhabitants, pro-Roman or sourly intransigent, could only wonder and wait.

We know little of Paulinus the man and soldier save what can be deduced from his deeds, both of commission and omission. The picture adds up to that of a professional soldier in his mid-fifties, singularly uncomplex, incorruptible, a stern disciplinarian, supremely confident of his ability to handle any situation by military means; but one distrustful of statecraft and bored by the chores of civil administration. It is a temperament that both created his difficulties and rescued him from their consequences.

His first eighteen months in Britain seem to have passed in the routine if exacting duties of a governor just arrived, getting his feet on the ground: at his desk in the newly built Praetorium in Camulodunum, bored and inattentive to the reports on civil matters— the state of the revenue, the progress of road-building, extra costs involved in the still uncompleted temple, labor requisitions and crop prospects—as laid before him by the procurator, Catus Decianus; touring the different legionary posts, inspecting the troops with a critical eye that missed little; and always on the move, from one place to another at a gallop, half a cavalry cohort ahead, half behind, over routes that were well paved, enduring Roman-built road at one stretch, slimy morass and peat bog, or rugged mountain trail, the next. And through it all, his mind was fixed on a distant campaign, required by imperial policy at home.

2

As a general rule, both in the expanding Republic and in the stabilized Empire, complete tolerance of the religious beliefs of subject peoples was taken for granted. So obvious to all Romans was this principle—with the possible exception of the two Catos to whom all things foreign were *ipso facto* subversive—that it was hardly ever called into question.

Only when a religion could be identified with doubtful loyalty to the State, or found to be a center of agitation against Rome, did it attract unfavorable attention from the authorities. This had happened to Judaism. The growing Christian sect was already at this time under suspicion of subversion, and in the northwest provinces the Celtic cult of Druidism, for identical reasons, had long been anathema.

Perhaps the mystery attaching to the forest rites of the Druids caused them to appear, in the eyes of Augustus and his successors, a menace more grave than mere barbarian superstition. Julius Caesar, the first of the Roman conquerors to come in direct contact with their practices and fanatic faith, thought they sacrificed human beings to the spirits of their war casualties. It may have been true. In any case, the Romans believed it and looked on druidical practices as horrible barbarian vestiges surviving in a civilized day. What seems certain, and probably adequate explanation of the reaction of the Romans, was that the Druid clergy as a whole fiercely resented and constantly opposed the advance into the Celtic world of Roman culture and civilization. Had the Druids come to terms with Rome it is wholly possible that their beliefs, worship, and faith, like those of the mystery cults of Greece and Asia, like the adoration of Egyptian Isis, might have become not only tolerated but fashionable in the cosmopolitan capital.

Augustus confined himself to prohibiting the celebration of druidical rites in Italy, leaving the Gallic provinces relatively free in their beliefs. Tiberius went further, doing his best to stamp out the religion in Gaul, possibly because he was convinced its votaries had instigated the serious revolt of the Aedui during his reign.

It was left for Claudius to forbid throughout the Empire the Druid practices and rites and to proceed, as circumstances permitted, to wipe out the cult with fire and sword. One result of his efforts was a continuous migration of Druid clergy and true believers from Gaul to their co-believers in Britain. Finding small welcome in the Roman Pale they were slowly driven to concentrate at their most holy of holies, the sacred oak groves and mysterious shrines of the island of Mona, now Anglesey, separated by the narrow Menai Strait from northwest Wales.

It can be inferred from Paulinus' first and daring campaign that the total suppression of Druid centers of subversion in Britain had been given a high priority by the Imperial policy-makers.

3

PRIORITY or not, there was much to do first. The tribes of Wales were still restive. The Silures in the south, undaunted by their many reverses, and the Ordovices in the north made no secret of their determination to resist the blessings of civilization. North of the provincial frontier, the Brigantes had still to be watched. In order both to cover the western flank of the Brigantes and to secure an advance base toward the Ordovices and the Druid shrines of Mona Island, Paulinus moved up Legio XX Valeria from its probable temporary base at Viroconium on the Severn to Deva, now Chester, on the Dee River.

The problems of Wales and the planning of the dangerous campaign to Mona may well have occupied Paulinus to a point where his temperamental distaste for civil administration led him to leave those matters, probably with a minimum of supervision, to his procurator, Catus Decianus.

There were others reasons of a more subtle kind to induce the Governor to leave Decianus much untrammeled. The Procurator, although nominally under the control of the Governor, was appointed by the Treasury back in Rome and possessed an independent channel of communication which through the Treasury could reach the Emperor. This semi-independence would suggest to any governor caution in handling his procurator, or indeed in too closely questioning the latter's official acts.

Decianus, too, had his responsibilities. One was the completion of the public buildings of the capital, the Temple to Rome and Augustus, the basilica, theater, and public baths. To complete these projects heavy drafts of labor and materials fell on the conquered Trinovantes —once the wards of Caesar. The collection of taxes, in money and in kind; above all, the rigorous enforcement of Roman law over actions left previously to individual inclination, or at most to the gruff command of a tribal king, operated on the turbulent Celts in a most unpleasantly restraining way. Under these combined lashes, administered and enforced with no modern notions of liberalism, disaffection smoldered among the Trinovantes.

Of themselves, these grievances might not have surged into violence. A spark was needed, which Decianus, in avarice wedded to stupidity, proceeded to supply.

North of the territory of the Trinovantes, holding most of what is now Norfolk with parts of Suffolk and Cambridgeshire, the powerful and populous Iceni, under their king Prasutigas, had remained loyal to their treaty of alliance with Rome, and were consequently beyond reach, except for a reasonable annual tribute, of the Roman tax-gatherers working under Decianus. Then in the winter of 60–61 A.D. Prasutigas died, leaving a widow, Boudicca—later romantically transformed to Boadicea—and two daughters.

Since the succession to his empty throne rested on the acquiescence of the Emperor in Rome, Prasutigas, perhaps to insure fair treatment for his people, left a will which divided his relatively great kingly wealth, much of it in lands and cattle, half to Nero and one-quarter to each of his two daughters. Boudicca received nothing, whether as the result of some intermarital animosity or according to normal Celtic custom does not appear.

Accretions to the Imperial Fiscus resulting from the testamentary dispositions of client kings were a matter of solid interest to Treasury officials back in Rome. The handling, transfer, and conversion of the imperial legacy into cash were all matters of intense interest to Roman traders, bankers, and land speculators on the spot. Decianus, as administrator, could also expect to benefit.

Driven perhaps as much by fear of censure in Rome for lack of thoroughness as by personal greed, Decianus proceeded ruthlessly to consolidate and list the legacy as a prelude to the conversion into money of the Emperor's portion. Since the estate consisted largely of land, livestock, and slaves, of personal possessions and little hard cash, conversion was necessarily slow.

In the process Decianus discovered that when Prasutigas allied himself with Rome, perhaps in an effort to carry his nobles along with him he had made various grants, mostly land, to his barons, being careful to list his grants in the treaty and have it accepted by Claudius. These grants, standing for some fifteen years, Decianus summarily revoked—an action hardly calculated to increase respect for Roman justice among these influential leaders of the kingless Iceni, however much it may have enhanced their understanding of Roman avarice.

Decianus further compounded the growing rage of the Iceni by informing the family and relatives of the deceased Prasutigas that they were to be held personally responsible for the full payment of the imperial legacy. When understandable delay occurred, Decianus took matters in his own hands and started offering properties for sale. The result was a descent on the Iceni lands, houses, cattle, and goods of a horde of Roman and Gallic traders, loan sharks, and even veterans, looking for auction bargains.

The outraged Iceni might have appealed to Paulinus. There is no evidence one way or the other, beyond his known personal integrity, that he would or could have overruled his grasping, tactless procurator. But Paulinus' long-laid plans for the conquest of Mona were at last complete. Even as Boudicca's angry protests were answered by a scourging, and by the rape of her two daughters—assailants unknown—Paulinus, accompanied by the Fourteenth Legion had already moved beyond his advanced base at Deva into the fastnesses of North Wales.

Beside him rode his aide,* a young tribune of aristocratic Gallic lineage and high ability named Julius Agricola.

4

IT COULD NOT have been easy progress. There was undoubtedly a track of sorts, worn by many centuries of Druid pilgrimages, a track caught between the sea on the right and lonely, wild, and forbidding mountains on the left. Two rivers, the Clwyd and the Conway, had to be crossed, together with lesser streams. The mountains, coming often close to the sea, provided many ravines out of which at any moment the fighting Ordovices might pour on the column. Over all was that air of brooding mystery, half foreboding, half the menacing presence of sullen Celtic gods which even two thousand years later still pervades these mist-filled hills and glens.

We can only estimate how many days were consumed in the march from Chester to the Menai Strait at present-day Bangor. The distance was about sixty miles, today a little more than an hour in a good car over a well-paved road. But in 61 A.D. when all around was enemy territory, when the road at best was a track, it was a dif-

---

* Tacitus (*Agricola,* v) uses the word *contubernio*—literally "tent companion"—best rendered as "aide-de-camp" here.

ferent matter. Allowing for frequent halts of the column while scout patrols fanned out ahead, around cliff faces and up ravines; for the times when the legion was called by sharp sudden blasts of the tuba to form line of battle against some alarm or attempted attack; for the imperative necessity of stopping early enough in the afternoon to construct a camp before darkness brought mystery and danger to the rampart's edge; for the protection of the slow-moving pack train carrying grain, fodder, lard, and perhaps some water essential to progress through this embittered desolate land; twelve Roman miles a day seems a reasonable estimate of progress. Paulinus and the Fourteenth might well have been a full week traversing the shoreline before reaching the strait.

Once opposite Mona, a day or even two was the minimum spent in construction of a base camp, in building boats and rafts to carry the infantry, and in reconnoitering for shallows in the strait by which the cavalry, at low tide, could cross. There was therefore no hope of surprise.

Tacitus gives so vivid a description of the crossing and assault that it appears likely he could have obtained the details only from an eye-witness—in all probability Agricola, Paulinus' young aide, later to become the historian's father-in-law.

The Druid priests and their thousands of followers, many refugees from Roman vengeance in Gaul, lined the shore awaiting the attack. While waiting, the fanatic, unyielding clergy called down the curses of their gods upon the impious Romans and in every possible way exhorted their faithful to that pitch of religious frenzy which multiplies bravery by disdain for life.

Paulinus' assault, in boats and on rafts, carried its own desperation. Over-water operations where no surprise is possible necessarily expose boatloads of men, momentarily helpless, to the full threat of shore-launched weapons. In terms of the distances effective at the time, the last fifty yards into the beaches of Mona may well have been for the legionaries a fearful test of stamina and morale.

But stamina and morale were what they had. Not for nothing had passed the endless days of training, the daily indoctrination in swift obedience to orders. This Fourteenth Legion was a fighting unit, brought to a high pitch by the alertness earned in the intermittent but often sudden guerrilla warfare to which it had for so long been subjected.

As Tacitus tells the story, the legionaries shrank instinctively back from the frenzied defenders, many of them women. This howling disorganized mob, waiting to thrust and hack and kill before they themselves were killed, presented no hope of easy victory. One does not have to be a child of twenty centuries ago to understand why the legionaries hesitated, nor how, recalled to duty, they obeyed the shouted orders of their officers and splashed ashore.

The issue was not long in doubt. The disorganized Druids simply could not stand against the firm discipline and proved tactics of the legion, tightly controlled by Paulinus. Once the foothold on the beach was gained, the troops swept across the island, slaughtering all they could find. Men, Druid priests, women, children, all were hunted down and killed without mercy.

Somewhere in the deep recesses of the oak groves, where the spreading branches were festooned with the sacred mistletoe, the Romans found the holy shrines of Druidism. The shrines they overturned, often enough on top of the slain defenders. The oaks they cut down or fired, watching with a kind of tired exaltation the end of superstition. For these men the only true gods were Jupiter Capitolinus, Greatest and Best; Mars the Avenger; the Bona Dea; the gods of Rome Eternal who had proved over seven centuries they could protect their own.

Paulinus had a right to savor for a moment the sweet, familiar taste of victory. Once again Roman troops under skilled leadership had proved their invincibility. But even as he sat his sweating horse, even as he received reports of the few Roman casualties, even as he issued orders for securing the island, a courier, fearing the dark and unknown trail, with only the sea on his right to guide him, was on his way from Deva with tidings of utter catastrophe.

5

THE ICENI had risen. Stung to desperation by the exactions of Decianus, fired by the exhortations of the indignant Boudicca, they had taken to arms. The Trinovantes, nursing their own grievances, had seen their opportunity and joined them. Gathering between the two tribes a force of about seventy thousand fighting men, they had taken and sacked Camulodunum, put all Romans and Roman sympathizers to death, often with barbaric cruelties, fired the town, and destroyed among the other public and private buildings the superstructure of the great temple. Its massive foundations of vaulted brick remained intact to provide, a thousand years later, the base for a Norman castle.

The destruction of the capital city had not been accomplished by the rebels without resistance. Hearing of the march on the city, Decianus, the procurator, gathered together what auxiliaries he could —about 200—and sent them to Camulodunum, there to be slaughtered in the final massacre. The Ninth Legion at Lindum Colonia had started south once the news reached its commander, Petilius Cerealis, an officer of whom we shall hear again. But from Lindum to Camulodunum was about 110 miles at a minimum, and longer by road. By the time Cerealis made contact with the insurgents, they had been able to gather fighting strength and fury. Overwhelmed, Cerealis was forced to retreat as hastily as might be to his fortress at Lindum. In the initial contact and later rear-guard actions he lost about 2,000 men, or one-third of his infantry strength.

Decianus, probably in Londinium, heard of the destruction of Camulodunum and decided all was lost. With unseemly haste, and surely as much of the treasury cash as he could quickly gather and transport, he fled to Rutupiae, took ship to the continent, and disappeared from history.

Probably but fragments of this information could have reached Paulinus at Mona. But there was enough to make clear that the settled part of the province was defenseless before the rebels.

The horrifying intelligence may have pricked Paulinus to an examination of his own responsibility for its occurrence. He had, obviously, overestimated the tranquillity of the Province. He had ignored, or tacitly approved, the brutality with which his procurator had gone about his exactions. In overconfidence he had denuded the Province of its ready reserve to carry out a remote and insignificant campaign against Mona. Whether or not these thoughts crossed his mind, he could not escape ultimate responsibility. No imperial governor could survive the loss of his province. The alternatives were clear. He must retrieve the situation, however desperate it might be, or die, if not in battle, by his own hand.

Reading the taut lines of Tacitus, we know only that Paulinus reacted with furious energy and decision. But the considerations of time and distance, of forces available, which he had to weigh are obvious. First, he himself, with the Fourteenth Legion was on Mona Island, 60 miles from Deva where the Twentieth, in combat readiness, backed up and protected his line of communications. Beyond Deva to Verulamium (by the not yet completed road to be known centuries later as Watling Street) was another 160 miles. The two legions at hand could not make the march in under two weeks.

Second, if he did not know then he was soon to discover that the bloody reverse visited on the Ninth Legion had so drastically reduced the combat effectiveness of that unit as to remove it from serious employment.

Third, there was Legio II Augusta, at Glevum, 80 miles south of the road junction where the Fosse Way crossed Watling Street.† The legion commander of the Second was away and the legion temporarily under the command not of a fighting general but of the praefectus castra, a promoted centurion named Poenius Posthumus. This, however, could not have worried Paulinus. Even a praefectus castra obeyed urgent orders.

If he could concentrate these three legions he would have a fighting force of about 18,000 infantry, supported by cavalry auxiliaries. The enemy strength was reported at 70,000. But they were not Roman soldiers. The Province was not yet lost; the issue still in doubt. But now time was of the essence and Paulinus could not wait for the legions to assemble. Giving the necessary orders, to be passed on to the Twentieth at Deva and to the Second at Glevum, Paulinus, with a cavalry escort, started for Verulamium and Londinium. So quickly did Paulinus and his cavalry move that before the Iceni and Trinovantes had turned from their pursuit of Cerealis toward the attractions of booty and slaughter in Verulamium and Londinium, Paulinus had reached the latter town. It would be interesting to know how long the haste-pressed journey took, over incomplete roads, through the territories of tribes if not yet hostile surely expectant, and in the last stages through areas where bands of the triumphant insurgents marauded at will. Without foundering the horses it could scarcely have been completed under six days, with no allowance for delays.

He found Londinium crowded with refugees and in a state of total panic. In the eighteen years since invasion, overconfidence

---

† At Venonae (High Cross), 12 miles SSW of Ratae Coritanorum (Leicester) and 66 miles NNW of Verulamium (near St. Albans).

had let the Romans concentrate on building the various towns to the neglect of fortifications. Both Londinium and Verulamium were unwalled, defenseless.

The tales of the refugees, reciting both fact and rumor of the sack of Camulodunum, were hardly calculated to calm the townspeople. Tacitus, again brief, says only that the rebels neglected no item of barbaric savagery in their days of victory and vengeance. Dion Cassius is more brutally explicit.

With tales of horror circulating in Londinium the sudden appearance of Paulinus from out of the distant west must have carried hysterical relief to the citizens. They were in for a rude awakening. If Paulinus did not already know, a cursory inspection showed the town as indefensible. The fact was decisive. His legions were at best still a week away. In addition, to commit them to the defense of an unwalled city was madness. Even had the city possessed a reasonable posture of defense, to maintain it against a siege would deny him the opportunity of meeting the insurgents in the open, on terrain of his own choosing, where the infinitely superior tactics of the legions could be counted on to procure that total victory which alone would restore Roman rule to the Province. We may believe that the harsh logic of the facts was reinforced by the temperament of a commander heavily endowed with pugnacity, now fighting for his honor, his career, and his life.

The laconic announcement of his decision cannot have failed to be received by the population with stupefaction and horror. The remark attributed to him by Tacitus, that "the loss of one town would serve the general good," was hardly tactful reassurance to those whose lives and property were involved in the sacrifice. Nor can his offer to receive within his legionary lines any townspeople who wished to go with him have had any general acceptance.

The decision could not have been an easy one. There were political overtones. The population of Londinium included, because of the banking and commercial activities located there, more than the usual proportion of Roman citizens. In that far-off day the dignity and property, let alone the life, of a freeborn Roman citizen were a first charge on the protective forces of the Empire. The repercussions of his decision to abandon the city, stirred to calumny by the frenzy of relatives, friends, and business associates of the inhabitants, might well bring about the termination of his career in disgrace. But he could see clearly what subjectivity and military ignorance denied to the vision of the citizenry; that an attempt on his part to defend the city would, by losing the entire Province, merely postpone their fate.

So, doubtless advising the burghers to remember their Roman pride and to organize as well as they could their own defense, Paulinus and his escort rode off, north and west. Somewhere along Watling Street he encountered the advance guard of his hurrying legions. Wherever the meeting took place, a new shock awaited him. Legio II Augusta, from Glevum, was missing.

Over the ages, it is impossible to reconstruct the motives or fears that led the craven Poenius Posthumus so flagrantly to disobey orders the urgency of which must have been apparent. Even more mystifying is his apparent failure to foresee the fate of his one legion when the insurgents, having wiped out Paulinus and his force, should turn their victorious attention to him. But examples through history, not excluding wars fought in our own day, will suggest that a timorous commander readily finds rationalization for inaction.

The failure of the Second Legion to appear at the rendezvous deprived Paulinus of about one-third of the force he had counted on. He now had on hand, to redeem the Province and his own honor, the Fourteenth and Twentieth Legions together with a few thousand auxiliary cavalry—perhaps in all, some 15,000 fighting men.

While Paulinus with his depleted forces was moving cautiously east, the insurgents, led by a triumphant and awe-inspiring Boudicca, had taken and destroyed Londinium, putting all inhabitants to death with a repetition of the barbaric cruelties of Camulodunum. Leaving the once lively town a smoking charnel house, to remain a bed of ashes (often uncovered in modern times by workmen digging into foundations in London), Boudicca led her force, now swollen with long trains of oxcarts carrying the booty of two cities, against Verulamium. The result was similarly total and horrible. Tacitus says that in the three destroyed cities not less than 70,000 Roman citizens and pro-Roman Celts lost their lives. Men might well have despaired of Roman rule in Britain. But Paulinus was not among them.

Moving warily east behind screening cavalry patrols, Paulinus sought not only the swarming, plunder-laden enemy but also a terrain which would meet his requirements. There can be no reason to believe that Boudicca and her council did not as eagerly seek out

Rutupiae: First-Century Houses near the North Wall

Expedition against Mona and revolt of the Iceni, 61 A.D.

1. Suetonius Paulinus, with Legiones XIV and XX, moves northwest from Viroconium; XX remains at the forward marching camp at Deva (Chester), while Paulinus with XIV proceeds to Mona, which he takes by amphibious assault.

2. The Iceni, under Queen Boudicca, rise in revolt; they are joined by the Trinovantes.

3. Petilius Cerealis, commanding Legio IX, moves south from Lindum against the rebels; he is defeated with heavy losses and retreats to his fortress.

4. Paulinus, learning of the uprising, hastens southeast along Watling Street with XIV and XX; II Augusta disobeys orders to join and remains in its fortress at Glevum.

5. The rebels capture and burn Camulodunum, Londinium, and Verulamium, with nearly total slaughter of the inhabitants.

6. Paulinus, with two legions and auxiliaries, meets the rebels northwest of Verulamium and totally destroys them.

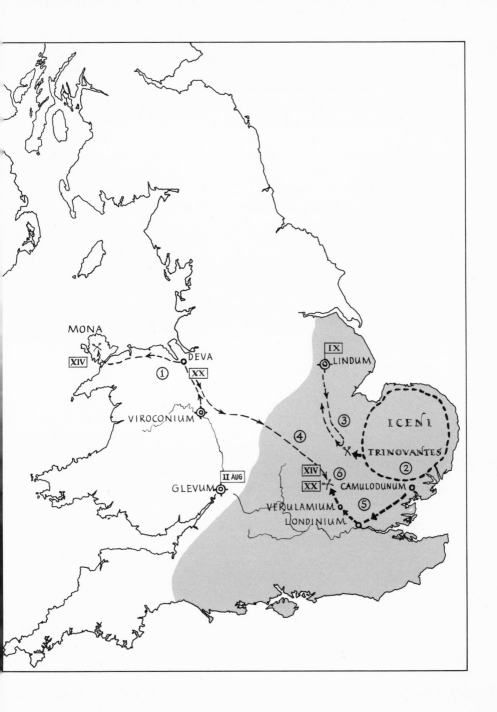

Rutupiae: The North Wall of "Richborough Castle," 85 A.D.

Maiden Castle: The Great Fortress of the Durotriges Stormed by Vespasian

the Governor and his remaining strength, for final success rested on his elimination. Once the Governor was defeated and dead the remaining troops at Lindum and the Second at Glevum—of whose defection the insurgents may not have known—would present no problem.

This conviction, which might or might not have been sound, rested on the fact that, years earlier, the loss of three legions at Teutoburg had sufficed to induce Augustus to give up the conquest of Germany. Surely the loss of an imperial legate and four legions, not to mention the destruction of three once flourishing towns in Britain, would have a similar chastening effect on Nero.

We do not know where the final encounter took place. Tacitus describes the location selected by Paulinus as a valley between rolling hills which protected his flanks, backed by a heavy forest in his rear, and in front an open plain suitable for the tactical maneuvering of his legions and cavalry.

To the insurgents, such a position might well have appeared but a trap for the Romans from which no retreat was possible. Boudicca's fighting Britons, swarming on the field behind their chieftains in war chariots, must have looked in amazement giving way to scorn and delight at the puny Roman force drawn up across the open ground. Behind the warriors came onto the far edge of the field the long, disorganized train of oxcarts carrying their women and children who, following Celtic and Germanic custom, accompanied their men to war. Each clumsy oxcart was additionally laden with such of the spoils and booty of three cities as the owner had been able to garner. This ring of oxcarts was to play an unforeseen role in the coming battle.

There may have been among the older, wiser heads of Boudicca's council an uneasy awareness of the turbulent lack of discipline in the force, of the nights of drunken revel following the destruction of the cities, of the ranting overconfidence, the boastful exuberance of their mercurial warriors. But any reservations or caution were lost in the general certainty of victory.

Meantime, the legions waited. We do not know how they were drawn up, save that following standard Roman practice the two legions would be side by side in line of battle, with the auxiliary cavalry stationed on both flanks. On the British side chieftains, wearing cloaks of deerhide and helmets into which bulls' horns had been affixed, moved among their tribesmen, driving the fighters away from their oxcarts and women, away from the drinking horns more than once that morning filled and emptied. By the combined processes of exhortation, pleading, and threat, a confused, wavering British line was formed, the foot soldiers falling in behind the plunging war chariots. With much shouting and braying of war trumpets the host moved forward against the last remnant of Roman power effective in Britain.

The Iceni and Trinovantes had had little share in challenging the conquest of eighteen years before. They had never suffered, as had the Welsh tribes and the Druids of Mona, the somber lesson taught by the legions in close combat. Even had they listened to the stories of veterans, survivors of the Catevellauni, who had followed Togodumnus and Caractacus to the Medway eighteen years before, had they been warned by those of the Durotriges who remembered the swath Vespasian and his Second Legion had cut through their country, the lessons could not have been learned, or put to use, in time.

Charging the Roman line, the inrushing Britons were met at close quarters by a deadly shower of spears, disabling their horses and throwing their ranks into confusion. Surviving so much, they were then confronted with the deadly formation of the cohort line, the *triplex acies*. The front line, charging with sword and shield, was only two men deep. The second and third lines of the cohort, holding the formation behind them, awaited the moment when the engaged front line began to tire. At a signal, the front line abruptly broke off action and dropped back, while the second line rushed forward to take its place. When the second line tired, the process was repeated by the third. In general, a Roman legionary fought at close quarters for not more than fifteen minutes before he was relieved by his replacement. The process was endlessly repeated so that the enemy foeman, brave and strong as he might be, fought on, meeting every quarter-hour a fresh, untired Roman, just as ferocious, just as ruthless in play of shield and sword as those before. Men had to be giants, and even more, thoroughly organized and disciplined giants, to withstand such an unending confrontation of fresh adversaries. Little wonder that fatigue induced despair, and despair the urge to flee while life remained.

As the legions by the use of this tactic bore relentlessly into the mass of Britons, the cavalry, through repeated charges and quick re-forming, broke up small nuclei of resistance on the flanks and prevented the flow of still-unengaged Britons toward the center. Slowly the rebels were thrown back on themselves, crowded into groups helpless for lack of room to wield their long Celtic swords. Too late they discovered that the ring of oxcarts, there to witness their final victory, was an obstacle to further retreat, a trap, self-cocked, waiting to spring against themselves.

No one, save possibly Paulinus, could have told when the battle ceased and the rout began, or later when the rout was stopped by the encircling wagon train and the slaughter of the trapped Britons began. No quarter was given. The legionaries knew well enough what atrocities these Celtic barbarians had perpetrated on the citizens of three Roman cities. They understood what would be their own fate had they been the conquered.

Somewhere in the final stages Boudicca disappeared, her chariot, early in the forefront of the battle, perhaps dragged off to temporary safety by her chieftains.

Tacitus says 80,000 Britons, men, women, and children, perished on this day of retribution. The number may be exaggerated, as many historians believe. However, since the insurgents constituted two populous tribes, and since families moved with the fighting men and were as ruthlessly cut down, the number given may not be too excessive. More to be questioned is Tacitus' statement that the Roman casualties suffered were a mere 400.

Sometime after the battle, word reached Paulinus of the death of Boudicca, either by her own hand or by her surviving escort eager to deny the pursuing Romans the satisfaction of her capture.

Another, distant casualty resulted from the battle. Across the island at Glevum, Poenius Posthumus, praefectus castra of the Second Legion, when word of the battle's outcome reached him, fell on his sword rather than face the fate surely in store at the hands of Paulinus.

6

FROM earliest times it had been unswerving Roman policy that military defeat must be avenged, and revolt cruelly, harshly, punished.

Paulinus, with his legions heavily reinforced by newly arrived replacements from the Rhine frontier, moved into the territory of the Iceni, laying waste farms and villages, confiscating livestock and property, seizing and selling into slavery all the inhabitants spared by his scouring soldiery. There is little doubt that his unrelenting rage, resting perhaps more than a little on his uneasy sense of his own personal responsibilty for the outbreak, would have depopulated the entire insurgent area if Rome itself had not called a halt.

The Imperial Fiscus had moved rapidly to fill the post of procurator, left vacant by the fleeing Decianus. The new incumbent was one Julius Classicianus,‡ of Cisalpine stock, married to the daughter of a Gallic chieftain who had played a major part in reconciling to Roman suzerainty his own tribe after a similar if less bloody revolt.

Shortly after assuming office, Classicianus seems to have protested to Rome against the too-merciless operations of Paulinus in the aftermath of victory. The protest, in Roman fashion, rested less on considerations of mercy and compassion than on the solidly pragmatic ground that a onetime rebel dead or sold into slavery would no longer pay taxes or earn tribute; and that the Province, if it were ever to become self-supporting, required a population to work its resources.

The Emperor's secretariat at Rome responded with that promptness which modern governments display when threatened with adverse effects upon the revenue. A prominent freedman of Nero's staff, a former Greek slave named Polycleitus, was sent to Britain to observe the situation and to make a decision in the name of the Emperor.

It happened that Polycleitus arrived at Gesoriacum on the Channel in time to cross to Britain on a ship carrying a draft of legionary replacements to Paulinus. Landing with them at Rutupiae, and treated with the ceremonies and honors appropriate to the Emperor's personal representative, he was mistaken by the defeated and demoralized Britons for a military commander in charge of the reinforcing contingent. If anything, the spectacle of an ex-slave commanding troops must have increased local amazement at Roman procedures.

‡ Parts of his tombstone, excavated in the City of London, are in the British Museum. The partial text reads, in translation: "To the Shades of C. Julius Fabius Alpinus Classicianus . . . Procurator of the Province of Britain . . . his sorrowing wife, Julia Pacata, daughter of Indus."

Perhaps the decision had already been made in Rome to remove Paulinus, and Polycleitus' diplomatic mission was to carry out the delicate task of conveying to Paulinus the notion that his military skill and undoubted pertinacity were more urgently required on other frontiers. In any event, Paulinus was relieved with honor and a new governor, Petronius Turpilianus, appointed to carry out the work of reconstruction.

There was, indeed, much to be done. Eighteen years of constructive work had been destroyed. If we can accept contemporary estimates, it would appear that nearly 150,000 on both sides had perished in the course of the insurrection—perhaps as much as 30 per cent of the province's population. In addition, trade and commerce had been rudely disrupted and a heavy blow dealt to the confidence of investors.

The surviving Iceni and Trinovantes were sullen, fearful, and nursing in abject terror the wounds inflicted by the flaying hand of Paulinus. The border tribes—the Silures and Ordovices in Wales, the powerful Brigantes in the Midlands—although escaping the consequences of the revolt, possibly because it was put down before they had time to join it, were apprehensive of the future, fearful of new and harsh restrictions on their liberties.

Beyond their borders other tribes, as yet untouched by Rome, heard in the harsh poetic Gaelic of their storytellers the tragic tale and pondered ways and means of succeeding where Boudicca and the Iceni had failed.

Nevertheless, the rule of Rome in the island was confirmed. The forced participation of the Britons in the great body of Western civilization, under the law and order imposed by Rome, was assured. Paulinus, for all his faults, had met and overcome a stupendous challenge. In so doing, he had set the course of British history for four centuries to come.

VI

AND THEN, AGRICOLA
62-85 A.D.

Whatever we have loved in Agricola, whatever we
have admired, abides and will abide, in the hearts of
men, in the ages of eternity, in the story of things
greatly accomplished.

—TACITUS, *Agricola*

1

THE SIX REMAINING YEARS OF NERO'S REIGN
were, for Britain, years of slow recovery. The aggressive policy of expansion which had led to the selection
of Veranius and Paulinus as governors had been
brought to naught by the upheaval and destruction of
the revolt. The obvious need was for a policy of con-
ciliation and reconstruction.

In sober fact, there was much to be done. Camulodunum,
Verulamium, and Londinium, the chief urban centers of Roman influence, had each to be rebuilt from ashes. Throughout the Province
the tribal populations must be assured of peace in order to get crops
planted, farmhouses rebuilt, the road system extended. Since Rome
was not conducting its Empire as an eleemosynary institution, it was
urgent that the Province be restored as soon as possible, not merely
to self-supporting status but to that level of production which could
create a surplus capable of metamorphosis into revenue for the Imperial Fiscus.

The governor chosen by Nero as Paulinus' replacement, Petronius
Turpilianus—we may wonder at his family relationship, if any, to

that contemporaneous Petronius Arbiter whose satirical humor has enlivened the intervening centuries—made clear quickly on his arrival at his post that his policy was the restoration of peace and the encouragement of concentration on the everyday business of earning a living, while greater affairs, like the extension of the Province, were to be held in abeyance.

The legions were left with little patrolling and no fighting in prospect. The Twentieth and the Fourteenth, honored by Nero with the official addition of *"Victrix"* to their names, could console themselves for lack of action by sneering at the Second and the Ninth for their absence from one of the greatest victories of Roman arms. Garrison life became routine and discipline inexorably relaxed. Turpilianus, far more the civil administrator than the general, left his troops to the care of the individual legion commanders while concentrating, with his procurator Classicianus, on the restoration of economic life. Turpilianus seems to have been moderately successful at this activity during his three-year term of office, in spite of Tacitus' snide remarks about the new governor.

In particular, probably to hasten export revenue, development of the mines of the west went ahead with vigor, especially in the effort to obtain silver, then mined in Britain as a by-product of lead ores.

Mining at this time, and for several centuries thereafter, appears to have been a government monopoly. Early pigs of lead from the mines of the Mendip Hills bear the imprint of the Second Legion,* to whose specialists supervision of the work appears to have been entrusted. Other mines were leased out to private development. Lead ingots bearing the mark of such a private entrepreneur, C. Nipius Ascanius, have been found, dating from this time or even slightly earlier (59 A.D.).

Slowly the three destroyed cities rose from their ashes, each more stately than before. The Temple to Rome and Augustus at Camulodunum was rebuilt on the unharmed foundations of the old. As a result of the lesson learned from the revolt, each city now was contained within walls. More forest land was cleared, much of it in the process of getting lumber for reconstruction. On the roads throughout the Province traffic increased as commerce gained. Slowly confidence re-

---

* One lead ingot, so stamped, found at St. Valéry-sur-Somme, France, indicates an overseas demand. Apparently the Mendip mines were in production by 49 A.D., five years after the conquest.

turned and with it new interest from the bankers, traders, and commercial houses of Rome.

After three years, Turpilianus was recalled. His administration must have found favor with the debauched tyrant in Rome, for although he fought no battles, stormed no enemy fortresses, conquered for Rome not one inch of ground, he was, on his return, awarded the supreme military honor of the triumphal ornaments.

He was succeeded by Trebellius Maximus, no soldier and less of an administrator than Turpilianus. He seems to have neglected the military side of his duties even more than had Turpilianus, for disaffection of some vague but dangerous kind was stirring in the garrison of the Province, centered in the Twentieth Legion at its fortress at Deva, under the command of Roscius Caelius.

It was the spring of 68 A.D., the 821st since the founding of the City. Back on the continent events were developing that were to bring to an end the rapacious comedy in which Nero had been his own most-applauded actor. The unsettlement resulting from his overdue demise and the lack of a clear procedure for the succession were to throw the Empire, for the first time in a century, again into the horrors of civil war. Even distant Britain could not escape the effects.

2

THE REVULSION and shame which the able administrators of the Empire suffered under Nero's excesses were felt particularly by C. Julius Vindex, governor of Gallia Lugdunensis, the great central province of Gaul, at his capital Lugdunum, site of the modern Lyons. Vindex was a descendant of one of the kingly families of Aquitaine which had received the *Ius Latii*—a kind of territorial citizenship—in the time of Claudius. His father had been a Senator of Rome. The background is important for it goes far to explain both his rebellion and the total lack of ambition or self-seeking he exhibited in its brief course.

The southern Gauls had embraced participation in the Empire with pride. To them, by and large, Rome had exhibited its greatness, its ineffable majesty, rather than the seamy side of city politics and life. They responded in major degree, by willingly carrying forward in their own province, the arts and graces of the civilization into which they had been accepted. In the best sense, they were more Roman than the Romans.

Vindex, child of this tradition, had risen on merit to his post as governor. We can understand his pride in this achievement, his loyalty to the imperial system which had given him opportunity, and the sore disillusionment, growing steadily to anger, with which he observed the morbidly insane excesses of Nero. To such a man, a clear distinction would exist between the eternal majesty of Roma Invicta, the universal state, and the satyrlike infantilism of the tyrant who held in his hands its enormous power for good or for bad. Additionally, as one proud of his Gallic ancestry, he may well have felt a sense of personal responsibility for the heavy tribute exacted from the people of his province, going, as he surely knew, not to the legitimate expenses of a world government, but to the fantastic extravagances of a power-mad egomaniac.

We do not know how long he pondered his distress, nor against what alternatives he weighed the actions open to him. However, in March of 68 A.D., with the enthusiastic support of the people and the garrison of one legion, he declared his province independent of Nero and stated that it would remain outside the Empire until a worthy Roman held the throne.

Casting about for such an individual, he wrote to Sulpicius Galba, governor of Hispania Tarraconensis (Northern Spain), offering his support if the latter would declare for the Imperial power. Galba, old, bald, and crippled with gout, let friends in the Senate back in Rome know that he too was disgusted with Nero but would proceed against him only as the champion of the Senate and People of Rome.

Vindex had struck a timely spark. Most of the European provinces now declared for Galba. But a difficulty developed with the unrest. Virginius Rufus (onetime guardian of the younger Pliny), another high-minded patriotic officer, governor of the Rhine frontier, sternly refused the offer of his legions to acclaim him Emperor in rival candidacy to Galba, and ordered them south against Vindex. Near Vesontio (present-day Besançon), the two governors met, and held a conference which apparently permitted Vindex to explain his motives to Rufus' satisfaction. The agreement they reached, however, was spoiled by some fighting between the troops of Vindex and those of Rufus, and in the confused situation Vindex, perhaps in despair, killed himself.

Back in Rome, leaders of the Senate, having first made sure of the support of the Praetorian Guard, proclaimed Nero deposed and Galba Emperor. Nero fled and, in possibly apocryphal dismay at the ingratitude of Romans, killed himself to avoid more condign punishment. Galba reached Rome after a journey from Spain under circumstances which must have been a severe drain on the strength of a sick man already over seventy. The stern measures he quickly instituted to recover for the Imperial Fiscus the enormous money gifts made by Nero to his favorites produced a whispering campaign against him in Rome, matched in its contumely only by the disgust of the Praetorians who had not received their expected bribes. A conspiracy against him grew rapidly, led by his onetime friend and counselor, Salvius Otho, formerly Governor of Lusitania (now Portugal). Meeting protests in person, Galba was murdered by the Praetorians, and Otho was declared Emperor.

This worthy lasted exactly ninety-five days before the ambitious and swinish Aulus Vitellius, governor of Lower Germany, marched on Rome with his hardy if avaricious legions. Otho, shorn of support, killed himself, and Vitellius mounted the throne, which to him, if records do not err, seems to have been merely a never-closing restaurant.

These world-shaking events at the center of Empire must have created a wild surmise in Britain, perhaps permitting the noted disaffection in the Army to come to a head. Tacitus says only that Trebellius, after escaping the wrath of the dissidents by hiding, later regained, at the cost of shame and humiliation, a precarious authority. There is other evidence that Trebellius, scared out of his wits, fled to the continent and appealed to the new Emperor, Vitellius. The latter, perhaps fully occupied with his own uncertain future, and with no time to spare for a governor who had abandoned his post, summarily removed him from office—probably *"cum ignominia"*—and dispatched one of his own supporters, Vettius Bolanus, to take charge in Britain.

Of this governor, Tacitus, continuing his epigrammatic disdain of governors who did not fight, says only that while the civil wars continued Bolanus did not worry the legions with discipline; that there was the same inaction in the field and the same rioting in camp, and that Bolanus, to placate the troops, surrendered any attempt to regain control.

There are good reasons to believe this terse judgment unduly harsh if not prejudiced. Bolanus had commanded a legion in the East under Corbulo, apparently with honor and perhaps with distinction, if we can judge from his being deemed gubernatorial material at all. And since Corbulo set mercilessly high standards for his commanders it is unlikely that any officer able to meet his requirements would thereafter in a more important post merit Tacitus' invidious scorn.

In addition, Bolanus was not without troubles in Britain. With a garrison reduced by the withdrawal of Legio XIV Gemina Victrix from Britain in 68 A.D., Bolanus faced new dissensions of a serious nature between Cartimandua and her rejoined, but still unpacified husband, Venutius. She now divorced him and added insult to injury by promptly marrying, perhaps to strengthen her position, the son of a powerful sub-chieftain of the Brigantes.

This act of womanly, if regal, independence seems to have stirred Venutius to a fury reckless enough to risk Roman intervention—which, in the light of the disruption of the Roman world, he may have discounted. He gathered his adherents from within the dissident elements of Brigantia, and aided by allies who could only have come from the northern reaches of Brigantian territory—that is, from the western Lowlands of Scotland—moved against his erstwhile wife's tribal capital of Isurium (now Aldborough), some fifteen miles northwest of York. During this action, Cartimandua, who was losing, was rescued, perhaps from immediate slaughter at the hands of her ex-husband, by auxiliaries, dispatched by Bolanus.

On the whole, Bolanus seems to have played a cautious and wholly understandable role, awaiting the outcome of the still unsettled situation in Rome. Although the appointee of Vitellius, he may have been too distrustful of the latter's staying qualities to take sides, either as an individual or as governor, when a powerful challenge to Vitellius' grab of power rose in the East.

3

In 66 A.D.—while Nero was in Athens, receiving the scoffing adulation of the populace attending the concerts where he sang his own compositions for their doubtful edification—the Judeans of Palestine had revolted against Rome. Vespasian, then about fifty-seven years old and a general with a high military reputation, was given the task of leading an army to end the rebellion.

Considerable pressure must have been brought on Nero to make this appointment on strict grounds of military merit; for tradition, or recorded gossip, often enough the same thing, has it that Vespasian, the rough Sabine commoner, fell asleep at the Emperor's performances. Lesser indiscretions had summarily ended the careers and lives of other generals, but Vespasian survived—if we are to believe Suetonius, by keeping out of Nero's sight.

The Judean revolt was a major rebellion, involving all of southern Syria and Palestine. In the years from 66 to 69 A.D., Vespasian, with energy controlled by caution, had reduced the insurgents to the last bitter, irreconcilable recalcitrants, holding the citadel of Hierosolyma (Jerusalem). The course of these operations, fought with increasing ferocity on both sides, was sufficiently absorbing so that he was able to remain aloof from events in Rome.

But the governors of the eastern provinces, under the leadership of Mucianus, governor of Syria, and the eastern legions, including those of Vespasian's Palestine army, were far from happy with the course of events that in the year 69 A.D. had left Vitellius temporarily Emperor. Casting about for an alternative, Mucianus descried in Vespasian the qualities needed, not only to wrest the throne from Vitellius, but to occupy it with honor and to conduct its affairs for the good of the City and Empire.

Following some negotiation, much intrigue, and some sharp fighting, Mucianus, at the head of the pro-Vespasian forces, won over the western legions and the Praetorian Guard. After less than a year in power the glutton Vitellius was killed and Vespasian acclaimed in his stead. The new Emperor, who had judiciously remained in Alexandria while the issue was in doubt, after leaving the siege of Jerusalem in the competent hands of his son Titus, proceeded by slow stages to Rome.

Vespasian's accession was meekly, perhaps gladly, confirmed by the Senate.† At the same time, it repeated the grim notice served on the Praetorian Guard by the Rhine legions of Vitellius that thenceforward its usurped nominating powers would be shared by the frontier armies. It was a precedent to have later baneful results. But at the time, after the disorder, slaughter, and destruction of the past year, it seemed only that Rome had discovered a master it could trust, a master in the truest sense the guardian of the people.

One might expect that these bloody disruptions of the public order, extending over some eighteen months, constituted a major threat to the stability of the Empire. On the whole, though, the governmental structure seems to have withstood the undoubted strain rather well.

While ambitious men contended the mastery of the state with arms, other military and civil officials were more or less placidly handling the daily details of government. Among the populace not directly caught in the fighting—as was Agricola's mother—men went about their work, largely unhampered and unthreatened. Lovers married, children were born, men and women reached the natural end of their years and were buried with filial respect. Trade carried on, crops were planted and reaped, the myriad affairs of upwards of one hundred million people continued largely undisturbed. There must have been uncounted millions who either did not know, or did not care about the struggles for the imperial office. But, says Tacitus, writing very much like a modern political historian rejoicing at the coming of his party to power, "when Britain, along with the rest of the world, was recovered by Vespasian, generals became great, armies obedient, and the hopes of the enemy languished."

Even before Vespasian's arrival in the City, Mucianus had taken certain administrative measures for the security of the Empire. Among others he dispatched the thirty-three-year-old Julius Agricola to command Legio XX Valeria Victrix, in Britain. In terms of Tacitus' evaluation of Bolanus, noted above, it is significant that Mucianus saw no immediate need for a change in governorship. It seems likely that Mucianus acted only to meet the known need of the Twentieth

† A fragment of the proclamation setting forth his powers survives.

for a stern disciplinarian to restore order. Agricola therefore arrived in Britain and took up his command under Bolanus.

When Vespasian could give attention to the affairs of the Britain he had originally helped to subdue—and undoubtedly apprised of the Brigantian disturbances led and maintained by Venutius—he dispatched there as governor one of the early adherents to his candidacy for the throne. This was Petilius Cerealis, commanding general of the Ninth Legion at Lindum during the Boudiccan revolt of 61 A.D. It seems likely that a factor in selecting him for Britain was not only his earlier knowledge of the island, but also his brilliant crushing of the revolt of Civilis in the Rhineland, just completed.

Vettius Bolanus was relieved, apparently with honor, for years later in the reign of Domitian, the poet Statius addressed to his son Vettius Crispinus, just starting out on his career, a friendly poem containing laudatory references to his father's achievements.

4

THE TEMPESTUOUS doings of Venutius, ex-king of the Brigantes, aided and abetted by tribes from the western Lowlands of Scotland, had put him and them beyond the pale of Roman alliance, making it necessary for Cerealis to teach them the harsh lesson demanded by steadfast Roman policy for contumacy. But before Cerealis could open operations he had first to make sure of his army. The rehabilitation of the Twentieth Legion under Agricola was presumably well in hand by the time the new governor arrived. Of the condition of the Ninth and the Second Augusta we know nothing and can only guess that to the men of the Ninth at Lindum, many of whose centurions remembered Cerealis from his days as commander, the mere word of his coming was enough to tighten discipline, renew arduous training, and in all respects prepare the troops to meet his exacting inspection.

As already noted, Legio XIV Gemina Victrix had been withdrawn from Britain in 68 A.D. The disasters and disorder of the disputed succession had seen it briefly in the service of Otho, under its old commander Paulinus, sharing in the defeat by the troops of Vitellius at Bedriacum in the Po Valley. Later the legion appeared as part of the permanent garrison of the Rhine frontier.

But its absence from Britain, which had induced caution in Bolanus, severely reduced the forces at the disposal of Cerealis. To bring the garrison up to its old level of four legions, he induced Vespasian to send to Britain from the Pannonian garrison Legio II Adiutrix. Since the transfer of an entire legion over such a distance, including the seaborne crossing of the Channel, took considerable time, and its acclimatization and refresher training in Britain even more, we can believe it was some months before Cerealis felt ready to move against Venutius and the intransigent Brigantes.

The newly-arrived Legio II Adiutrix, together with the long-established Legio II Augusta in the southwest, were left to guard the Province, while Cerealis began operations with the Ninth Legion, his own old command, and the Twentieth, from Deva, under Agricola.‡ Cerealis' first move was to advance the Ninth Legion from its long-occupied fortress at Lindum north to a new fortified base camp at Eburacum (York), only some fifteen miles southeast of the Brigantian capital at Isurium (Aldborough). From this general area an ancient track led northwest across Stainmore and Cumberland to a point near Carlisle, thence across what is now the Scottish border into Dumfries. Evidences of an early line of Roman marching camps along this track seem conclusive evidence that it was the route followed by Cerealis.

‡ The naming and numbering of Roman legions can be confusing to the present-day reader. Originally, it appears, legions were numbered in sequence— I, II, and so on. But during the civil war between Octavianus and Marc Antony, each side raised legions and numbered them consecutively. Following his triumph, when he assumed the name Augustus, Octavianus deactivated many legions but kept some of Antony's, partly as a gesture of reconciliation and partly because they were excellent fighting units. Those legions with identical numbers were then distinguished by the addition of names. Legio II Augusta, for example, bore that name because it had been on the Emperor's side during the civil war. Legio II Adiutrix was created by Galba and confirmed by Vespasian later.

The proliferation of legions bearing identical numbers continued for many years. By the time of Alexander Severus (222–235 A.D.) there were four First Legions, five Second Legions, two Fourths, two Sixths, two Tenths, and two Twentieths, besides others. The picture is made no clearer to the modern eye by the fact that legions with different numbers might have the same name. There were, for instance, both Legio II Augusta, here mentioned, and Legio III Augusta, an entirely different unit created during a reorganization of the African garrisons by Augustus and for nearly three centuries stationed at Lambaesis, the present-day Lambesi, Algeria. For details, cf. H. M. D. Parker, *The Roman Legions* (Oxford, 1928).

Tacitus says many battles, sometimes bloody battles, were fought in this campaign, although he neither locates nor describes them. But ruins of Celtic hill forts with formidable defenses of dry stone show signs of destruction dating from this period, lending confirmation. Also, it seems probable that the intractable Venutius, understanding how little mercy he would receive from Cerealis, would have resisted to the best of his power wherever local strong points permitted hope of a successful defense.

We know from Tacitus that Agricola, leading the Twentieth, participated in this campaign, in the process earning the approval of Cerealis. We do not know whether his role was that of a separate but co-ordinated command, working up the western flank of Brigantia, with the enemy thus pinched between two powerful forces, or whether the Twentieth was incorporated with the Ninth in a two-legion column.

The earlier record of Cerealis, indicating a boldness and dash in his leadership, a willingness to adopt less cautious but more efficacious tactics, allows us to lean to the belief that Agricola was ordered north through Lancashire, Westmoreland, and Cumberland, maintaining close liaison with Cerealis on the east, until the two forces, meeting at or near Carlisle, closed a ring of steel around nearly the whole Brigantian territory.

A phrase in Tacitus saying that "Cerealis often gave him part of the army to command, to test him; sometimes on the strength of the issue, increased his forces" bears out this likelihood. It is easy enough to imagine the General conferring at some guarded rendezvous with his young and aggressive division commander over a planned assault on the western flank which might require temporary reinforcement by auxiliary units from the main column. Further confirmation of the separate movements of the two legions may be inferred from the fact that the marching camps located by archeologists on the York-Carlisle road are of a size suited to the accommodation of one legion and a few alae of auxiliary cavalry, but not large enough for two legions.

That something like this happened is substantiated by the discovery, at the lowest level of Roman Carlisle, of pottery typical of the Cerealis period. Luguvalium, or Carlisle, later to become the western anchor of Hadrian's Wall, almost certainly dates its Roman origins from this time. Its location, close to the inward tip of Solway Firth

DIS
MANIBVS
C·IVL·I·FA·BAIPINI·CLASSICIAN

TWO LINES OF THE INSCRIPTION ARE · HERE LOST,
GIVING DETAILS OF HIS EARLIER CAREER.

PROCPROVINCBRITANN
IVLIAINDIEILIAPACATAINFELIX
VXOR

Tomb of Julius Classicianus, Procurator of Britannia, 61–65 A.D.

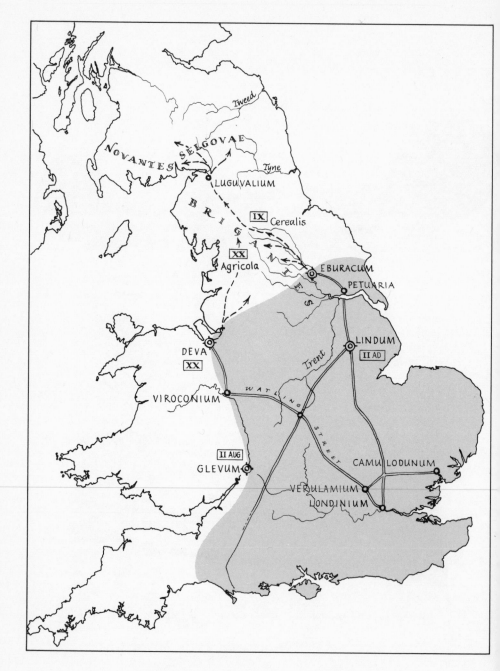

Conquest of the Brigantes by Cerealis, 71 – 74 A.D.

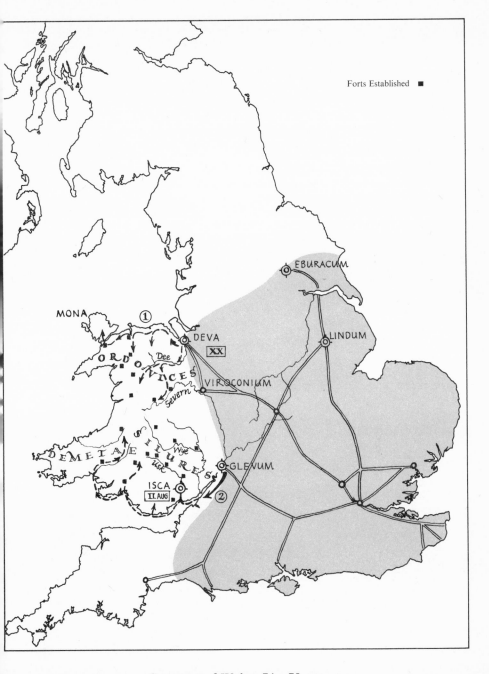

Conquest of Wales, 74 – 78 A.D.

1. Conquest of the Silures by Frontinus, 74 – 77 A.D. II Augusta moves from Glevum to new permanent fortress at Isca Silurum.

2. Conquest of the Ordovices by Agricola, 78 A.D.

Verulamium (St. Albans): The Amphitheatre

Isca Silurum (Caerleon-on-Usk): Roman Earthworks

and to the Eden River, establishes the site as a suitable one for the erection by Cerealis of a guardian fort strong enough to insure the hard-won submission of the Brigantes.

What happened then? Certainly the majority of the once-allied territory of the powerful if internally divided Brigantes came under direct Roman control. But we remember that Venutius, in his bid for power against his former wife, enjoyed the help of allies, already noted as almost surely coming from across the present Scottish border. No Roman commander, from the founding of the City, ever thought of being magnanimous when it came to dealing with those who had assisted in rebellion against Rome. Nor can we believe that Cerealis, within the limits of his power, could be any exception to this nearly inexorable rule.

We may believe then, that Carlisle did not represent the limits of Cerealis' advance north, as one might infer from a superficial reading of Tacitus' *Agricola*. The Novantae of Galloway, and the Selgovae farther north in Lanark and Peebles, the most likely source of Venutius' allies, were by that policy clearly marked objectives of Roman punitive attention. And later evidence indicates that the territory of the Brigantes themselves did not end at or near the Solway-Tyne line, but extended north into Annandale, Dumfries, parts of Roxburghshire, and even into Selkirk. If so, Cerealis, embarked on the subjugation of the Brigantes and the condign punishment of their allies, would have been failing in his duty had he not moved deep into the western Lowlands of Scotland, there to establish the rough lesson that to irritate Rome was always an economic and too often a mortal risk.

However, it is obvious that the lesson, so painfully learned, only reached the tribes farther north and east as it was passed on by word of mouth. Otherwise it is hard to explain how Tacitus, even while diligently at work glorifying his father-in-law's military achievements, would have to write that it was not until the latter's fifth campaign season (82 A.D.) that he encountered tribes theretofore unknown.§

Also from Tacitus' perhaps unconscious veracity, we know that the second, third, and fourth campaigns of Agricola in Scotland

§ For a full and reasoned treatment of Roman advances into Scotland prior to Agricola, cf. "Agricola and his Predecessors" and "First Roman Contact with Scotland," Ch. II and IV, *Roman Britain and the Roman Army,* by E. Birley (Kendal, England, Titus Wilson & Son, 1961).

(79, 80, and 81 A.D.) required no fighting worth mentioning, but
were chiefly devoted to consolidation of territory, to the building of
forts and roads, and the general activities to be expected of an army
operating in an area already subdued and probably cowed.

When with all this evidence is combined the general contemporaneous attitude in Rome that Britain up to Caledonia had been
subdued in the time of Vespasian, rather than in the reign of Domitian
when Agricola was doing most of his far-north campaigning, it is
difficult, if not impossible, to doubt that the pacification of the Lowlands, at least up to the Forth-Clyde line, was the work of Cerealis,
perhaps carried on after the transfer of Agricola to Rome in 72 A.D.,
and before his own replacement as governor in 75 A.D. by Sextus
Julius Frontinus, an able, even remarkable general who, copying
Caesar and forecasting modern styles in generalship, wrote books.¶

In spite of, or perhaps because of, his literary bent, Frontinus was
also a man of decisive action. The expanded province he inherited
from Cerealis had accepted the futility of resistance and was well on
its way to becoming a stable and flourishing section of the Empire.
Only on its borders was there still attachment to the old lawless life
of the tribes, possibly intensified in temptation by the growing wealth
and beckoning booty piling up within the Roman Pale.

The noisiest and most intractible of the still-unconquered Britons
south of Forth-Clyde were the two hill tribes of Wales, the Silures in
the south and the Ordovices in the north, whose territory had so far
presented insurmountable obstacles. Frontinus fixed on the Silures as
the first objects of his close and unwelcome attention.

Because of the wildness of the countryside—much of it still covered by the Forest of Dean—direct overland action from the fortress
of Legio II Augusta at Glevum (Gloucester) was, if not impossible,
at least unduly hazardous. So Frontinus moved by sea down the
Bristol Channel—one wonders what his sailors thought of the great
tidal bores that twice each day enliven the estuary—landed his troops
on the Welsh coast, and quickly seized the fertile plain of Glamorgan.
We may suppose this operation to have had the secondary objective

¶ Two survive: *Strategematicon*, Liber IV, a treatise on the art of war,
referred to by the much later Vegetius as an authority for his own classic; and
De Aqueductibus Urbis Romae, an architectural and engineering work on the
City's water supply.

of depriving the Silures of their major food-raising territory, thus forcing them back and up the valleys of the Usk and the Wye.

Once the littoral was secured, Frontinus boldly moved his legionary base forward from Glevum to Isca Silurum (Caerleon-on-Usk) || where he initiated construction of a permanent walled fortress, destined to be the home station of Legio II Augusta for more than three hundred years.

Operating from this base, Frontinus was able to move north and west, passing the Black Mountains into Brecknockshire in mid-Wales. The lands of the co-operative, or at least not hostile Demetae —who may have watched with a sardonic glee born of many earlier injuries the flagellation of the Silures—in Pembrokeshire and Carmarthenshire were encircled rather than penetrated by a road system initiated by Frontinus, who continued his campaign against the Silures perhaps as far north as the valley of the upper Severn. Beyond, the mountains of Montgomery made that approach to the territory of the belligerent Ordovices an undue risk. The chastened Silures were left under control by a system of roads and small garrisons at intersections and other defensible points which, by controlling any road movement of the indigenous population, made rebellious concentration impracticable.

He then retraced his steps to Caerleon, and thence moved north to Viroconium (Wroxeter), and from there on to Deva (Chester) at the mouth of the Dee River, where he started enlarging the earlier marching camp of Paulinus and Agricola into a permanent legionary fortress of monumental stone for Legio XX Valeria Victrix, although it is likely that its first occupant was Legio II Adiutrix.

It seems clear that from this base in already pacified country (lead ingots produced in mines from the Deceangli territories of Flintshire have been found dateable to 74 A.D.), Frontinus intended to follow against the Ordovices the same tactics which had proved so successful in subduing the Silures; that is, a movement into their territory from the river valleys and partition of the land into small areas, controllable by fortlets and traffic patrols; together with such military lessons in the superiority of Roman arms as would discourage, if not totally prevent, later eruptions.

|| "Caerleon" appears to be a Celticization of *castra legionis;* "Usk" the modern form of *Isca.*

But in 78 A.D., before this campaign could get under way, Frontinus was recalled. The new governor, fresh from the honor of the consulship at Rome for the year 77, was Gnaeus Julius Agricola; thus sent on his third tour of duty in Britain, this time with full responsibility and power, together, perhaps—in reaffirmation of Nero's earlier policy of expansion in Britain—with orders from Vespasian to proceed to the conquest of the entire island.

It is worth noting that in general, according to Roman imperial policy, legates sent as governors of the frontier provinces requiring garrisons of more than one legion were older men, experienced soldiers and administrators in their fifties or above. That Agricola, at the age of forty-one, should have reached so high a position in the imperial hierarchy as the governorship of Britain and command of four legions is, at the very least, evidence of the high confidence placed in him by Vespasian.

5

THE BIOGRAPHICAL essay which Tacitus, early in his writing career, produced in admiration and respect for his father-in-law is one of the few of his prolific writings to survive intact the destruction and neglect of the long ages following the collapse of Rome. To this fortunate chance we owe not only a beguiling portrait of a sturdy and dedicated soldier and proconsul, but also a detailed picture of events in Britain during the years 78–85 A.D.

The picture is far from complete. Tacitus' ideas on geography were vague,# far less informed than was Greek knowledge of two hundred years earlier. He displays a cavalier disinterest in distances, times, places, all apparently too mundane to interrupt his loyal preoccupation with, as he says himself, "the vindication of my father-in-law, Agricola."

It is this professed purpose that induces caution in following his story. In view of many recent military memoirs, we need not be unduly censorious if the careful selection of material, the ambiguous phrase, and the implication designed for favorable inference add up

For example, he thought that Hibernia (Ireland) lay between Britain and Spain.

to a portrait of virtue and military excellence unconfirmed by contemporary opinion.

Then too, perhaps with propagandistic intent, as well as to add to the stature of Agricola, Tacitus' *Life* is to a great degree a polemic, extolling the ancient aristocratic virtues, assailing corruption in office, deploring the tyranny of emperors—he wrote in the reign of the tolerant Trajan—and in general bemoaning the loss among his fellow citizens of those high concepts of duty and public honor with which his art clothes Agricola. Yet it is good to know that for Tacitus, even if exaggerated in example, the Stoic virtues—*gravitas, pietas, constantia, virtus,* and *disciplina*—the Roman virtues which had nurtured the City's rise to world dominion were still admired, still sturdily held as proper standards for Roman behavior, over eight hundred years after the founding of the City.

We can lose perspective in sticking to Tacitus, who pretended to none himself. Quite aside from his overlaudatory picture of Agricola, there are serious omissions. In his strictures on the corrupt emperors before Vespasian, including also Domitian as a reversal to Neronic viciousness, there is no recognition of the efficient and largely impersonal process by which, with perhaps fewer errors than would occur among us today, competent governors were sent out year after year to rule the provinces with, on the whole, remarkable integrity and often high ability.

Tacitus records, for example, that Agricola received his first commission as a military tribune from Nero, without giving either that worthy or his military secretary credit for the discerning selection which put Agricola on the first step of a senatorial career. He admits great governors were appointed by Tiberius and Claudius, even by Caligula and Nero, but sees in this consistent policy no balancing factor against the emperors' individual and fascinating vices.

He ascribes Agricola's relief from the governorship of Britain in 85 A.D. as due wholly to the suspicious jealousy of Domitian, without giving weight either to the fact that Agricola had held the assignment for more than twice the normal term of three years, or to the equally relevant truth that Domitian's troubles on the Danube frontier made impossible the support, in either logistics or manpower, of any further offensive operations of Agricola.

In echoing his father-in-law's complaint that he was denied higher appointment in the imperial service—Agricola evidently expected either the governorship of Syria, the highest gift among the overseas assignments; or failing that the less onerous, but hardly less honorable, choice of the provinces of Africa or Asia—Tacitus ignores the perfectly honest and understandable point of view of the Emperor's secretariat in Rome: that Agricola's victory over the Caledonii was in truth a minor affair compared with battles won and lost on other frontiers; and that since for better or for worse all of Agricola's frontier experience had taken place in Britain, he could be considered a British expert only and lacking the rounded experience on the widespread frontiers of the Empire considered essential in the highest positions.**

Yet despite special pleading and moral indignation—as Dr. Will Durant puts it, "no moralist should write history"—or perhaps because of them, Tacitus in his life of Agricola gives us an unforgettable picture of a proconsular Roman, governing his province, consolidating its frontiers, building roads and forts, protecting the inhabitants, dispensing justice, stamping out corruption, encouraging the economy, fighting an occasional battle, and steadily inducing by force of character and power of example first reluctant, then wholehearted acceptance of the Pax Romana.

6

WITH THESE reservations we may now follow Agricola's tour of duty in Britain as related by Tacitus, additionally modified by the discoveries of modern archeology.

The long passage from Rome to Britain—by sea to Massilia where years before he had shown too great an interest in philosophy; then by overland stages through Gaul to Gesoriacum; then once again by sea to Rutupiae; and by land over the new Roman road to Canterbury, and on through Rochester to the Thames bridge at Londinium—would surely have provided ample time for reflection on his new responsibilities.

Perhaps his thoughts on touching British soil went back to the horrible days of Boudicca's revolt, when the fate of the Province hung from so desperately tenuous a thread. If so, surely he recalled the

** Cf. Birley, *op. cit.*, Ch. II, "Agricola and his Predecessors."

lessons he had then learned from Paulinus in tenacity, courage, indomitability, and cool calculation under stress. Along with these lessons, fundamental, never-to-be-forgotten elements of his military education, there was, we may believe, a mature appreciation of Paulinus' errors and neglect of civil affairs, major contributing factors to the revolt.

Perhaps there was in Agricola's Gallic ancestry a sense of kinship with this island people, an appreciation of their innate love of freedom, producing an attitude which Tacitus described as "a willingness to discharge their imperial obligations provided there was no wrongdoing in the process; for their subjection to Rome, while complete enough to earn obedience, did not imply slavery."

There can be little doubt that Agricola, before departing Rome, was briefed, to use modern nomenclature, on all known developments in Britain up to the time of his appointment. In any case he would have learned from Frontinus, who, following strict policy, was not allowed to leave Britain until his replacement arrived, of planned operations against the Ordovices, which it would be Agricola's first duty to carry out.

The area was familiar to Agricola from his earlier service in command of the Twentieth at Deva. No time, therefore, need be wasted in overcautious reconnaissance. And following so able a general and administrator as Frontinus, Agricola may well have been aware of the necessity to impress his personality and leadership on both provincials and border tribes as soon as possible.

A tactical error of the Ordovices in ambushing and nearly wiping out an ala of auxiliary cavalry gave Agricola his opportunity. The Ordovices, theretofore unconquered and consequently brash, could hardly have chosen a worse time for their exhibition of Celtic exuberance.

Agricola was barely installed as governor when he started west and at Deva ordered into action his old command, Legio XX Valeria Victrix. With this main force, supported by auxiliary cavalry, he promptly invaded the mountain territory of the Ordovices, advancing perhaps along the valley of the upper Dee, perhaps along the coast and inland via the valleys of the Clwyd and Elwy. Caught in their mountain lairs and hillside farms before they had any chance to concentrate, the Ordovices, after a short campaign, disappeared from history.

To make his point abundantly clear, Agricola then returned to the north coast and perhaps with taut memories of his last visit to the area turned west to the Isle of Mona, repopulated since the attack by Paulinus seventeen years earlier. The islanders, enjoying a vicarious freedom in the happy illusion that Roman power was far away, were speedily disabused. They, as Tacitus puts it, "coming to the conclusion nothing was impossible to men who fought this way, . . . petitioned for peace and surrendered the island to Agricola."

The effect of this venture on the provincial population must have been condign. This new governor, this Agricola, instead of spending his time in Londinium, living in luxury, entertaining and being entertained by the wealthy and influential of the city, had stopped for a few days only, then disappeared into the mysterious but surely hostile west. Thence, after a period, had come news of his victories, no doubt magnified en route. This was obviously no man to try to cozzen, to dupe, to inveigle with polite nothings while one plotted behind his back. Any notions of rebellion, or even the hope of studiously innocent non-co-operation, crumbled before this harsh precedent.

Surely too, as word of the extinction of the Ordovices went north with the peddlers and itinerant traders through the territories of the recently subdued Brigantians and their allies of the Lowlands who already knew the hard hand of Rome, caution and even despair extinguished hope, thus playing a major role in insuring a minimum of opposition when it came time for Agricola to move north.

The North Wales campaign over, Agricola seems to have returned to Londinium—or to Camulodunum—where he gave his attention to administrative matters, and seems, as a start, to have drastically overhauled his own headquarters. He then took a direct and doubtless stern interest in the functions and performance of the procurator's office, stamping out peculations and abuses, which, as he had good reason to remember, could be a main source of dissatisfaction among the inhabitants.††

There is a passage in Tacitus, by no means clear in its ramifications, which still manages to suggest the kind of official chicanery Agricola found and stopped. The provincial government was always a ready purchaser of agricultural products, chiefly perhaps grain and

†† Agricola, possessing the confidence of Vespasian, could afford to be more exacting in his control of the procurator than other governors.

leather for the needs of the Army. It was, therefore, standard practice, not alone in Britain but generally throughout the Empire, that a major proportion of cantonal taxes could be paid in kind. This governmental readiness to accept commodities in tax payment was augmented by the general shortage of coin, perhaps at this time not so aggravated as in later ages. Payment of taxes in grain and its abuse by officialdom is the subject of Tacitus' story.

The wheat so obtained by the government was stored in government warehouses pending delivery to the garrisons; or as surplus might permit, to be sold for government revenue. At some point beyond the acquisition of food reserves required principally for the Army, it appears that the farmer had the option of paying the rest of his tax in coin and keeping his grain to sell for his own profit and risk on the open market. Venal tax agents of the procurator's office seem to have preferred the latter method of payment, possibly for the obvious reason that money sticks more easily to greasy hands than does grain, and is more susceptible to concealment. So, to make it more difficult for farmers to deliver grain, some of the agents appear to have conceived a process as ingenious as it was dishonest. Collection points were established at inaccessible locations around the countryside, and the hours when grain would be received were set at times most inconvenient to the farmer. If persistence in delivery overcame these obstacles, the farmers often enough found the collection points arbitrarily closed with no officials on hand to weigh their grain and issue the appropriate receipts. The farmers so treated were thus forced to sell their grain on the open market, where the excess of supply naturally enough depressed the price, giving the agents who had engineered the swindle another opportunity for personal profit.

Tacitus indicates that Agricola swooped down upon this practice, thereby earning both the gratitude of the farmers and the resentment of officials denied what time and prior immunity had raised to the level of rightful perquisite.

Interfering with the extortions of tax-gatherers and their allied Roman traders had in the last days of the Republic and under some Emperors often enough earned for honest proconsuls contumely and false charges in Rome, ending frequently in their recall and trial for malfeasance. But Agricola, sure of the support of Vespasian, was in a position to make his reforms stick. The result was happy. The provincials, freed from official peculation, settled down to learn Roman ways, with not only a desire for the luxuries of civilization but also, doubtless, an eager interest in learning, not to circumvent but to practice for themselves, some of the more highly developed systems of graft. It is possible, of course, that the tax agents and traders, after a period, discovered in their enforced rectitude a novel ease of conscience.

We must, I think, consider Tacitus' report of vigorous operations in the summer of 79 A.D. as essentially a flowery description of a consolidation of control established by Cerealis' earlier conquest of Brigantia and Agricola's own of North Wales. The description of the process by which forts and Roman garrisons were placed for the adequate policing of the territories is almost exactly that followed so successfully by Frontinus in his operations for control of the Silures of South Wales. Tacitus speaks of no battles fought; and the sudden raids he mentions need have been no more than the unannounced appearance of reconnaissance units before a village; for, Tacitus implies, when the natives were sufficiently overawed—as well they might be— Agricola was at pains to describe to them the attractions of peace. Coming from a Roman governor, these attractions could well be many, even if always implicit was the threat of what would happen if they proved insufficiently popular.

With the approach of winter Agricola reverted to the task of civilizing his province. The paragraph in which Tacitus describes the Governor's methods was in fact a policy handbook in general use throughout the Empire for the Romanization of newly acquired subjects. The same procedure, less succinctly expressed, is evident in Caesar's treatment of the inhabitants of Cisalpine Gaul and of Gaul beyond the Alps (now Provence), and extended, as soon as subjection was complete, to the Rhine.

Nevertheless, the process is worth discussing in some detail, both for the light it throws on Roman realism, and for its contemporary interest as Western civilization meets the problem of rudimentary and barbaric peoples, under the euphemism of "undeveloped nations" ascending into demagogy. It is set forth in *Agricola 21:*

> The winter which followed showed the soundest of plans developed to lead a people habituated to war, by appreciating comfort, to practice peace.

Put less cynically, the problem was to get the Britons, wedded to their tribal organizations and therefore to their engendered bellicosity, to accept Roman concepts of order, of safety of person and property under law, not by continued coercion but because after practice they would find in the daily exercise of those concepts a way of life preferable to what they had known before. It is the less-appreciated side of Roman expansion, less interesting than the endless story of ruthless conquest and cruelty, that for long ages of Roman rule the process had gone on, among both civilized and barbarian peoples, slowly building over the centuries the concepts of a universal peace, a unified economy, and a common body of law, flexibly adjusted to regional traditions, under which all mankind could live together in concord. That the attempt did not succeed everywhere detracts less from the majesty of the concept than from the assumed wisdom of man.

> . . . he would exhort individuals and help communities to build temples, forums, market places, houses.

In spite of the panegyrics on rural life we find in Virgil, Horace, and other Latin poets, Roman civilization, as already noted, was essentially urban. Its foundation, the length and breadth of the Empire, was the village, town, or city—the *vicus, oppidum, urbs, colonia,* or *municipium*—each with its carefully defined degrees of self-government, each a settled community with its temples to both local and Roman gods, its forum for public meetings and the exchange of goods, its basilica for local government and the courts, its wine shops and baths for gossip as well as lubrication of inner and outer man; its houses, shops, and small manufactories. In such communities generation after generation of families lived and died.

It was clearly Agricola's duty, during his term of office, to foster the creation and extension in Britain of this urban civilization, given its early example in the building of the provincial capital at Camulodunum. Before the coming of the Romans the tribal organization of Britain hardly knew the town, nor could the residence of the tribal chief be reasonably described as a capital. Undoubtedly earlier governors, carrying out the same imperial policy, had made some progress, but in fairness to Agricola, it is about in his time that the cantonal centers began to change from what at best were aggregations of huts into splendid, if small, Roman cities—with streets crossing at right angles, a basilica, forum, baths and temples, shops and markets, serving as a center for the entire tribe. From these beginnings developed in time cantonal capitals such as Calleva Atrebatum,‡‡ now an archeological ruin near Reading, which was once a prosperous crossroads town as well as the canton center of the Atrebates; Corinium Dobunorum, now Cirencester, in the Cotswolds, aforetime the thriving center of the British wool trade; Ratae Coritanorum, now deep beneath the streets and houses of modern Leicester; Viroconium Cornoviorum, now forsaken under the shadow of the Wrekin; Venta Silurum in Wales; and others, both living and dead.

Along with the development of the tribal capitals went the growth of other urban communities destined to more or less permanent existence as settlements of varied folk: Londinium; the once Roman coloniae, or settlements of veterans; Camulodunum, Glevum, and Lindum (now Colchester, Gloucester, and Lincoln); the two fortress towns of Deva (Chester) and Eboracum (York); and the watering resort of Aquae Sulis (Bath), as fashionable in late Roman times as it again became in the eighteenth century.

> . . . he praised the energetic, rebuked the indolent, and competition for his praise, rather than force, became an incentive.

The high prestige, let alone the near autocratic authority, of the Emperor's deputy in Britain was no mean instrument either of coercion or of persuasion. As in our day, praise from on high, publicly bestowed, was as great an asset, prestigious as well as financial, as public admonition was a liability. No governor, let alone one as intelligent as Agricola, could have been unaware of the influence his mere words exerted. Yet it is likely enough that competition for the Governor's favor, or fear of his displeasure, existed only among that chieftain class which had most to gain by co-operating with a dominance they were powerless to escape. Among the lesser folk of the tribes, sticking stubbornly to their mother tongue and Celtic customs, certain in their racial confidence, persisting to this day, that they knew better how to order their affairs than could any foreigner, it seems improbable that Agricola's efforts merited serious consideration.

‡‡ Calleva excavations show Period I occupation circa 45–64 A.D.; Period IIa, 65–100 A.D. Cf. *Roman Silchester,* by George C. Boon (London, Max Parrish, 1957).

. . . he began to train the sons of the chieftains in a liberal education.

The then current generation of tribal leaders within the Province had been coerced into obedience. But if the Britons were ever to be truly Roman, the next generation must be so educated as to insure their willing, if not enthusiastic, participation in civilization. It was therefore essential to any long-term program of assimilation that the youthful aristocracy be instilled with the worth of Roman values, with a grasp of Rome's ecumenical mission.

Agricola seems to have brought to Britain to initiate this educational experiment a schoolmaster and rhetorician, Demetrius of Tarsus. What methods were used to insure regular attendance, let alone understanding, at the sessions held by this Greek pedagogue, to whom Latin was surely a secondary and inferior tongue, while the Celtic dialect was beyond the serious interest of a scholar, remain unreported.

. . . he gave preference to the native shrewdness of Britons over the more studious but less enterprising Gauls.

Although Tacitus does not precisely so indicate, this must have applied to public employment in the always growing civil service of the Province. However necessary it had been in the early stages of the occupation to import bilingual Gauls with a knowledge of Roman administrative procedures, the sooner they were replaced by qualified Britons, the sooner a cause of exacerbation would be removed and the Britons so employed would acquire a vested interest in maintenance of the Roman status quo. Tacitus records the success of the policy:

As a result, the nation which used to reject Latin came eagerly to seek fluency in that language.

The civil service was not alone the source of eagerness to learn Latin. An additional stimulus to its use was the recruiting of young Britons into auxiliary cohorts of infantry—Cohors I Brittonum soon appears on the Army list—where drill commands, nomenclature, and the pithy phrases of drill field and barracks demanded quick acquaintance, if not with the classic prose of Cicero at least with the simple and often scatological vocabulary of the camp. We may believe too that a demand quickly developed among the merchants and traders of Londinium and the port towns for clerks able to read and write Latin as well as to keep accounts in its cumbersome number system.

> The wearing of our dress became a distinction, and the toga fashionable.

Surely a Briton of that day was carrying sycophancy rather far in dispensing with his warm trousers and jerkin of fleece in favor of tunic and toga. But then, the toga, an oversize garment, could conceal beneath its stately folds any reasonable number of warmer, indigenous items of apparel.

> . . . little by little the Britons fell into our charming way of life, enjoying the lounging rooms, the baths, and the convivial banquets . . .

Tacitus could not refrain, even in eulogizing his father-in-law, from completing his description of Romanization with his customary sardonic lash:

> . . . deeming these things culture instead of the chains which bound them to slavery.

7

As the summer of 80 A.D. approached, Agricola again took to the field, moving north. It is difficult to trace his movements. Tacitus writes:

> The third year of operations opened up new tribes while the clans were ravaged right up to the estuary of the Tanaus.

Who were the "new tribes" and which estuary is the Tanaus? The point has been made that "new tribes" means some not theretofore receiving the military attention of the Romans, although not unknown to them, since Tacitus reserves the phrase *ignotas gentis* for those encountered in Agricola's fifth campaigning season. These "new tribes" seem to be the Votadini, who lived north of the Tyne with villages and grazing grounds reaching nearly to the Firth of Forth, and perhaps some eastern septs of the Selgovae, who, as earlier noted, very likely were rudely chastised, in their western territories at least, by Cerealis. But what of the estuary of the "Tanaus"? If by this is meant the Tay, as most modern authorities seem to agree, it is surprising that Tacitus should report Agricola's sixth campaign season (83 A.D.) as operations against tribes settled "beyond Bodotria," the clearly identified Roman name for the Firth of Forth.

If Agricola did indeed reach the Tay estuary in his third campaign, and without battles or even annoyance by the enemy, but suffering from "savage weather," he was close to the northernmost point he is known ever to have reached. The legionary fortress of Pennata Castra, at Inchtuthill on the Tay, is believed of his construction, either in this or a later year.

Yet he had time in this year to plant forts and garrison them with a year's reserve of provisions. It seems probable that these forts, or a majority of them, were those he placed along the early Roman road called the "Stanegate," between Carlisle on the west and Corbridge (Corstopitum) on the east, to protect the eastern crossing of the Tyne. This seventy-mile stretch, protected by the rivers Tyne and Irthing, is the narrowest part of the island until some hundred miles farther northwest the Firth of Forth (Bodotria) and the Firth of Clyde (Clota) reach inland to within thirty-five miles of each other. This line of forts, or fortified camps, evidently meant to be held through the winter, probably by auxiliary troops, and in communication with each other along the roadway of the Stanegate, effectively secured the Province from encroachment while also sharply separating the restive Brigantes from their former allies to the north.

Yet the puzzle remains. If we assume that Agricola's main base, from which operations started, was the fortress of the Ninth Legion at York (Eburacum) a reconnaissance in strength as far as the Tay would involve a foray of something over two hundred miles, with approximately only the first seventy-five through the pacified country of the Brigantes and the Parisii of York and Durham. Thence, from Corbridge north, there was the road to make passable for the legions, security detachments to be assigned to keep it open, and supplies to be forwarded under guard; while in the meantime the construction, manning, and supplying of the Stanegate forts was being carried on.

It seems unlikely that Tacitus' "Tanaus" can be read as a corruption of "Tinea," the Roman name for the River Tyne and its estuary, which appears in no geographical source until the seventh-century *Ravenna Cosmography*. To assume so much would indicate that Agricola got no farther north on the east than Tacitus implies Cerealis had on the west a decade earlier. Yet it does tie in with the construction of the forts and road of the Stanegate, and if, as Tacitus states, Agricola selected the location of each fort himself, he must have spent much of his time in that summer of 80 A.D. in the immediate neighborhood. If so, it is difficult to see how he could lead his forces, even without serious opposition, 125 miles further into the approaches of the Highlands where he encountered the "new tribes."

Perhaps, in recognition of Tacitus' invariably dim notions of geography, the reference to "Tanaus" meant Tweedmouth, a mere fifty-odd miles beyond Corbridge, over ground that Agricola—if we are to believe Tacitus, with some confirmation from archeology—was to move with some resistance during the following year. Given the weapons and effective operating radii of the day, fifty miles, or two to three days march, was about as far as a prudent commander would venture into hostile territory without a secured forward base of operations. This base seems to have been the line of the Stanegate.

Yet, Tacitus describes the next year's campaign (of 81 A.D.) as being spent "in consolidating territory previously reconnoitered" and proceeds to make clear that he means all the land up to the thirty-five-mile gap between the Firths of Forth and Clyde, including the territories of the Dumnonii, as well as those of the Votadini and the Selgovae. Apparently, during this summer he constructed a series of forts along this line, backed up by others in the area between that forward bulwark and the Tyne-Solway line of the previous season.

Tacitus reports battles fought in this campaign, but typically, fails to locate them. Later archeological excavation has disclosed native hill forts at various places throughout the area, some showing evidence of having been attacked and partly demolished at a very early stage of the Roman occupation. Those at Birrenwark in Dumfrieshire, Arbory Hill in Lanark, North Eildon in Roxburghshire, and Taprian Law in East Lothian are some which might have been sites of more or less desperate attempts to arrest Agricola's advance. On the other hand, it is possible that they fell to Cerealis as he sought out for punishment the Lowland allies of the Brigantes.

In any case, the enemy, says Tacitus, meaning those who either lived beyond the Forth-Clyde line or had fled there, was in effect moved to another island. The significance of this phrase appears to be that the northern tribes, prevented from land forays south, could reach Roman territory only by water movement over either of the two firths.

Before Agricola could move safely north of the new forward line —unless of course he had already ventured to the Tay in the preceding year—there was still behind him, south of this line and westward, the Galloway peninsula with the contiguous lands of Dumfries, Lanark, Renfrew, and Ayrshire, sparsely populated by a tribal aggregation called the Novantae, to be explored and brought within the encompassing power of Rome. This was the task set for the summer of 82 A.D.

Yet again geographical vagueness protrudes. Starting his description of the summer's activities, Tacitus writes:

"In the fifth year of campaigning, *having crossed in the first ship,* he subdued in repeated and victorious battles tribes up to that time unknown."

Crossed from where to where? Tacitus goes on in the next sentence to talk about the garrisoning of "that part of Britain which faces Hibernia" (Roman name for Ireland), says the latter island lies between Britain and Spain and commands the Gallic Sea, and gives the next two paragraphs to a discussion of Ireland and of Agricola's belief that he could conquer it with one legion and a few auxiliaries.

Does Tacitus mean to imply that Agricola crossed to Ireland? It is true that from Portpatrick on the Rhinns of Galloway in Wigtown —known to the Romans as Novantorum Peninsula—across to Island Magee just north of Belfast Lough is under twenty-five miles. On a reasonably clear day the shoreline of Hibernia looming in the west could easily have excited Agricola's interest.

But if a crossing to Ireland is implied, there is no historic, traditional, or archeological evidence to support it. And indeed, Tacitus himself implicitly denies it when he reports Agricola's consideration of the possibilities, and the Irish quisling held "for use as opportunity offered." With the paraphrase of Agricola's opinion that "such a conquest would help to secure Britain, because with Roman troops everywhere the hope of liberty would disappear," Tacitus dismisses entirely the year's campaigning.

What then, are we to think of the crossing by the "first ship"? There is, of course, the possibility that Agricola had been called to the continent during the winter for conferences of one kind or another and returned as soon as navigation to Britain opened with the coming of spring. However, there is no independent confirmation of such a journey, and as a general rule at this time, governors were expected not to leave their provinces during their terms of office, except to conduct forward operations against the barbarians.

Modern air photography and some archeological exploration have disclosed the existence of marching camps, signal stations, and other evidences of Roman presence in this period, dominating the lines of communication from the south counties of Galloway north through Ayrshire and Renfrew. If, in fact, the summer's work consisted of establishing Roman control of this area, the crossing by "first ship" begins to make sense, since the land approach to the Galloway peninsula through swamps and the rugged Rhinns of Kells presented serious hazards easily by-passed, as did Frontinus in South Wales, by a ship movement from the south shore of Solway Firth across, say, to Wigtown Bay or any other point on the north shore.

So, we may believe, passed Agricola's fifth campaign, of 82 A.D., marching and countermarching, subduing, without serious battles, the perhaps sparse population of the western Lowland counties.

The projected invasion of Ireland resolves itself into an evening's speculation, after dinner perhaps, from a tent near Portpatrick, where in the long summer evenings of that latitude the twilight persisted even after the sun had set behind the distant but beckoning shore. Neither then nor under any subsequent Roman governor was Hibernia disturbed by Roman attention. For better or for worse, the island was left to its intertribal quarreling, to its brigandage and raiding, to its Druidism and Celtic way of life; all so stirringly related in the Gaelic literature of later centuries, centering on the incredible doings of Finn MacCool in the south, and on the Homeric glories of the Knights of the Red Branch in the north. While consolidating control of Galloway and the area north to the Firth of Clyde, Agricola seems to have sent the ships which had carried his forces across Solway on an exploration of the west coast of the Highlands. Perhaps hoping to emulate both his own amphibious flanking action of this season and that of Frontinus earlier in Wales, he was searching for an area where he might land his troops on the coast and engage from the rear the savage and warlike Caledonians of the Highlands.

Even in summer today, a coastal voyage between the mainland and the encroaching Inner Hebrides has its hazards. Whatever geographical knowledge was gathered on this voyage by Demetrius of Tarsus who accompanied the expedition—we must believe his school for young British aristocrats was merely enjoying a normal summer vacation—would have been annotated with horrendous tales of steep-cliffed islands, of giant waves driven in from the west on rock-strewn shores, of deep and menacing fiords slicing into forbidding mountain country with no ascertainable passes, of fog and rain and sudden vicious storms. Whatever the details, they seem to have been sufficient to discourage Agricola from any foray into Caledonia from the west.

So, to progress farther north, he found it necessary to return to the east. As autumn approached and the fleet with its awestruck crews returned to Solway Firth, he seems to have sent it south to safe harbor with directions to rendezvous the following spring in the Firth of Forth.

Presumably making sure that his auxiliary garrisons, now interlacing the whole Lowland countryside between the Forth-Clyde line of forts and the Stanegate, were adequately drilled, rationed, and instructed in their tasks for the coming winter, Agricola returned to the Province there to observe the advancing Romanization of the populace, to clear the administrative paper work—as formidable in the Roman Army as in ours—and to plan his next campaign in Scotland.

This operation, beginning in the spring of 83 A.D. was a joint army-navy penetration of "the tribes beyond Bodotria," although, as already noted, it is not impossible he reconnoitered the same area in 80 A.D. His route of march has been traced along the south bank of the Forth to a river crossing near Stirling, thence northeast up the valley west of the Ochill Hills toward Perth. Moving without serious resistance, although perhaps aware of gathering forces of the Caledonian tribesmen at a distance, he reached the Tay where, on its east-flowing stretch near present-day Dunkeld, he built, either in 83 or 84 A.D. if not earlier, a strong legionary fortress, Pennata Castra, now part of a golf course at Inchtuthill. This massive fort, occupied briefly by Legio XX Valeria Victrix, proved to be the farthest north of sustained Roman penetration, although temporary camps, probably of reconnoitering detachments of cavalry and infantry, have been identified as far north as Glenmailen in Aberdeen.

It is possible that these farther camps may not have been built by Agricola but are evidence of later, deeper penetration by Septimius Severus.

As Agricola advanced toward the Tay, surely with a wary eye cocked on the river-cut passes through the brooding Grampians on his left, the fleet coasted along the shoreline, entering deep into the Firth of Forth then out again, edging around Elie and Fife Ness, past the moors that were to become the sacred shrine of golf at St. Andrews, and into the Firth of Tay.

Prearranged contact between the fleet and the army appears to have taken place at frequent intervals, partly for supply of the army, partly for transmission of reports to Agricola on the lay of the land north and east, with what information about settlements or enemy bands might have been garnered from the ships. Tacitus speaks of these meetings; of joint camps sheltering infantry, cavalry, sailors, and marines together. He writes in contemporary terms of interservice rivalry, of arguments, boasting, and exaggerations of burdens borne by each service while the other was presumably enjoying a carefree vacation at government expense. We may believe the partisanship and bickering as vehement and unresolved as in our own day.

This year's incursion into the north of Scotland failed to enjoy the apparent immunity from serious resistance of earlier campaigns. For reasons unknown to us, but perhaps connected with the desire to cut as wide a swath as possible, Agricola's troops advanced in three separate but mutually supporting columns, each setting up at night its own defensive camp. This procedure too, as Tacitus implied,§§ may have been a first attempt by Agricola to lure the wary Caledonians into an attack on what the tribesmen could have deemed a minor force. If so, it succeeded, for one summer night, during the short hours of semi-darkness of those latitudes, the camp of the Ninth Legion—perhaps woefully understrength, for Tacitus speaks of it as the weakest of the three—was stormed by the Caledonians, who apparently forced the ramparts and were hard at work inside the camp trying to exterminate the Ninth when Agricola appeared leading detachments from the supporting columns. The Ninth, taking courage from the assistance, fought back with renewed vigor until the

§§ Tacitus (*Agricola*, xxxiii) has Agricola later address his troops: ". . . they [the enemy] are coming; they have been dragged from their coverts."

enemy, assailed in the flank, broke and fled to the safety of the Grampian passes, there to take stock of this lesson in tactics and to plan for greater and more organized resistance. They could not have been expected to grasp the fact that a major battle, involving as much as possible of Caledonian manpower, was exactly what a Roman general would have sought.

Agricola's problem lay in the nature of the terrain, as centuries later it posed problems to the English forces of the Duke of Cumberland. The gently sloping land of Stirlingshire and eastern Perth, and beyond the Tay the countryside stretching north through Angus and Kincardine to Aberdeen, presented no serious obstacles to Agricola and his tough, disciplined troops, particularly with naval support. But to the west and north the curving rampart of the Grampians presented a forbidding prospect, penetration of which would be at the constant risk of ambush with no certainty of ever bringing the tribesmen to battle. Thus, while Agricola could occupy the Lowlands of the east coast, and maintain them by a string of forts built from Inchtuthill south, with outpost forts far up the valleys of the Earn, the Almond, and the Teith, there could be still no assurance of peaceful, constructive occupation so long as the Caledonii of the western wilderness retained their raiding proclivities.

The answer was to entice the tribes to unite and attack him in force. In a pitched battle any Roman general could count on superior Roman discipline and tactics to allow him to wipe out by either slaughter or capture the flower of tribal manpower. Perhaps this was the object Agricola sought in exposing the Ninth Legion as a decoy. If so, it was a near thing, and with a little less Roman luck he might well have lost a third of his force and suffered a defeat which would take a lot of explaining in Rome.

However, the opportunity, if sought it were, did not arrive until the following year, when an unconscious ally appeared in a Caledonian chieftain whom Tacitus names Calgacus. For this tribal upstart Tacitus expresses the praise he reserves in general for barbarian chieftains so myopically parochial as to challenge his own Empire's gift of civilization. In a surely apocryphal speech to the Caledonians, Calgacus is allowed to coin Tacitus' famous if cynical description of Roman expansion—". . . they make a desolation, and call it peace." But before Calgacus' oratory could induce the clansmen to a common effort, Agricola had troubles of his own.

Among the auxiliaries attached to his legions was a cohort—about battalion size, perhaps five hundred men—of Usipii, recruited from a Germanic tribe inhabiting the right bank of the lower Rhine. At one of the points of contact between the army and fleet, this unit, brought to mutiny by considerations now lost to history, stole three vessels of the fleet and set off by themselves. To get free for their adventure in piracy they had first to murder their praefectus, or commander, a Roman of the equestrian order, and those centurions and legionaries detailed among them as a cadre for training and instruction. This they proceeded to do, thus perpetrating a crime against the Roman military system for which no exculpation would ever be possible.

Once off with the pirated ships, the mutineers seem to have coasted south, landing occasionally to raid, but suffering in the process until, according to Tacitus, they were driven to cannibalism within their own ranks. This last seems improbable, in view of both the paucity of possible source for the historian's knowledge and the later rich booty garnered by the Saxons in their seaborne assaults on the same coast.

Eventually some survivors among them seem to have managed to cross the North Sea to Holland where they were captured by the Suevi and the Frisii living there. So they ended their essay into freedom as slaves. Some few perhaps were sold across the Rhine into Roman hands where, if identified, they had the chance, in lingering, horrible hours on the cross, to regret their ill-conceived and worse-managed defection from the Roman Army in Scotland.

So serious and unusual an event as a mutiny in a Roman military unit must have had its repercussions outside Britain, and quite possibly in Rome itself where, in the immemorial way of higher headquarters, the responsible commander would be looked on as at least presumptively to blame. On this, Tacitus is silent. Yet it is wholly possible that the occurrence became, in the Army files in Rome, a question mark which played its part in Agricola's later failure to receive high appointment.

During the winter of 83–84 A.D. the ambitious chieftain Calgacus managed to form some sort of confederation of the Scots tribes capable of putting in the field an army strong enough, in their own minds at least, to defeat the persistent Romans. So, when in the spring of 84 A.D. Agricola brought north his Legio IX Hispana and Legio II

Adiutrix with auxiliaries, to junction with the Twentieth—which in all probability had spent the winter at Pennata Castra—he was not long in discovering a major concentration of tribesmen hovering on the high ground to his left and west, awaiting the conflux of courage and opportunity to attack.

Thanks to Tacitus' disinterest in geography we do not know where the battle he called that of "Mons Graupius" was fought. For generations confusion was caused by the error of Puteolanus, who published the first printed edition of *Agricola* in 1475 A.D., at Milan. In this edition he rendered the name "Mons Grampius," creating a startling equivocation with the name of the whole mountain chain, a name which otherwise does not appear in history until some two hundred years later. Yet his error may well have been the source from which seventeenth-century geographers derived "Grampian."

Various locations have been suggested, including that of the Pass of Killiecrankie, scene of a long-celebrated victory of the Highland clans over the English 1,605 years after Agricola's "Mount Graupius." A local tradition holds that the seventeen-hundred-foot peak of West Lomond in the Ochill Hills was the scene of a great battle between the clans and the Romans. Actually, this seems too far south for the great battle of 84 A.D. However, its proximity to the remains of a Roman fort found at Ardoch, halfway between Stirling and Perth, might indicate that the local tradition is concerned with the attack on the Ninth Legion of the previous year.

Thirty thousand Caledonii and allied tribesmen, says Tacitus, were gathered in possession of high ground when Agricola approached with an army of three legions, 8,000 auxiliary light infantry, and 3,000 cavalry. Among the auxiliary cohorts were new formations of Britons recruited and trained in the Province; perhaps that Cohors I Brittonum later to achieve distinction and the prize of early Roman citizenship for bravery in battle under Trajan in the Dacian War.

The numbers of the opposing forces do not appear as unbalanced as Tacitus suggests. If Agricola's legions were near full strength of 6,000 men each, his total force came to about 29,000 men. If the Caledonii did in fact number about 30,000 the numerical odds were about even, making attack by the tribesmen suicide rather than effrontery.

Under the circumstances, and undoubtedly influenced by the

nature of the terrain, Agricola was fully justified in following the precedent of Cerealis (from whom he may have learned it) in holding his three legions as reserve in front of his camp and placing the conduct of the battle in the hands of the auxiliaries.

The picture of the battle left us by Tacitus displays an unruly swarm of clansmen rushing down from the higher ground, massed in such depth that only a few at one time came in contact with the confident, waiting cohorts. Once again, as in so many other battles around the Roman world, the vicious Roman short sword proved its superiority in close combat over the longer, pointless blade—very like the later Highland claymore—which, good for slashing and cleaving only, became useless in melee. Slowly the auxiliaries bit into the center of the Caledonii, pushing it back.

Under this remorseless pressure, the front of the clansmen, such as it was, spread sideways threatening to outflank the Roman line. This danger Agricola met with his flank cavalry, four squadrons of which were able to cut their way through the packed mass and, reaching the Highland rear, pounce on thousands of warriors who had not yet struck a blow for freedom.

As a result, the battle quickly degenerated into a Caledonian rout. Night and satiation in killing, says Tacitus, ended the pursuit.

Total casualties, we are told, were 10,000 clansmen and 360 Romans. Among the latter was the luckless Aulus Atticus, praefectus of an ala of auxiliary cavalry, carried by his tumult-maddened horse like an English king of later years full into the middle of the enemy. Borne on winds defying the intervening centuries we can still hear the admiring shouts of those troops who thought his charge reckless bravery, giving way to ribald laughter as they guessed the truth.

Although what we may assume to be Agricola's full purpose— to wipe out the male population of the Caledonii, both as fighting men and as potential fathers of another generation of troublemakers —may have failed of complete realization, the victory effectively broke resistance, drove the discouraged survivors back into the trans-Grampian fastnesses, and secured the coastal plain. All in all, it was a victory for disciplined troops over mob courage comparable to the later butchery at Culloden.

Evidently in preparation for another year of campaigning which would take him to the northern extremities of the island, Agricola, while some of the summer and early fall of 84 A.D. remained, sent his fleet north to explore and report. Although Tacitus speaks of this reconnaissance as "circumnavigation" of Britain, it seems likely that the fleet got no farther than to permit its admiral and ship captains to recognize some landmarks noted on the previous voyage up the west coast. Perhaps Cape Wrath, on the northwestern extremity of Scotland, might have been recognized as the farthest north of the earlier hazardous exploration of the channel between the Inner Hebrides and the west coast.

In fact "circumnavigation" in our sense of the term cannot be inferred if this voyage alone (and not the combination of the two in succeeding years) was meant, for Tacitus indicates that the fleet returned to the harbor from which it had started, the unlocated "Portus Trucculensis," as Agricola marched slowly south, leaving the Twentieth behind him at Pennata Castra and the line of communications forts and the Forth-Clyde barrier garrisoned by auxiliaries. It is possible, but wholly improbable, that this fleet anchorage could have been on the west coast of Britain, or even very far south on the east.

Nevertheless, such a voyage of exploration and discovery, edging along the Scottish mainland past Rattray Head, turning west into Moray Firth, northeast again to Duncansby Head, negotiating the perils of Pentland Firth with the Orkneys wave-washed to starboard, was for the time, and the state of navigational knowledge, a considerable achievement. These ships had no compasses. The fleet commander or his Greek sailing masters might have had considerable knowledge of practical astronomy to guide them, but still could hardly have failed bewilderment at the different aspects of their well-known stars in these northern latitudes.

Additionally, affecting masters and crews together, the superstition and ignorance of the day could hardly fail to generate dread of the unknown waters. On the other hand, had present-day directions of the *North Sea Pilot* been available at the time, it is likely enough the sailing masters would have refused to go at all:

> Before entering Pentland Firth, all vessels should prepare to batten down, and the hatches of small vessels ought to be secured even in the finest weather, as it is difficult to see what may be going on in the distance, and the transition from smooth water to a broken sea is so sudden that no time is given for making arrangements.

As it was, Tacitus reports no ship losses, leaving us with the impression that these skilled mariners found no terror in a northern counterpart of the long-familiar Scylla and Charybdis.

This campaign of 84 A.D. climaxed the career of Julius Agricola, patriot, general, and administrator, who was recalled by Domitian before the spring of 85 A.D. to Rome, there to live out his remaining years in the bitterness of inaction. We cannot quite believe him the paragon of all the Roman virtues, as his son-in-law drew him. Perhaps he fought no battles beyond the near defeat of 83 A.D. and the victory of Mount Graupius, which, reported to Rome, may well have been deemed a minor squabble when measured against the costly and not too successful wars fought with the Chatti in North Europe, or with the dangers posed by Decebalus across the lower Danube.

Nevertheless, in seven years, even if most of them were spent in consolidating the work of his predecessors, he had extended the boundaries of the Province into Scotland. We cannot criticize a general who achieves his aims without unnecessary bloodshed. In the process he had carried the glory and fear of Rome to their farthest north; there pacified unruly tribes whose inaction during the next generation is adequate proof of his success; and yet left behind, in the south, a new generation of Britons who held themselves Romans, schooled to carry some part of the responsibilities of Empire as well as to enjoy the pleasures and luxuries of a rich and many-faceted civilization.

For Agricola's epitaph, we may stand with his son-in-law, for once gentle and kindly:

> . . . that which we have loved and admired in Agricola rests and must forever remain in the hearts of men, through ages yet to come, in the tale of great things dared and accomplished. Full many of the heroes of old oblivion has buried, their fame and repute forgotten. But Agricola, whose tale is here unfolded, will live forever in the heritage of our children.

Thanks to Tacitus himself, and to an accident of preservation, he here wrote more truly than he could have hoped.

VII

THE PROVINCE
85-120 A.D.

. . . Laud we the gods,
And let our crooked smokes climb to their nostrils
From our blest altars. Publish we this peace
To all our subjects. Set we forward: let
A Roman and a British ensign wave
Friendly together . . .
— SHAKESPEARE, *Cymbeline*

1

FOR OVER THIRTY YEARS AFTER AGRICOLA'S departure, Britain has no written history. The old adage allows us to hold it, perhaps, a happy time.

A literary scrap here and there intrudes upon the silence. Juvenal mentions that Domitian would be glad to hear of the death of a British king called Arivaragus; and that storming Brigantian forts was routine work for centurions bucking for promotion to primipilus. But Juvenal mentions no dates and may have been talking about Agricola's tour of duty. In fact, the remark may rest on a tour of duty the satirist himself performed in Britain, as prefect of the First Dalmatian Cohort.*

Suetonius, the gossip columnist, records the execution by Domitian of a former governor of Britain of senatorial rank, one Sallustius Lucullus, for some petty nonsense involving the naming of a new type of lance. This bit of capricious tyranny should probably be dated late in Domitian's reign, both on account of his increasing

---

* During which he seems to have acquired a taste for British oysters.

savagery as he grew older, and from other indirect evidence placing it after Agricola's death in 93 A.D. Since Domitian was murdered in September, 96 A.D., the sudden demise of Lucullus would seem to have occurred within this three-year period.

Confirmation of this timing may be found in the presence in Upper Moesia, in 103–105 A.D., of a special kind of unit, a *pedites singulares Britannici,* or British governor's honor guard. Perhaps this was the unit armed by Lucullus with his fancy lance, abruptly shipped to the northeast frontier of the Empire when Lucullus was recalled.

But all this carries much conjecture. What we do know is that the defense forces of Britain were seriously reduced in the period immediately following Agricola's recall, to meet the major threat posed by Decebalus of Dacia.

During the later years of Agricola's governorship, Domitian's military advisors in Rome had undoubtedly queried the large numbers of auxiliary units required by Agricola to win and then police the newly pacified territory of Britain. They may well have been slightly mollified by the drafts of British recruits organized into auxiliary cohorts and after training or even some combat experience under Agricola sent to the continent to bolster the Rhine-Danube frontier; but it is doubtful that these accretions balanced Agricola's requirements.

Then too, far more important than the auxiliary units were the legions. Long-standing imperial policy resisted temptation to increase the total number of these powerful commands, although various Emperors had found it necessary from time to time.† Domitian had in-

---

† The intermediate changes in the legionary order of battle are instructive by their paucity. Augustus' reforms and reduction of the Army left it with twenty-eight legions. Of these, three (XVII, XVIII, and XIX) were lost in Germany in 9 A.D., stricken from the list, and never again reactivated. Two legions (XV Primagenia and XXII Primagenia) were added by Caligula or Claudius prior to 43 A.D., bringing the total to twenty-seven. Nero organized Legio I Italica, and later, in 68 A.D., Legio I Adiutrix from the fleet marine force at Misenum. Galba activated Legio II Adiutrix, which we know was sent to Britain during Cerealis' governorship.

Vespasian cashiered four legions (I Germanica, IV Macedonica, XV Primagenia, and XVI Gallica) for their role in the Civilis revolt, and in their place raised two new ones (Legio IV Flavia Firma and Legio XVI Flavia Firma). Domitian activated another, Legio I Minerva, but lost V Alauda, a Gallic creation of Julius Caesar's, in his Danube campaign, leaving, at the end of his reign, a total of twenty-nine. There were later additions and losses but it is nevertheless a fact that for the first two centuries of the Christian era, the regu-

creased the total number to thirty with his activation of Legio I Minerva. Even so, the four legions stationed in Britain represented just under 15 per cent of the legionary force available for Empire defense. Domitian's advisors, ceaselessly scanning the defense requirements of ten thousand miles of frontier, may properly have considered this too heavy a commitment of legionary force to a distant and not yet profitable island province. It is not surprising that they may well have looked on the island garrison as a first priority reserve to meet any urgent requirement in a troubled frontier area. King Decebalus, a most formidable adversary, supplied the requirement by invading Moesia within a year after Agricola's departure from Britain. A quick result was the ordering out of Britain of Legio II Adiutrix, probably in the summer of 85 A.D.

Domitian, starting to move against King Decebalus, was delayed by the abortive revolt of Antoninus Saturninus, governor of Upper Germany, whose two legions acclaimed him Caesar. This imperial irritation, although soon put down by loyal troops, allowed Decebalus time to prepare for Domitian's offensive. The Emperor's first expedition was defeated with heavy Roman losses for which nevertheless Domitian demanded and obtained from an obsequious Senate a triumph on his return to Rome.

Legio II Adiutrix never returned to Britain. Twenty-five years later, in the time of Hadrian, the Army list showed it on the Danube frontier stationed at Aquincum, the modern Budapest. Its withdrawal from Britain, however great the continental need, posed serious problems in frontier adjustment to Agricola's successor.

The Legion's station had been at Deva (Chester) from which it patrolled not only North Wales but also Cheshire and Lancaster on the west flank of the still-restive Brigantes. This area could not be left vacant. With some reluctance but facing imperious necessity, the governor ordered the Twentieth Legion back to Deva from its far-north fortress of Pennata Castra on the Tay. The result was that the defense of the Forth-Clyde line and its forward outposts devolved upon auxiliary units.

Militarily, it seems to have worked for at least a generation, if we are to judge from the absence of any reports of difficulties in Britain during this period. The success may be ascribed less to the re-

---

lar Army of Rome varied only by 20 per cent. (Cf. H. M. D. Parker, *The Roman Legions.*)

sistance the widely dispersed auxiliary garrisons could offer than to the exhaustion of the Caledonii and their allied clans so roughly handled by Agricola at Mons Graupius. But politically, the move was far-reaching in its negative results.

The auxiliaries perforce left in Scotland were far from the civilizing agents the legion, with its corps of trained specialists, represented. The Latin spoken by the auxiliaries, drawn from Germanic, Pannonian, Thracian, and Spanish tribes, was not their native tongue. Thus a fundamental requirement of advancing Romanization, the common use of Latin, could not be met in any great degree among the tribesmen whose conduct the auxiliaries regulated.

For the few Roman officers commanding the auxiliaries, the administrative and peacetime burdens—conducting courts, supervising road construction, maintaining fortifications, intensifying training, engineering of one sort or another, meeting medical demands from troops and civilians alike, assuring water supply, arranging for adequate rations—the thousand and one quasi-military activities at which the officers and men of the legions were old hands, must have been so excessive and time-consuming as severely to limit the continuous contact and amiable if firm relations with the tribal peoples which alone, by force of example, could induce their acceptance of the Roman way. The inevitable result was the failure to give to the population of the Lowlands a personal stake in the preservation of Roman rule, Roman order, and Roman law in Scotland. In later years the Province and the Empire were to pay again and again for this failure.

To protect his Scottish outposts the governor made other dispositions, among which we may note the expansion of the Agricolan camp at Trimontium (Newstead) into a major fortress. Only indistinct ramparts now remain of this bulwark and main support, north of the Cheviots, for the line-of-communications road from Corbridge to Pennata Castra on the Tay. Located near a bend of the Tweed where the gaunt remains of Dryburgh and Melrose abbeys and Abbotsford, once the home of Sir Walter Scott, now tell mutely of so much later history, the fortress seems to have been constantly garrisoned, except for a short period around 100 A.D., for long centuries as the focal point of Roman defense of the Lowlands. For much of this time its garrison was the Ala Petriana Milliaria, a thousand-man regiment of cavalry, one of only twelve in the entire Roman Army, and the only one of its kind in Britain.

In the meantime the road system was developed throughout the area. Not only was the Great North Road extension, later called Dere Street, more heavily fortified; but another, starting at Deva on the west, heading north through Warrington at the root of the Mersey estuary, thence close to Preston in Lancashire and on through Brougham to Carlisle and through Carlisle into Dumfries, across Lanark near Abington, and then northeast to join Dere Street at the Forth, was strengthened and improved into a main thoroughfare. An offshoot went northwest to the Clyde anchor of the Agricolan line of camps between Forth and Clyde. Slowly, connecting roads were built, crisscrossing the whole area north of Carlisle-Newcastle through the Lowland country. Patrols and traffic control stations at crossroads prevented any great concentration of the tribesmen, as had been done earlier by Frontinus in Wales, and by Cerealis in Brigantia.

This pacified area had now to be covered and garrisoned by a seriously depleted force, backed up, from far in the rear, by the legions in their fortresses at Eburacum, where the Ninth was based, and Deva, where the Twentieth, perhaps rejoicing at its return to comparative civilization, had settled in. Legio II Augusta was held at its far-west base, Isca Silurum (Caerleon-on-Usk) to watch South Wales.

Whatever the reasons, whether resting on Agricola's decimation of the hardy Caledonii, the general futility of resistance, or the well-planned measures of control taken by Agricola's successor, the system worked. For over a generation, for all we know to the contrary, the northern and western frontiers of the Province remained at peace.

2

IN THAT portion of the province south and east of the early boundary —the Severn-Trent river line—a new generation of Britons had reached maturity, a generation which had never, in the old Celtic freebooting sense, known liberty. Persons born in the year of Plautius' conquest were, in 85 A.D., the year of Agricola's departure, forty-two years old, long accustomed to family responsibility and even approaching the end of the short life span granted by the rudimentary sanitary and medical conditions of ancient times. They had grown up, in most cases married, and reared offspring under Roman law, firmly held in their behavior to Roman ideas of public order. The ambitious among them were fluent in Latin, at this time already a colloquial dilution of Cicero's elegance or Caesar's austere prose. In most cases they were bilingual, retaining command of their mother Gaelic as an essential means of communication with the rural districts and the lower classes in town.

But their future was with Rome. We cannot doubt that an overwhelming proportion of the British upper classes—by which, at this stage, is meant the family groups of the old tribal chieftains—subjected for their entire lifetimes in varying degree to the civilizing processes so blandly ascribed by Tacitus to Agricola but which were in fact standard Roman policy in taking over a barbarian province, wholly accepted, participated in, and advanced, for themselves and their children, the Roman way. Indeed, within their purview, they knew no other. Economic advantage and normal ambition, at every point of contact, fortified this acceptance. Advancement in either wealth or dignity was impossible outside the Roman complex.

The tribal capitals, encouraged, if not initiated, by Agricola, potential urban centers theretofore generally unknown to the Celtic polity, grew in population, in commerce, in material dignity, as their centralizing function was accepted by the tribes.

Although, after a slow start, the growth of the towns was steady, it was also limited, with Londinium a sole exception. The Britons, then as now, seemed less than gregarious, preferring the life of the countryside to that of the town. The economy and agricultural methods employed encouraged the accumulation of land, at least by those Britons with some capital. As these country estates became viable, the landowners, drawing on Roman building methods and adapting Roman architecture to the climate, built farm and estate houses of all sizes, known to later generations of amateur archeologists as "villas." These houses, some quite elaborate, and nearly all possessed of a hypocaust or means of heating at least some of the rooms against the rigors of a British winter, were no rural pleasure domes, but the centers of intensively cultivated and frequently (in all respects except for luxuries) self-supporting agricultural estates. The sturdy

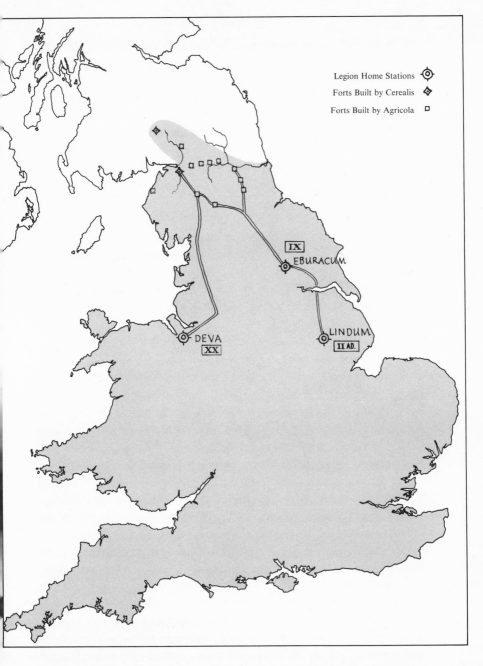

Legion Home Stations ◉
Forts Built by Cerealis ◈
Forts Built by Agricola ▫

IX
EBURACUM

DEVA
XX

LINDUM
II AD.

Agricola's first northern campaign, 79 A.D.; consolidation of
Cerealis' conquest of the Brigantes.

Agricola's northward reconnaissance, 80 A.D.; Legio XX advances
to Pennata Castra, II Adiutrix is transferred to Deva.

Note: It is not certain whether Agricola reached the Tay in this year or
later, or when the forts here shown were built.

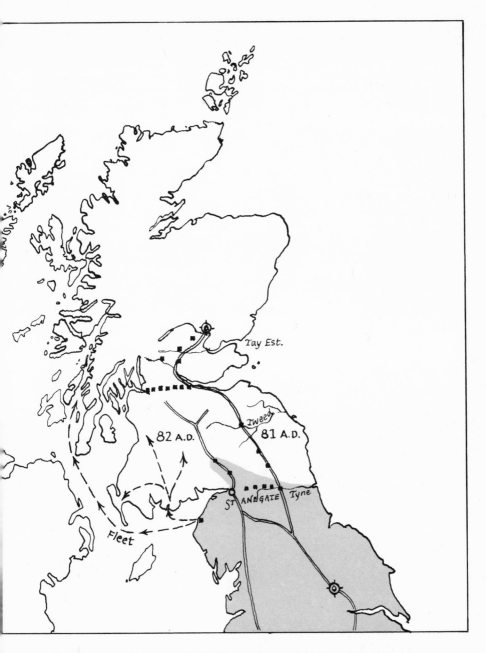

Agricola's movements, 81 and 82 A.D.: consolidation of eastern lowlands and erection of forts on Forth-Clyde line, 81; consolidation of
western lowlands and fleet reconnaissance of western coast, 82.

Agricola's campaigns against the Caledonii, 83–84 A.D., with fleet
scouting the east coast, culminating in victory at Mons Graupius.

foundations of these houses, often with elaborate mosaic floors in various states of preservation, have sufficiently survived wanton destruction and the passage of centuries to permit identification. They are found throughout southern England, with concentrations in Somerset, Gloucestershire, Kent, Hampshire, and the home counties.

The tribal capitals served their purpose as the years passed, although perhaps not to the degree expected as they seldom grew above 6,000 in population.‡ Calleva Atrebatum, cantonal capital of the Belgic Atrebates, has been shown by painstaking excavation to have been at this time still quite a small town; built within the old Belgic defenses which enclosed an area of about ninety acres, with streets, or rather paths, wandering haphazardly and some fifty or sixty houses or buildings of various sorts. It did have, however, a substantial bath house with a very impressive portico supported by eight columns, the beginnings of a forum-basilica, and three or four small temples —all built probably before the end of the first century. The time of rebuilding in strict Roman fashion, with streets laid out at right angles, was to come later, not before the second century.

Most of the progress in Romanization at this time was confined, with a few exceptions, to the southeasterly portion of the Province. Wales, Brigantia, and the Lowlands remained areas of military occupation, populated by tribes which had not yet accepted, even if obliged to endure, Rome. Beyond Eburacum with its town growing up about the Ninth Legion's fortress, Roman civilization fell rapidly away. The moors and the forests, the tilled fields and pastures remained in hands that clung to the habits and thoughts of their Celtic forebears, submissive but noncommittal before the passing of patrols or the swift canter and jingling of harness that gave notice of a cavalry ala riding north on the business of Rome.

Even within the Roman Pale many villages existed, perhaps throughout the entire four centuries of Roman occupation, quite untouched by the imported civilization. Examples are found in Salisbury Plain and in the Fens—regions in which the villa system is rare —of these backward but largely self-sufficient communities, living by agriculture, grinding their own grain, and possessed only of agricultural implements and crude pottery. It is perhaps silent evidence

‡ Corinium Dobunorum (Cirencester), center of the wool trade and in the second century A.D. second largest town in Britain, might at its peak have had a population of ten to twelve thousand.

of the efficacy of Roman policing methods that these sites have yielded no weapons of any kind.

It was inevitable, no doubt, in Britain as in other remote parts of the Empire, that the Romanization impressed by the conquerors was itself transmuted in greater or less degree to produce a people who were neither Roman nor Celtic, but something in between, exhibiting underlying Celtic customs and traditions with a superimposed gloss of civilization. Even then, the Romanization existed in gradations, with undoubtedly the major absorption of Roman ideas taking place among the aristocracy and from them suffering progressive dilution, to villages like those noted, where there is no evidence of any Romanization at all.

In a certain sense these gradations might be expected from the very flexibility of Roman control and the methods by which the civil side of the government was established. Within the overriding requirements of the provincial government, the tribal capitals were self-governing, permitting to their residents a very high degree of individual freedom and dignity. Each tribal area was governed by the order of decurions (*ordo decurionum*), generally numbering about one hundred of the principal landowners, educated citizens, aristocracy, and tribal leaders. From among the *decuriones* a tribal senate was selected, called the *ordo splendidissimus,* to all of whom it was customary for the governor to grant Roman citizenship when they assumed their responsibilities.

From among the splendidissimi four working officials—two senior, the *duoviri iuredicendo,* and two junior, the *duoviri aediles*—were annually elected. These were the day-to-day working officials of the tribal capital and its dependent territory. The elections were democratic enough, if one recognizes the severe limitations of the franchise, but there can be little doubt that candidates who for any reason were personae non gratae to the governor had little chance of gaining office and much less of long retaining it. Rome extended its civic freedoms to strengthen dominion and to simplify administration, not to obstruct either.

The senior duoviri sat as local judges in both civil and criminal cases. Major causes could be appealed to the procurator's courts, or in really serious litigation, to the governor himself. Cases involving Roman citizens went, of course, directly to the jurisdiction of the procurator's courts, and carried the right of appeal to Caesar himself.

The junior duoviri were responsible for town and shire administration; for the building, repair, and maintenance of public buildings; for roads; and for other public works and responsibilities, including the often onerous burden of maintaining the rest house (*mansio*) and relays of horses for the use of the imperial couriers.

Provincial taxes were initially set by the procurator, who seems about this time to have shifted his offices from Camulodunum to Londinium because of the latter's superior location. Taxes were based on a careful census of persons, landed property, cattle, slaves, and other wealth assessed by tax-appraisers called *censitores*. The taxes were two: *tributum soli,* a land tax; and *tributum capitis,* a head tax. Every five years the senor duoviri carefully revised and adjusted the individual assessments. Because of the importance of this task and its immediate repercussions, not only on the revenue but on civilian morale, the officials elected in these critical years were called *duoviri quinquennales.* Roman policy saw to it that election to these offices was held as a high honor.

The collection of taxes in cash or in kind, preserving from democratic laxity this delegation of taxing power, was the inexorable legal responsibility of the whole body of decuriones. The responsibility was real, and if collections for any reason failed, the decuriones were expected to make up any deficit from their personal resources. In the nature of men the system appears not only sound but administratively inexpensive.

For long centuries the tax burden seems not to have been unduly onerous. Later, as imperial problems brought about the severe restrictions and heavy imposts associated with the centralized controls set up by Diocletian, the situation of the citizen, caught between a failing economy and a rapacious government, became desperate.

Aside from the tribal capitals, various degrees of authority and self-government were granted towns and cities of Britain as was done throughout the Empire. Glevum, Camulodunum and Lindum, being coloniae, had special privileges because of their concentrations of veterans, all Roman citizens. Londinium, perhaps because of the multiplying activities of the provincial government centered there, seems to have been held in the status of oppidum, with limited rights of self-government. Only Verulamium appears to have reached the high civic status of a *municipium,* self-governing with few limitations. Eburacum (York) in later years became a colonia, and Professor

Eric Birley has pointed to evidence that Deva (Chester) at some time prior to 212 A.D. ceased to be classified as a minor town of the Cornovii, whose cantonal capital was at Viroconium, and was granted some status of its own—whether colonia, urbs, or oppidum is not clear.

There were other arrangements, examples of Roman political flexibility. The client kingdom of the Regnenses in Sussex, Hampshire, and Surrey retained complete local autonomy, at least for the lifetime of its king Cogidumnus. His loyalty to Rome was recognized by the rare bestowal on him of twin titles—*Rex et Legatus Augusti in Britannia*—probably by Claudius. These honorifics signified that Rome recognized him not only as an independent king but also as a Roman citizen holding within his domain the legal authority of a Roman praetor. Undoubtedly this imperial honor was treasured by Cogidumnus for its prestige. That it also placed squarely on his shoulders responsibility for maintaining Roman law and practices in his kingdom may have been less obvious but surely more the meat of these sonorous titles.

There is no record of another client king so honored as Cogidumnus. This may be due to the chance that has preserved a dedication stone of a temple to Neptune and Minerva in his capital of Noviomagus (Chichester), giving his name and titles, rather than to the absence of other chieftains within the Province similarly honored for recognizing the futility of opposition. However, Prasutigas, King of the Iceni, was equally loyal to his treaty with Rome up to his death in 60 A.D.

Within this subtle complex of control the Pax Romana held undisputed sway. Trade increased as people learned to desire luxuries theretofore unobtainable, by the simple process of seeing them displayed at the town markets. The widespread use of Roman money both simplified commercial transactions and increased the velocity of turnover. Prosperity, destined never to reach a level we would deem more than modest, grew slowly as the fruits of earth, the simple products of farm, pasture, orchard, and mine, were exchanged for the niceties of civilization. Wine from the continent, with that of Italy preferred to the less expertly developed wines of Gaul, early became a major item of import and seldom seems to have lacked buyers. Samian pottery, house furnishings, silverware, and other appurtenances of civilization entered the ports as leather, wool, grain, and metals were shipped to the continent. A brisk internal trade in oysters delighted Roman epicures and Celtic appetites in about equal proportion.

The Roman roads, in spite of local cost of upkeep, contributed to the increasing integration of the island economy. Surveyed originally in terms of military need, and carrying always a priority for military traffic and the imperial courier service, they were still able to accommodate increasing amounts of civilian and commercial traffic.

For the wealthier classes at least, the roads provided an ease and celerity of travel hitherto unknown, thus opening new vistas of experience and breaking down parochial bigotries. Not the least of attractions to Britons from afar were the hot springs of *Aquae Sulis* (Bath) about this time enclosed in stone buildings of Roman architectural design, forerunners of a later magnificent expansion.

On the whole, the Province seems in these closing years of the first century A.D. to have been developing quietly, in peace and order, undisturbed by events across the Channel. The generation born at the time of the conquest grew old and in its turn was gathered to forefathers who had not known Rome. Governors came and went, leaving no new conquests, nor any notable tyranny to mark their names in history. Children were born, grew up learning to speak and write Latin, and reached manhood with its cares. To the west and north the guardian legions and ceaselessly patrolling auxiliaries maintained the provincial frontiers, even while the soldiers who had known Agricola completed their terms of service, were mustered out, and retired to the various coloniae while their places in the ranks were taken by young citizens of Rome, a majority born in Britain and many in all likelihood sons of veterans. Legion commanders and other senior officers arrived in Britain from the continent carrying the Emperor's commission, to serve their tours of duty and to depart to new assignments around the Empire. We know of one, at least, from an altar at Deva, bearing the resounding name of T. Pomponius Mamilianus Rufus Antistianus Funisulanus Vettonianus, who commanded the Twentieth for a term in the late 90's before going on in the hierarchy to the consulship in Rome in the year 100. We may believe the years of his assignment in Cheshire a welcome breathing spell between harsh and bloody wars on the continent.

3

So PASSED quiet years in Britain. Meanwhile, in Rome, the once able Domitian, whose early years as Augustus had carried out the promise of the honest and efficient administrations of his father Vespasian and his brother Titus, turned crafty and suspicious under the weight of fear. Perhaps the abortive rebellion of Saturninus, back in 86 A.D. had been a blow both to his confidence and to his self-esteem, for it was about then that the vicious qualities appeared in him which were to spell for Rome another period of capricious tyranny reminiscent of Caligula and Nero.

As his fears grew to frenzy and his suspicion waxed universal he brought about his own end by including his wife and immediate staff in his distrust. Their daggers acted in self-preservation, ending Domitian's life before he could terminate theirs. The last of the Flavian line died violently in 96 A.D., a sorry caricature of the wisdom, firmness, common sense, and earthy humor of his father Vespasian—and indeed, of his own early promise.

The Senate, acting for a change surprisingly like its old Republican self, selected as Emperor one of its own, a Roman gentleman of stainless reputation and proved integrity, Marcus Cocceius Nerva. Possibly because the entire Roman world remembered with horror the slaughter and destruction which had attended the contested succession to Nero, no rival candidates presented themselves. Nor did either the Praetorian Guard or the frontier legions propose a candidate to be seated in blood. Nerva, already old when he assumed the imperial responsibility, died after a short reign of sixteen months at the age of sixty-six, but not before he had adopted and proclaimed as his son, heir, and successor the general commanding the Rhine defenses, Marcus Ulpius Traianus.

Trajan, as he is known to us, was Spanish-born and the first non-Italian to hold the Principate. He was primarily a fighting general of considerable pugnacity, whose first move after settling affairs in Rome was to mount an offensive against King Decebalus of Dacia, who had inflicted such a humiliating defeat on Roman arms under Domitian. Because of the demands on military manpower this campaign beyond the Danube necessitated, Britain was not long in feeling its effects.

Trajan appears to have taken no legions from Britain but he must have withdrawn many cohorts and alae of auxiliaries. Some few we can trace. A Cohors II Batavorum is among the units listed as suffering casualties, inscribed on a monument set up by Trajan after the Dacian war was won. Another the identification of which is defaced, but which included soldiers certainly of British origin, is mentioned on the same memorial. We know that Agricola at his battle of Mons Graupius had had four Batavian cohorts, of which by 100 A.D. only one was left in Britain. And we know that Trajan honored Cohors I Brittonum, earlier withdrawn by Domitian, with the title *Ulpia Torquata Pia Fidelis* and a grant of Roman citizenship to its personnel for bravery in Dacia.

Many other units must have been withdrawn, for quite suddenly, within a few years of 100 A.D. all the garrisons north of the Cheviots, and perhaps down as far as the Tyne-Solway line were pulled out of their stations. In effect, all the territory north of Tyne-Solway won by Cerealis and Agricola was abandoned. As a natural result, courage and enterprise blossomed anew among the tribes which neither time nor attention, inclination nor opportunity had permitted to become Romanized. A new generation among the Caledonii edged out from behind the Grampians, scouted the now deserted camps and fortlets, paced the unpatrolled roads, and dreamed of a day of vengeance.

Some arrangements for maintaining the peace of the frontier were incumbent on the governor faced with such a diminution of his forces. There may have been halfhearted political alliances entered into with the Lowland tribes, the Selgovae and the Votadini and others, aimed at protecting their lands as well as the frontier of the Province from the Highland clans. In the absence of evidence, whatever arrangements the governor made worked for a few years.

There was some troop movement in the opposite direction; whether reinforcement of the depleted garrison or merely a routine switch of units is hard to determine. In any event, Cohors II Asturum, a partly mounted unit, attested in Germany in 80 and 89 A.D., was moved to Britain sometime between 89 and 105 A.D. The accident of preservation of the evidence in this instance might indicate that there were other units moved into Britain which cannot be traced.

Perhaps to compensate for the reduction in force, perhaps merely to advertise his intention to maintain the island province, Trajan authorized new construction in stone for the legionary fortresses. In stately, even monumental, architecture, new permanent barracks; an impressive Praetorium, or headquarters, a palatial house for the legion commander, ample, even luxurious baths; an amphitheatre outside the walls; granaries, stables, bake ovens, recreation facilities; and elaborate mess halls and hospitals replaced the older makeshift establishments at Isca Silurum, Deva, and Eburacum. Similar reconstruction was undertaken at auxiliary forts in Wales. No provincial watching or laboring on their construction could doubt that Rome was in Britain to stay.

Yet trouble of some kind was on its way. An inscription found at York testified to the constructional work on the stone fortress during 108 A.D. It is the last dated evidence of the existence of the Legio IX Hispana Triumphalis Macedonica, the proud possessor of 170 years or more of Roman military glory, veteran of the conquest under Plautius, of the Boudiccan revolt, of Agricola's far-north campaigns. From this point on, the legion disappears from history.

We do not know what happened. There is evidence of a severe British war, perhaps in 117–119 A.D., perhaps attended by earlier outbursts of a lethal character. Vague evidence indicates it might have been centered in the southwest of Scotland, beyond the Solway-Tyne line. Fronto, who wrote history while teaching the future Emperor Marcus Aurelius rhetoric, has come down to us in a fragment which says only that the casualties suffered by the Romans in Britain at this time were as great as those suffered in the Jewish revolt of Hadrian's later reign.

But there is also fragmentary evidence of trouble during Trajan's reign, which ended in 117 A.D. The evidence rests partly in two diplomas (retirement certificates, carrying citizenship unless previously granted) of *Cohors I Cugernorum*. On the first, issued in 103 A.D., the cohort's designation is unadorned. But by 122 A.D., when the next diploma is dated, the title has become *Cohors I Ulpia Traiana Cugernorum Civium Romanorum,* indicating that sometime prior to Trajan's death in 117 A.D. the cohort had performed so gallantly in battle as to win not only the honorific *Ulpia Traiana*—a sort of "Trajan's Own"—but the much more tangible reward of an advance grant of Roman citizenship to its personnel. One might reasonably suspect that since Trajan was campaigning in distant Mesopotamia from the spring of 115 on, he could spare little attention to affairs in Britain, so that possibly this action he so lavishly rewarded took place before then. On the other hand, even if in the press of affairs in the East he still had time to act favorably on a British governor's report and recommendation, we may assume at least a year passed before the papers could be prepared and catch up with him. Perhaps 115 or 116 is the latest date this action could have taken place. It is unlikely that the cohort was moved from Britain to earn its honors on the continent, for it is later, in the second half of the second century, listed as the garrison of the Hadrianic fort of Brocolita (now Carrawburgh).

The second bit of evidence of serious trouble in Britain in Trajan's time rests on a tombstone found in Cyrenaica, west of Egypt. This records the death of a certain C. Julius Karus, a native of Narbonne in southern Gaul, serving as a military tribune of Legio III Cyrenaica while leading a mixed detachment of that unit and of Legio XXII Deitoriana, both then making up the legionary garrison of Egypt, on a recruiting expedition into Cyrenaica.

But the tombstone also goes into details on Tribune Karus and proves that this officer was quite a combat leader. For it records that, while in command of Cohors II Asturum, partly mounted (which we have already noted as having been moved to Britain from Germany sometime prior to 105 A.D.), Tribune Karus had been awarded "in the British War" the *Corona Muralis,* the *Corona Vallari,* the *Corona Aurea,* and the *Hasta Pura.*

The award of these decorations to a relatively junior officer for one campaign is scarcely duplicated in Roman military records that have come down to us. A reasonably analogous occurrence today would be for a battalion commander in the Korean War to win the Congressional Medal, the Distinguished Service Cross, and at least two Silver Stars, and live, not only to tell the tale, but to serve later in higher duty on the other side of the world.

Trajan, on the record, was far more lavish in the award of decorations than was his successor, Hadrian. There is, therefore, a presumption that the gallant deeds of Karus in Britain while in command of the Second Asturians were performed, not only while Trajan was still Emperor, but early enough so that he could act on the forwarded recommendations.

Then there is the recruiting mission to Cyrenaica during which Karus died and was mourned by his troops, who took the trouble to erect his tombstone. It is unlikely this mission could have taken place after 115 A.D., for in that year the Jews of Cyrene rose in revolt, massacred many of the non-Jewish residents, and were put down only after Trajan sent an expedition under Marcius Turbo. It is difficult to believe that Cyrenaica, after that convulsion, would appear sufficiently attractive as a recruiting ground to justify a detachment being sent the long road from Egypt for that purpose.

We may conclude then that sometime between 105 and 115 A.D. there was a severe outbreak of hostilities in Britain which expanded into the full-scale war of 117–119, in which it has long been assumed that the Ninth Legion itself was almost totally destroyed and erased from the Army list. That this loss of a legion occurred then is the view held by nearly all scholars of Roman Britain until very recently. But this view was cogently questioned by Professor Birley in 1948. His argument rests on epigraphical evidence.

In examining inscriptions recording the careers of two senatorial officers, one L. Aemilius Karus, governor of Arabia, 142–143 A.D., and L. Novius Crispinus, commander of Legio III Augusta (the garrison of Africa and Numidia), 147–149, Professor Birley makes clear that their earlier but undated service as military tribunes of the Ninth Legion could not have taken place as early as 120 A.D. A third inscription, to a Marcus Cocceius, son of Severus, a praefectus castra of Legio X Gemina, records his service as primipilus of the Ninth. Again, so early a date for this high position as the year 120 seems improbable.

Yet if the Ninth was not destroyed in this period, something happened to it,§ then or later, for by the reign of Marcus Aurelius it is missing from the Army list of legions and stations then compiled. Under what circumstances, when, or where the legion disappeared, we simply do not know.

Trajan's conquests of Dacia and the East, where he annexed to the Empire the new province of Mesopotamia after defeating the

§ In 1953, Professor I. H. Richmond writes: "That the legion was cashiered there is no doubt, and it seems evident that this fate, at the hands of the disciplinarian Hadrian, followed an ignominious defeat." In what may be partial acceptance of Professor Birley's views, Professor Richmond goes on to say; ". . . Some of its officers at least, survived." Cf. *Roman Britain*, I. H. Richmond, Penguin Books, London, 1953.

Parthians, strained not only the military resources of the Empire but also a sturdy heart and vigorous constitution worn out in the service of Rome. He did not survive the journey back from the Persian Gulf, dying at Selinus, in Asia Minor, in 117 A.D.

His successor, whether by recognized merit or woman's guile, or a combination of both, was Trajan's nephew, Publius Aelius Adrianus, also of Spanish birth, and surely one of the ablest as well as most complex personalities to enliven the ancient world. Soldier, poet of sorts, philosopher, disciplinarian, engineer, architect, lover of things Greek both glorious and disreputable, monumental builder, incorrigible traveler, and conscientious, responsible Emperor, Hadrian—with the two successors he personally selected—was to raise the Roman Empire to its zenith in splendor, prosperity, and majesty.

VIII

THE FRONTIER
120-196 A.D.

Hang out our banners on the outward walls;
The cry is still "they come!"
—SHAKESPEARE, *Macbeth*

1

WHETHER OR NOT THE NINTH LEGION was destroyed at this time, the interest of the new Emperor in Britain and its problems is attested by vigorous measures he took for the strengthening of its garrison, as soon as continental conditions and the security of his own position permitted.

Somewhere about 120–121, Hadrian ordered Legio VI Victrix Pia Fidelis, from the garrison of Lower Germany into Britain.* A strong detachment from XXII Primagenia in Upper Germany seems to have accompanied it. And a vexillatio from VII Gemina, on duty in Spain, soon followed.

It was this major reinforcement of the provincial garrison that convinced many students of Roman Britain that the Ninth had met its fate in the disturbance of 117–119 A.D., since so massive a move-ment could scarcely be understood except as an essential replacement. If, as has been suggested, this view is no longer tenable, some other

---

* Professor R. G. Collingwood, in 1953, wrote: "The VIth Legion, Pia Fidelis, which Hadrian brought over to replace the IXth, an unfortunate unit, once severely cut up in Boudicca's rising, and once in Agricola's campaigns, and again, beyond recovery, in a rising early in the reign of Hadrian."

explanation of the dispatch of the augmented Sixth Legion to Britain is necessary. It is possible, and worth exploring, that this movement followed not from any urgent need to replace the vanished Ninth, but from a general regroupment of frontier forces around the Empire's borders, in accordance with Hadrian's developing concept of a coherent, long-term frontier policy.

The departure of the Sixth and its reinforcement from the Twenty-Second had obviously weakened the Rhine defenses. To make this loss good, Hadrian moved Legio XXX Ulpia Victrix, a creation of his predecessor and uncle, Trajan, from Upper Moesia (the area south of the Danube mouths) into Germany. The selection of this command would seem to indicate that Trajan's conquest and annexation of the trans-Danubian province of Dacia had not only moved the frontier far forward of Moesia, but had so pacified the area that its garrison could be safely reduced by one legion.

But these correlated movements of whole legions were but a minor readjustment within the basic frontier policy which, with much ex post facto deduction, we may believe Hadrian had put together. The policy may be stated as follows:

ONE: On each frontier establish a clearly identifiable boundary, either natural or Roman-constructed, which will mark beyond any doubt the line "separating the Romans from the barbarians."

TWO: Defend this line by forts and patrols far in advance, employing auxiliary troops, operating from bases on the line itself or close behind it; farther back, to provide a deep defense or forward support as needed, erect the permanent fortresses of the garrison legions, housing the invincible shock troops and major civilizing agents of the Empire.

THREE: Establish on this boundary line ports of entry and departure, where cross-boundary traffic in either direction may be closely controlled, and customs duties, where applicable, collected by *numeri* (a special force of frontier police); by this means any attempt to infiltrate the boundary can be controlled and the danger of large concentrations of enemy gathering on cultivated Roman territory behind the line be severely limited.

FOUR: Encourage by all possible means the growth and development of Roman life and civilized ways, right up to the line itself; this is crucial to the long-term success of frontier maintenance.

Such a co-ordinated policy, to be persisted in over a long period, seems to have been born in Hadrian's mind as a means to mitigate, if not entirely solve, a majority of the difficulties which in prior years had harassed the Roman frontiers.

The fourth element of the policy, the requirement for full economic growth and social development up to the boundary itself, is at once the most vital part of the whole and that most characteristic of Hadrian, the builder. If successful, its benefits would be manifold.

As new residents—perhaps for the most part veterans, entitled to settle on land grants made by the government as a law suit in Justinian's *Digests* indicates—occupied and tilled farmlands close to the frontier, the surplus food they raised would become available to feed the garrisons. This would not only provide the settlers with an assured market, but also would present the government with a major saving in transport charges. With the economy of the settlers so assured, they in turn would supplement the moderate demand for manufactured goods and services created by the extraneous needs of the regularly paid soldiers. To meet this demand towns—vici— would grow up, near the forts but accessible to the settlers, populated by merchants and purveyors of one kind or another. The townsfolk themselves would be in need of farm products, thus further increasing the prosperity and interdependence of the border area.

Moreover, after a term of years, the human fertility of the settlers and townsfolk might be expected to produce annual crops of sons peculiarly fitted, both by their knowledge of the locality and a natural desire to perform their military service close to home, for enlistment in the local forces. Thus, not only would the government's recruiting problems be eased, but the manpower so gathered could be expected to show greater discipline in camp and determination in battle.

Lastly, a perhaps overoptimistic but by no means unjustified hope for such a policy might rest in the contrast between their own rudimentary existence and the civilized life the barbarians from beyond the line could not fail to observe when on market days they were permitted to cross the boundary and trade their products for the sophisticated merchandise of Rome. Out of this commercial intercourse a desire for emulation of the Roman way could be expected to rise, from which in time voluntary Romanization of the barbarians would follow, thus extending the area of the Pax Romana.

Only by the presupposition of some such imperial policy on the part of Hadrian does it seem possible to explain archeological evidence uncovered in Britain, along the *limes* (boundary) of the Rhine-Danube frontier and, most definitively, along the recently excavated and studied "Fossatum Africae"—the line of road, ditch, and watch-towers which at the Sahara's edge delimited the southern boundary of the imperial provinces of the two Mauretanias.

It is clear that such a forward policy depended on the ability of Rome to maintain the military initiative, to do what fighting might be necessary forward of the boundary, to inculcate in the outland the notion and belief that the boundary itself was inviolate, that behind it Rome and the Romans lived in the majesty of the Pax Romana. If the day should ever come when the military initiative was lost, then—then—but who of Hadrian's time, including the Emperor himself, could ever have conceived such a day might come? Had not Rome, Republic and Empire, held the military initiative ever since the founding of the City, over eight hundred years ago? Were not Rome's armies invincible, its provinces secure, its civilized life an example to copy, not an object of pillage? Lose the military initiative? Impossible!

We cannot hold Hadrian responsible for a lack of foresight denied to us in our own time. As Professor Birley put it in his detailed treatment of this point of view ("Hadrianic Frontier Policy," *Carnuntina*, iii [1956] pp. 25–33): "If the policy did not prove successful in every respect, and if on some frontiers it had ultimately to be abandoned and a withdrawal made to a line chosen primarily for military reasons, that is not to say that Hadrian must be denied due credit for an impressive contribution to the record of large scale planning."

2

IN 122 A.D. Hadrian went in person to Britain, perhaps arriving at about the same time the Sixth Legion was completing its movement. He stayed less than a full year, and probably not more than a few months. We may assume he first took time to examine—with that meticulous attention to detail and penetrating insight into over-all principle his biographers found so remarkable in an Emperor—all aspects of the Province's political and economic life, as well as its defense.

Beyond these and associated duties, self-imposed activity in every imperial province, his major business in Britain was to make a decision about its frontier. There were various solutions to be considered, many factors to be weighed.

To reach an unassailable natural frontier would require conquest of the entire island, with even then a watch kept on the Orkneys to the north, on the Hebrides and Hibernia to the west. To achieve as much might have been the original intent of Nero in sending Veranius, and of Vespasian in approving and supporting the advance of Cerealis and later that of Agricola into Scotland. Hadrian must have been aware that lack of means, resulting from urgent troop requirements on the continent, had forced Domitian to curtail Agricola's conquests. Undoubtedly the prospect of conquering all of Britain would have appealed to Trajan had not his campaigns in Dacia and the East pre-empted his attention.

But Hadrian was no expansionist. One of his first acts on succeeding Trajan had been to relinquish control of the latter's recent conquest of Mesopotamia. Hadrian seems to have had a keener insight into the limitations of the imperial resources than had his predecessors. Perhaps closely related to his formulation of a consistent frontier policy was his realization that those resources in manpower and in costs were already close to the breaking point while little had been done to make the border areas economically viable. Thus the solution of complete conquest, if considered—and it is possible that the earlier decision to send over the Sixth Legion was so connected—was discarded.

Another alternative solution, surely weighed in all its ramifications by Hadrian if we can take his abandonment of Mesopotamia as precedent, was to withdraw entirely from Britain, setting the western boundary of the Empire on the Channel as it had been in the days of Augustus and Tiberius. By so doing he would be able to strengthen his continental frontiers by the island garrison—perhaps fifty thousand legionaries and auxiliaries, worth their weight in gold if stationed along the Rhine and the Danube. Such a drastic solution was not without attraction to an extremely intelligent man charged with the security of civilization. Aside from the massive reinforcement of the continental frontiers, abandonment of Britain would relieve the imperial Treasury of a substantial annual deficit, since, if we are to

Hadrian's Wall near Borcovicum (Housesteads)

Roman-British Silverwork: Bowls and Spoons from the Mildenhall
Treasure

Roman-British Tesselated Floor: From a Villa at Withington

Roman-British Silverwork: "The Neptune Dish" from the Mildenhall
Treasure

Roman Bath at Aquae Sulis (Bath)

believe Appian,† costs were not yet balanced by incoming revenue from the Province.

Yet total abandonment was a solution which in Hadrian's sense of imperial responsibility, if ever seriously considered, had to be discarded. The southern portion of Britain had been Roman for nearly eighty years—the better part of a century. Over this span of time a major investment had gone into the island, an investment in military lives as well as in the constructive efforts of road-building, the encouragement of cantonal towns, the establishment of colonies of veterans, the draining of marshes, the improvement of agriculture, the rise in metals production, and the development of trade. It was a serious investment, all in all, and if not yet profitable might soon be expected to return dividends. After all, Britain was potentially a rich and fertile island, adequately if not thickly populated by an energetic, hard-working people, docile under fair treatment, resentful only of patent and continued injustice (as Tacitus remarked, unaware that he was describing national characteristics which have persisted to our times).

Unlike the flatlands of Mesopotamia, exposed to the incursions of the well-organized and aggressive Parthian Empire, and therefore an interminable *casus belli,* the southern portion of Britain was defensible against the more or less opportunistic, if frequently formidable, raids from the still barbaric northern tribes. Further, and perhaps determinative, the abandonment of the island, as word of the decision, surely magnified in rumor and in hope, spread swiftly through the hostile peoples and nations around the Empire's borders, would be taken as evidence of imperial weakness so severe as to invite calamity. The dangers thus engendered might prove far more costly than any resultant savings in manpower or financial resources.

If, therefore, neither total conquest nor total abandonment were feasible, some middle ground had to be found on which to base a solution within the newly formulated frontier policy.

Hadrian's decision may be briefly stated. The seventy-odd-mile stretch of high ground north of Tyne and Irving running from Tyneside on the east to Solway Firth on the west would be suitably marked as the northern boundary of the Province. Its defense would

† He wrote: "The Romans hold the most important part of Britain, but do not need the rest of it, for even the part they do occupy is not profitable."

lie to the north, in the territory once pacified by Cerealis and Agricola but now a center of unrest. South of the marked boundary Roman life and customs, civilization and peace would unfold right up to the boundary itself. So far the writ of Rome would run. Beyond it? That would be up to the tribes.

The question immediately arises: Why did Hadrian select this line when he surely must have known that less than one hundred miles to the northeast a line only half as long, between Forth and Clyde existed, already marked by the abandoned forts of Agricola?

The many and diverse elements under consideration and the mental processes involved in the making of Hadrian's decision are, of course, lost to history. But some factors, brought to light by archeology, are evident.

First, the territory north of Tyne-Solway extending to Agricola's northern line had been abandoned by the forced withdrawal of garrisons in Trajan's time. And, as noted, Hadrian was reluctant to expand the Empire's boundaries. Additionally, the serious British war of 117–119 had almost certainly been fought in this territory, chiefly in the western section, and Hadrian could well have thought this area still so troublesome as not to warrant inclusion in the Province. That his sense of danger from Southwest Scotland existed is proved by the special pains he took to strengthen and defend the approaches to the western end of his selected boundary.

Second, there was still much work to be done in the territory of the Brigantes, south of the line, if, in following his policy, Romanization was to move forward. Undoubtedly in the Pennine chain stretching north and south there were still obdurate hillmen of the Brigantians who would take plenty of watching. And further, the whole area south of the proposed boundary, but north and west of the old provincial line of Trent-Severn, would take years to bring to settlement, on farms and in towns, by a population wedded to the Roman way.

Combining these two considerations alone it is easy to imagine Hadrian's deciding that enough was enough; and to move farther north for the sole reason of shortening the line involved more immediate trouble and more long-term problems than it was worth.

In any event, the decision was so made and it would constitute in its development a vital factor in the life of Britain for more than three hundred years.

3

ONCE DETERMINED on a course of action, Hadrian allowed no mean vision, no pettiness of execution, to detract from the monumental achievement of his purpose. This was no less than the building of a mighty wall as boundary marker across the waist of England from Pons Aelius (Newcastle-on-Tyne) to a crossing of the Eden a mile or two north of Luguvalium (Carlisle) and thence along the southern shore of Solway Firth to Maia (Bowness).

The plan of the Wall as first devised called for a stone rampart 10 Roman feet (approximately 9½ English feet) thick and 15 feet high, with a battlemented parapet 5 feet high on the north side. At intervals approximating a mile a small fortlet would be built, with a gateway through the wall to the north, housing detachments of customs and frontier police (numeri) to control trans-wall traffic. Between each two fortlets (now known as milecastles) would be set two watchtowers rising above the Wall, with access to a sentry path on the top.

As the planning moved west, the lack of suitable stone in Cumberland forced a change in construction. From Camboglanna (Birdoswald) to its western terminus, the Wall was to be built of turf instead of stone and concrete, necessitating a base 20 feet wide to compensate for the lesser solidity of the material.

The Wall was not conceived as a fighting platform. Nor, indeed, as a military barrier; for its location as it crossed the waist could not, in many places, be considered sound from a purely tactical point of view. It was, as Hadrian intended, simply a boundary marker, with gateways permitting control of cross-wall traffic.

If the wall was to be defended, that defense would take place in enemy territory north of the Wall. The auxiliary units assigned to this task would be stationed in the Stanegate forts, established by Agricola, behind the Wall, and on the west and east, in outpost forts commanding the approaches.

Under the supervision of Hadrian's governor, Platorius Nepos, the work was organized in typically Roman fashion. Detachments of the Twentieth, Sixth, and Second Legions were moved north. Within each legion each cohort, and within each cohort each century, was assigned its own portion to build. As each century finished its work, it placed an inscribed stone to mark its responsibility for the construction inspectors.

Inscriptural evidence and architectural idiosyncracies identify the share of these three legions in the work of constructing the stone wall. There is no record of the participation of the Ninth Legion. If this legion was not destroyed in the war of 117–119, as Professor Birley has indicated, why are not its inscriptions found on the wall? Professor Birley advances two suggestions. One is that the Ninth was employed in building the turf wall beyond Birdoswald, where its centurial inscriptions, being on wood instead of stone, would have had little chance of survival through the centuries. This suggestion has to be weighed, because the cutting and placing of turf blocks into a solid rampart has its own specialized technique at which the legions, but not the auxiliaries, were adept. And, as Professor Birley notes, *tegulae,* or roof tiles, marked with the stamp of the Ninth Legion have been found at Carlisle, obviously the natural base for work on the turf portion of the barrier.

Alternatively, Professor Birley suggests that the Ninth, being most familiar with the forward territory, was assigned to guard the construction while in progress. We simply do not know. The presence or absence of the Ninth Legion in Britain at this time remains a mystery. It is a mystery, however, which could be solved overnight by a fortunate archeological discovery almost anywhere within the Empire's old boundaries.‡

Beside the legions, other technicians were brought up as the need developed. Personnel of the Classis Britannica, the Channel Fleet, for example, did construction work at Onnum (Haltonchesters, where Dere Street goes through the Wall), built extensive warehouses at Condercum (now Benwell), and even put up a stretch of the Wall itself. Cohors I Aquitanorum must have been a unit highly trained in construction work, for they are recorded as having done building at Brocolita (Carrawburgh) in 130–132 A.D. and at Navio (Brough, in Derbyshire) in 158 A.D.

The work of preparing the foundations and some of the actual construction was nearly complete when for some reason unknown

‡ E.g., a tombstone, votive inscription, altar, or other memorial giving in detail enough of the career of an officer of the Ninth to permit inference of its fate; or an Army Station list, circa 120–130 A.D.

to us the plans were changed. It seems to have been decided to reduce the base thickness of the Wall from about ten feet to eight, and to extend its eastern terminus some three miles beyond Pons Aelius to the townsite now known, appropriately enough, as Wallsend. The Romans, then or later, called it Segedunum.

This change in plan came too late to catch some of the faster work gangs, resulting in stretches of "broad wall" interspersed with the more usual "narrow wall." Nevertheless, with other modifications of a minor nature the Wall, as originally conceived, appears to have been completed in about five years, or by 127 A.D. In the eastern portion it was in truth a monumental construction in the best Roman manner. The north and south facings of the Wall were of dressed stone, the interior rough fill held together by concrete and mortar. Far enough in front of the Wall so as not to weaken its foundations, a deep ditch was dug, the earth from the trench being thrown up into a berm south of the ditch, the straight inner side of berm and ditch being angled so that observation of the ditch bottom was possible from the sentry walk on the Wall itself. A road, called the "Military Way," south of the Wall gave access to milecastles and watchtowers.

Yet even while the building of the Wall was in progress, a further major change was decided on. Perhaps the understandable uproar and unrest the very construction of this barrier created among the tribes being shut off to the north was a military threat which the auxiliary units, based on the Stanegate forts from Corstopitum (Corbridge) to Luguvalium (Carlisle), were too far away to handle with dispatch. They may, too, have been too weak in numbers to meet the increasing bellicosity north of the Wall; and if they were to be reinforced by new units, suitable permanent stations must be provided.

In any event, new forts were built along the line of the Wall all the way from Segedunum (Wallsend) to Maia (Bowness). In this system two of the Stanegate forts, already situated close to the Wall line, were included to provide a total of seventeen major fortresses, each capable of holding one or more alae of cavalry or cohorts of infantry. The confusion in planning caused by this alteration is evidenced by archeological discoveries. The fort at Borcovicum (Housesteads) was completed before the Wall building details arrived, while at Aesica (Greatchesters) the work on fort and Wall went on concurrently (although the fort proper does not appear to have been completed until 127 A.D.). At Brocolita (Carrawburgh) the Wall seems to have been completed before work on the fort began.

Perhaps an indication of the tactical problem faced in the course of this construction is the large cavalry fort Petriana, which took over the Wall defense at Stanwix, just north of the old Cerealis-Agricola fort at Carlisle. This huge establishment covering better than nine acres not only guarded the high road from the south, but provided quick support for the outpost forts of Blatobulgium (Birrens) and Castra Exploratorum (Netherby). The fort's name was taken from the unit stationed there, the Ala Petriana Milliaria, the thousand-man cavalry regiment which under its earlier five-hundred-man status had been based at Corstopitum (Corbridge) at the eastern end of the Stanegate, and later was to move to Trimontium (Newstead) beyond the Cheviots. It appears certain that the commander of this ala was by seniority the over-all tactical commander of all forces north of the Sixth Legion at Eburacum. It already has been noted that in the entire worldwide dispersion of the Roman Army there were but twelve of these powerful cavalry commands. Its position at Stanwix therefore establishes the importance the authorities attached to holding down the barbarian exuberance of southwest Scotland.

The completion of this chain of Wall forts, and their garrisoning by auxiliaries probably moved north from supposedly pacified Wales and Brigantia, as well as from some of the Stanegate forts, still did not mean the Wall was to be defended *in loco*. The forts were bases only, secure from molestation, easy to supply via the Military Way, from which combat units could quickly move north to engage and dissipate any observed threat. Undoubtedly the units based in these forts were actually occupied primarily in regular and interlocking patrols far north of the Wall, returning only at intervals determined by the need for rest, rehabilitation, and what recreation might have been available.

Referring back to the Ala Petriana at Stanwix, it is worth noting in connection with these patrols and the ability of the Romans to reach any threatened area quickly, that its capability, typical of Roman cavalry, to cover better than fifty miles a day gave it a radius of action comprising nearly the entire Lowlands of Scotland as well as those parts of Cumberland and Northumberland north of the Wall. Without discounting either the irritation or the hardihood of the Lowland tribes, we can well believe that the appearance of an advance patrol of this entire command in any troubled area would induce caution in the boldest enemy of Rome.

There remains for discussion the last major addition to the Wall complex, the so-called *Vallum*. Historians and archeologists of Roman Britain were for generations in agreement that this wide and deep ditch, south of the wall proper, was an earlier construction than the Wall itself, a first approximation at establishing a marked frontier. Since World War II, however, further investigation has established that the Vallum was in fact the last modification of the overall design and was constructed primarily to restrain curiosity-seekers, tourists, smugglers, and other nuisances *south* of the Wall from interfering with the orderly control of traffic through the Wall and with the movements of both supplies and garrisons in convoy along the Wall length itself on the Military Way.

If, as seems likely, there were still dissident and predatory Brigantians hiding in the Pennine hills, the Vallum could delay and channel any raids they might attempt against the Wall proper. On the whole, though, such ventures would seem both rare and hopeless; so the Vallum's primary function appears to have been to restrain at a reasonable distance those friends of incoming tribesmen from beyond the Wall, along with peddlers, merchants, pickpockets, promoters of cock fights, prostitutes, and other undesirables eager to gain entry to the forts and milecastles.

This was Hadrian's Frontier. The Wall itself—with its fortresses; milecastles; watchtowers and connecting roadway; the rearward Vallum; the flanking fortresses on the east at South Shields and Jarrow and on the west beyond Bowness through Beckfoot, Maryport,§ Burrow Walls, and Moresby at Solway mouth ¶—is without question the mightiest monument to Roman rule in Britain, and one of the most impressive to be found anywhere the Pax Romana crowded on the footsteps of the pioneer legions. So much of it as has survived the passage of nineteen centuries still eloquently bespeaks the organizing genius, the technical resources, the money, and the

---

§ Possibly the port from which Agricola sailed to Galloway in "the first ship" of the season (cf. Ch. VI); the lowest strata there show evidence of an Agricolan fort.

¶ An inscription unearthed there shows that the fort was constructed by the Twentieth Legion during Hadrian's reign, after 128 A.D. In this year Hadrian received the honorific *"Pater Patriae."* Inscriptions lacking the "PP" after his name therefore can be dated 117–128 A.D., those with it, 128–138 A.D.

skilled labor Rome could marshal to the design and construction of an imperial project; to the grandiose, even majestic, implementation of an imperial policy.

4

THE FRONTIER seems admirably to have served its designed purpose in the years after its construction and manning. Whether there was in fact any saving in over-all military manpower may be questioned. The economy, if it occurred, took place far south of the Wall complex in country where, at least for a time, the greater sense of general security engendered by the majestic frontier seems to have rendered wide military surveillance unnecessary.

In Wales at this time the interlocking net of small forts and road patrol stations, designed to control the movements of the inhabitants, seems to have been largely denuded of troops. Only the great legionary fortress at Isca Silurum (Caerleon-on-Usk), with perhaps skeleton detachments of Legio II Augusta, remained a guarantee of the peace in the west.

Similarly, the network of posts and traffic control stations established more than fifty years earlier by Cerealis and Agricola in Brigantian territory were at about this time either vacated or reduced in strength as the units theretofore assigned to them were moved up to garrison the Wall and its rearward supporting forts at Papcastle, Old Carlisle, Old Penrith, Brougham, Kirby Thore, and Whitley Castle; and to the east in Durham, Binchester, Lanchester, Ebchester, and Chester le Street.

Thus the countryside south of the Wall and its approaches became relatively free of traffic controls for at least a while. The resulting mobility accorded the population, while undoubtedly stimulating trade, also made it possible for the stubbornly intransigent hillfolk of the Pennines to dream again of long-forbidden pillage, even if a generation was to pass before awakening courage met opportunity.

It has been emphasized that Hadrian's frontier policy rested on the need to settle and civilize the areas reaching up to the frontier itself. It seems now clear that the measures taken by Hadrian established confidence in the permanence of Roman rule with the result that before long new settlers and retired veterans were moving into the fertile lands and pastures of Yorkshire and Durham on the east, and the Lake District on the west.

Earlier historians of Roman Britain, as a general thing, drew a clear distinction between the settled Romanized province east and south of the Severn-Trent line and the exclusively military nature of the occupation north and west of that line. But in recent years new excavations, based on the results of air photography by Dr. K. St. Joseph have established beyond reasonable doubt the progressive growth of farms and population centers in the northern counties. It appears that this growth, small and even slow at first, gained both in size and momentum as the years passed, and continued well into the fourth century A.D., establishing this facet of Hadrian's frontier policy as, in Britain at least, a signal success.

The examples found by archeologists are many and their over-all significance is unmistakable. After the Wall fort of Petriana was established at Stanwix, for example, the older military site of Luguvalium (Carlisle) was opened for civil settlement and grew to a sizeable town of some seventy acres, much of it now buried beneath the modern city. Ten miles southwest of Carlisle a village grew up around the cavalry fort at Olenacum (Old Carlisle), marked by roads and substantial buildings obviously erected with every expectation of permanence. A reference in Nennius indicates that this town retained its identity and existence well into Saxon times. All through this part of Cumberland, air photography has disclosed traces of old and certainly Roman-British farmsteads, in addition to civil settlements, sometimes of considerable size, near the once purely military stations.

The modern town of Maryport, on Solway Firth, site of the flank fortress of Alauna, has yielded inscriptions indicating a polyglot civil population, including one at least referring to a Christian. The size of this civil settlement, coupled with major warehouse installations on the water front, may well indicate a thriving seaport plying a commerce based primarily on seaborne supply, up the Irish Sea, for the westward stations of the Wall.

The same growth of civil population is exhibited in Westmoreland where the Eden Valley forts of Brocavum (Brougham), Verterae || (Brough), and Bravoniacum (Kirby Thore) are all contiguous to settlements of solid construction much more extensive

|| Constructed by Calpurnius Agricola, ca. 162 A.D.

than the few notion shops, wine emporia, brothels, and gaming houses which could count on support from the military garrison alone.

On the east, along the main Roman highway later called Dere Street, Cataractonium (Catterick), in Yorkshire—now perhaps better known for its racing season than for its ancient origins—and a whole string of sites in Durham have yielded traces of substantial civil settlement.

Nor was this steady growth confined to the immediate hinterland. Along the Wall itself, rearward of the Vallum, not only at Corsopitum (Corbridge) which later grew into a major ordnance and quartermaster's base for the eastern stations, but at such intermediate sites as Borcovicum (Housesteads), Cilurnum (Chesters), and Vindolanda (Chesterholm), the existence in post-Hadrianic times of substantial housing and shops is now proved, awaiting only further excavation to make clear the details of their construction and extent. Doubtless the same tendency to develop a related civil community occurred at the other fortresses of the Wall.

With this slow growth and advancing settlement, wealth in the forms of agriculture, mining, manufacture, and commerce steadily increased although never, perhaps, at the rate achieved in Gaul. The population of Britain, sensing the stability and security of the Province south of the Wall, became ever more Roman, reaching out for the benefits, if not eagerly accepting the responsibilities, of participation in a world state. It seems probable that the Britons, finding unity with the many disparate races and religions of the Empire in common adherence to a law, a far-flung free-trade area, a single currency, administered by a government generally just and seldom unduly harsh, accepted their membership in the Pax Romana with swelling pride.

Yet if Britain participated to the full in the general peace and prosperity of the Empire under Hadrian, it was not without the troubles inherent in its frontier status. In 132 or 133 A.D. some serious trouble broke out in the southwest of Scotland beyond the Wall. The threat presented enough difficulty to the patrolling auxiliaries and supporting forces on the Wall to demand the personal attention of the governor, Julius Severus, and reinforcements from the continent, referred to in inscriptions as an *"Expeditio Britannica."*

We do not know if Severus, the outstanding general of his day, was on duty in Britain when the rising took place. If so, it would seem that some advance warning had reached Hadrian, portentous enough to warrant his sending so distinguished and capable an officer to take charge. If not already on the island, his prompt dispatch to handle the problem is prima-facie evidence of the seriousness with which it was regarded in Rome. It is possible that it was in this fracas that the Ninth Legion was defeated and so thoroughly decimated that Hadrian deactivated and removed it from the Army list. In any event, Severus seems to have handled the outbreak with the competence expected of him. Certainly by 135 A.D. the situation was again in hand for in that year, when the Jewish revolt broke out over Hadrian's building of a new pagan city, Aelia Capitolina, on the site of Jerusalem, abandoned since 70 A.D., the Emperor had no hesitation in recalling Severus to take command in Palestine.

Three years later, in 138 A.D., Hadrian died, after twenty-one years of constructive rule, at the age of sixty-two.

He had tightened the organization and unity of the Empire left him by Trajan, relieved it of overextension in Mesopotamia and Scotland, rebuilt the Treasury surplus, created and adorned many cities, developed the civil service into a permanent and rather efficient bureaucracy, reorganized the Army, selected his generals with care while constantly trying their capacities in assignments of increasing responsibility, and stabilized the Empire's frontiers under a far-seeing policy. Along with this transitory bequest to posterity he left a wistful little poem which has outlived all his other achievements.#

Nevertheless, the Empire he handed over to the gentle but wholly resolute Antoninus Pius was at its peak in wealth, prosperity, world prestige, general well-being, and unchallengeable power. From the Wall in Britain to the Caucasus Mountains and the Euphrates River; from the Rhine, the Danube, and the Black Sea to the Second Cataract on the Nile; to Sahara's edge; and to the mighty Atlantic

Animula, vagula, blandula,
   Hospes comesque corporis
   Quae nunc abibis in loca,
   Pallidula, rigida, nudula,
   Nec, ut soles, dabis iocos.

   Soul of mine, pretty one, flitting one,
   Guest and partner of my clay,
   Whither wilt thou hie away,
   Pallid one, rigid one, naked one,
   Never to play again, never to play.
   (Quoted from *Caesar and Christ* by Will Durant.)

rollers beating on the coast of Mauretania Tingitana the Pax Romana reigned. Its conferred economic benefits, a marked absence of racial prejudice, and a total religious tolerance broken only by doubts of the loyalty of small bands of stubborn and noisy Christians, all combined to create among upward of one hundred million diverse peoples a felicity beyond all ancient and much modern parallel.

5

IN 139 A.D. the Emperor, Antoninus Pius, sent into Britain as governor the general and consular Lollius Urbicus, who, as a member of the staff of Hadrian, had been decorated in the Palestinian war. Surprisingly, the actions taken by Urbicus soon after his arrival in Britain indicate orders from Antoninus Pius to restudy and re-evaluate the social and military significance of the Hadrianic frontier, and to take such steps as might seem desirable for the improvement of the Roman position in Britain.

When Lollius Urbicus arrived in Britain, the frontier complex of the Wall had been operative for a little over ten years. In a sense it had justified its building, although the costs in labor and materials may well have seemed excessive to a fresh mind and objective approach. We have no evidence of unrest south of the Wall in this period and much to the contrary of peaceful progress. Nevertheless, as the troubles of 132–133 A.D. had proved, requiring the military prowess of Julius Severus to repress, beyond the Wall in the territories of the Novantae, Selgovae, Votadini, and Caledonii, the establishment of the marked frontier had not yet brought the hoped-for results.

Perhaps implicit in Hadrian's conception of the frontier was the thought that the tribes beyond, seeing before them a barrier impenetrable save for individual and peaceful barter, would give up their bellicose propensities and after a time seek to emulate in their own areas the procedures, the order, and the rule of law which had produced so striking a felicity south of the frontier.

While this concept possessed, as later centuries were to show, a long-term validity, it failed adequately to assess the immediate irritation produced in the north by the very fact of the Wall itself. It also failed to appreciate that the northern tribes, freed of close Roman surveillance, were able to plan in concert, to act in combination, and in general to hatch mischief of which Rome, to avoid becoming the victim, must supply the deterrent.

An ever-present factor, perhaps impressed on Urbicus by the Emperor's military secretariat, was the continuing need of the imperial defense forces for new manpower. The wild Scots tribes beyond the Wall had had ample time, since the days of Agricola's punitive efforts, to raise and nourish in the hope of vengeance a whole new generation of young males. From the Roman point of view these young savages could be vastly better employed, even to their own individual benefit, in defending the Rhine and Danube frontiers rather than be left undisturbed to harry and annoy the guardian cohorts of the Wall.

Whatever his mandate and the over-all considerations impelling him to action, it is clear that Lollius Urbicus, early in his term of office, determined to move forward once again in the paths of Cerealis and Agricola and to establish such a control of the Lowlands as would obviate the threat against the frontier which, starting in Trajan's time, had grown increasingly troublesome and costly. He started by reopening the Stanegate fort of Corstopitum abandoned when the Wall fortress of *Onnum* (Haltonchesters), three miles northeast, was erected at the crossing of the Great North Road (Dere Street) through the Wall. The work was done by Legio II Augusta in 139 and 140, as attested by inscriptions, and consisted mostly in the construction of large stone granaries, the only conceivable purpose of which seems to have been for use as a major supply depot to support a movement in strength north along Dere Street.

In 142 A.D. Lollius Urbicus was ready and moved out beyond the Wall. Apparently without serious resistance he reconquered the south of Scotland and re-established the northern positions of Agricola. Then, on the thirty-five-mile line of the old Agricolan forts, from Carriden on the Forth to Old Kilpatrick on the Clyde, he built a new frontier, a barrier of turf rather than stone but in many respects a more formidable barrier than Hadrian's southern creation.

The milecastles and watchtowers of the Wall were not copied. Instead, nineteen medium-sized fortresses, each capable of maintaining a cohort reinforced by cavalry, not more than three miles apart, provided protection for the rampart and allowed quick reinforcement of any threatened action. A deep ditch was dug on the north side to make access to the rampart difficult. To protect the open western flank from across-Clyde forays, Urbicus built forts at Bishopton and Lurg Moor in Renfrew on the south shore of the Clyde estuary and extended a road through the Pass of Darvel to the Ayrshire coast. On the east, also to forestall flanking attack, Urbicus moved beyond the rampart, garrisoned anew at least some of the Agricolan forts north to Stirling, and spread his occupation east through Fifeshire, thus denying the use of that countryside for the marshaling of hostile tribes, including one now heard of for the first time, the Maeatae.

This massive turf rampart, extending from sea to sea across the narrow waist of Scotland, with its supporting fortresses, flanking protection, and advance posts, thus became the far-north frontier of Rome. Historians have named it the Antonine Wall to distinguish it from Hadrian's earlier frontier to the south. Like much of the frontier construction of the Roman Empire, its sheer mass has defied the ages and can still be traced, in grassy mound and steep sloping ditch—a mighty rampart warning all barbarians beyond that here began Rome and civilization.

It is not known how many willing or unwilling recruits were rounded up during the advance of Urbicus and his army through the Lowlands of Scotland and on to the Tay. Some, perhaps the majority so enrolled, were demanded as drafts from tribes which had acknowledged defeat and unconditionally surrendered. But shortly after this time, new, partially trained contingents of Brittonni began to appear for duty on the Rhine frontier near the Neckar.

Yet it is doubtful if any major saving of manpower, so far as total Roman military commitment in Britain is concerned, could have been achieved by this advance. Professor Birley has shown (in "Some Military Aspects of Roman Scotland," Dumfriesshire and Galloway Transactions, xxxi, 1954) that the total garrison of the Hadrianic frontier, including outposts, flanking and rearward supporting posts, must have been of the order of 21,500 men, and that the new dispositions north of the Wall required a minimum of 18,000. While a majority of the northern forces may well have been taken from the Hadrianic frontier, there is evidence that the latter installations, although perhaps in many cases reduced to mere housekeeping detachments, were not simply closed down.

Perhaps more important than the source of the northern garrisons was their disposition as established by Lollius. Only about 6,000 appear to have been required to man the forts along the Antonine Wall. Another 3,000 would be the minimum for the outpost stations north to Inchtuthill. The balance, 9,000 men, were placed in the new forts or Agricolan reactivations, along Dere Street north of Haltonchesters and through the Lowlands. Professor Birley raises a pertinent and still unsolved question:

> But half that large force—equivalent in strength to the combined armies of the two Mauretaniae— ** was deployed for control of the security zone in the first instance and only half was specifically looking north toward the untamed tribes of the Highlands. Here surely, we have the strongest of hints that there is still a serious gap in our knowledge of Scotland in Roman times; for where is the archeological evidence for a population large and warlike enough to hold down as many troops as were required to garrison and defend the rich and populous province of Mauretania Caesariensis, or its sister province of Tingitana?

As the forward movement of Lollius was consolidated and the Antonine Wall became operable, the Hadrianic barrier naturally fell into disuse. Many of the gates through the Wall appear to have been kept open, while at convenient points causeways were built across the Vallum and the dyke marking the Wall's south edge was cut to permit easy access to the Wall itself. Farther south the network of small forts and traffic control points in the territory of the Brigantes, abandoned in the heyday of security following the building of the Hadrianic Wall, remained empty, indicating that the authorities were wholly satisfied the pacification of that area was completed. They had still to reckon with the British temperament.

6

HISTORY is silent on the immediate causes of the serious and prolonged disturbance that flared in the Brigantian country, both north and south of the Hadrianic Wall, in 155 A.D. Whatever the causes, real or demagogic, the absence of occupying troops, permitting the Brigantian populace the more easily to gather in numbers, was surely a significant factor in the severity of the outbreak.

** Cf. p. 87.

From archeological studies and recorded troop movements, it is possible to put together some indication of the revolt's strength and extent. An inscription at Corstopitum (Corbridge) records a dedication to Mars the Avenger for casualties suffered and avenged by a detachment of the Sixth Legion. So, obviously, the insurrection had to be serious enough to bring this command north from its base at Eburacum (York). But there is a further record of reinforcements for all three legions being landed at the Tyne, dispatched from Germany. So it follows, not only that at least a part of both Legio XX from Deva (Chester) and Legio II Augusta from Isca Silurum (Caerleon-on-Usk) had been brought north, but that the fracas had been deemed serious enough by the authorities in Rome to warrant instructions to the Rhine command to send help. On this evidence alone, it is clear the then governor, Cn. Julius Verus, had his hands full and probably was unable to check the revolt until his reinforcements arrived.

The wide extent of the damage done by the insurgents is indicated by the reconstruction found necessary after 158 A.D. when the revolt appears to have been finally stamped out. The governor, Julius Verus, who had borne the brunt of the fighting, was recalled and a new governor, possibly—on the strength of an imperial rescript issued by Pius and a diploma recovered at Camulodunum—a certain Lentulus Verus. Whether or not that was his name, he seems to have lasted not more than two years and to have been replaced by Statius Priscus, fresh from the consulship of 159, an officer who had risen steadily from a promising start when he was decorated for bravery while a legionary tribune in the Palestinian war. He must have been held in high repute as a general, for in 162 he was recalled to take a command in the East, against the Parthians. He was replaced as governor of Britain by Calpurnius Agricola, whose name we find attached to much of the reconstruction.

The work included the rebuilding of the Hadrianic outpost fort of Blatobulgium (Birrens) in Dumfriesshire and the construction of a new fort at Navio (Brough in Derbyshire), far south of the Wall but so close to the extensive lead mines of the Peak District as to suggest that, if the revolt itself did not reach that far, at least the convicts working the mines seized the opportunity to create trouble on their own account. Two other destroyed forts south of the Wall— Mediobugdum (Hardknott in the Cumberland Hills) and Bremetan-

Roman Wall on Tower Hill, London

Corstopitum (Corbridge): Colonnade at the Granaries

Hadrian's Wall: A View near Winshiels Crag

Hadrian's Wall: Abutment near Chester's Bridge

nicum (Ribchester in Lancashire)—had to be rebuilt and an additional fort built at *Veterae* (Brough in Westmoreland). In effect,
these measures indicate not only the severity of the revolt but also
that Calpurnius found it necessary to reoccupy much of Brigantia.

Archeological study has proved that in addition to this reconstruction and new building north and south of the Wall, the supply depot
of Corstopitum (Corbridge) and the Stanegate fort of Vindolanda
(Chesterholm) both underwent substantial reconstruction at this
time. If the reconstruction at Corstopitum was required as a result of
damage done by the insurgents, it is reasonable to believe that the extensive depot, with its granaries and ordnance shops, was from the
first outbreak a priority target, and that its capture and pillage, by
making supplies available, materially prolonged the rebellion.

In the course of the troubles it was found necessary for the
Romans to abandon the forward areas won by Lollius Urbicus. But
with the revolt quelled, and necessary steps taken to prevent its
recurrence, Calpurnius Agricola moved forward again, and reoc-
cupied all the area, including the Antonine Wall and undoubtedly
some of its forward outposts. One step he took suggests the tactical
problem he faced. It was absolutely essential to maintain the line
of communications with the Antonine Wall along Dere Street in the
east. To guarantee its security, Calpurnius expanded the Agricolan
fort at Trimontium (Newstead) and moved into it from Petriana
(Stanwix) on the west line the thousand-man cavalry unit sporting
the resounding title of *Ala Augusta Gallorum Petriana Bis Torquata
Milliaria Civium Romanorum.*††

This movement placed this powerful command not only squarely
on the main line of communications to the north, but midway in the
Lowlands, rather than on Hadrian's Wall itself as it had been at
Stanwix. Since its commander was the senior officer north of York, it
appears part of Calpurnius' purpose to place him at a central point,
important in itself, but one from which his immediate and highly
mobile force could move anywhere in the Lowlands on short notice
to break up reported concentrations of unruly tribesmen before they
had a chance to get organized.

Calpurnius also remanned the Hadrianic barrier, at the obvious

†† "Augustus' Own Petrian Cavalry Regiment of Gauls, Twice Awarded the
Honorary Collar [a sort of unit citation] and Granted Roman Citizenship, One
Thousand Strong."

cost of weakening the Antonine Wall's garrisons and its supporting network both north and south.

The thoroughness with which Calpurnius Agricola went about his task, involving so much laborious construction and relocation of troop units, would seem to indicate beyond cavil that, in the eyes of Rome, Britain was important and would be held as far north as the Antonine Wall, even at the considerable cost in military manpower so entailed. The result seems to have justified the decision. For at least another generation following Calpurnius, there was, if not peace in North Britain, at least no uproar worth contemporary mention, or comparable to the greater challenges to the security and well-being of the Empire developing along the Danube frontier, in the East, and within the body politic itself.

7

WHEN MARCUS AURELIUS, the Stoic philosopher, succeeded Antoninus Pius in 161 A.D., the mass of the Empire's population appears in retrospect to have been as contented as people ever are, and a majority proud of their participation in so stable, so seemingly eternal a society.

The immensely long borders (over three times the length of that between Canada and the United States) were vigilantly defended by alert, disciplined troops under commanders who with rare exceptions were competent and experienced practitioners of the military art.

The Law, somewhat less confused after Hadrian's codification, while stern, approached justice in its administration. Punishment for individual crimes was harsh, discouraging petty larcenies and minor felonies. Malefactors of great wealth, able to retain high-priced legal talent, fared better, as with us.

Politically, for all but slaves, freedom on a local scale was real. Citizens and provincials vied in adorning and beautifying their city or cantonal capital and the contributions of philanthropists to the public welfare were on a scale not approached again before the establishment of the great eleemosynary foundations in the United

States. Even slaves were protected by a watchful law holding firmly in check the rapacity or arbitrary brutality of individual owners.

On larger, imperial issues the people had no say, and willingly or not followed the policies of Emperors who, in Marcus Aurelius' words, believed in and tried to establish "the idea of a state in which there is the same law for all, a policy of equal rights and freedom of speech, and the idea of a kingly government that most of all respects the freedom of the governed."

Yet for all this felicity, dangers lurked, some external, some unseen, others cloaked in the most innocent of guises.

The decisions of the Emperor on imperial policy and all too often on matters of petty detail were handed down and eventually enforced by a proliferating bureaucracy already exhibiting that built-in rate of useless increase we know as Parkinson's Law.

In the older cities—Alexandria, Antioch, Rhodes, Cyrene, Carthage, Ephesus, and others—as well as in Rome itself, a noisy, turbulent proletariat demanded by incessant rioting blackmail in the form of free bread and circuses. In Rome, mob and decadent aristocracy vied with each other in devising raids on the Imperial Treasury. The supposedly elite corps of the Praetorian Guard was again developing an unhealthy sense of its own power, unmotivated by devotion to the State, and restrained only so long as able Praetorian prefects, loyal to the Emperor, could maintain discipline.

Perhaps since the days of the first Augustus, the Empire as a whole had been suffering a continuous and insidious loss of manpower. No one factor could be assigned as the primary cause, while many contributed, their additive effects remorseless and irreversible, even if, in those days of inadequate statistics, at first hardly noticeable. The policy-directed infertility of the huge slave population; the widespread practice of infanticide; the burdens of matrimony which could hardly compete with the license of bachelorhood; the flight of small farmers from eroded lands to the city, there to fester in unsanitary swarms—all these and other influences combined with the normal low life expectancy of ancient times to produce a fluctuating but persistently shrinking population—imperceptible at first, but obeying the demographic law of geometric growth and decline.

In 165 A.D. to all the underlying factors was added a virulent acceleration. The legions in the East, under the over-all command of

Lucius Verus, the playboy brother of Marcus Aurelius, had been embroiled against Parthia since 162. In the course of the campaign the troops contracted a contagious disease which by contemporary description of its symptoms and lethality was either the bubonic plague or a savage strain of typhus. This unwelcome guest the legionary hosts brought back with them to the cities of Syria. Spreading out from the crowded slums and warrens, the epidemic quickly infected wide areas of the population. With extraordinary rapidity the sickness spread over the Roman world, working its deadly way for fifteen years before burning out. There are no records left of the casualties, nor any way of estimating their extent, save perhaps by extrapolation from the known fact that in the city of Rome alone, two thousand died in a single day.

The northern provinces, including Britain, seem to have suffered least. One interesting result of the plague was a notable increase in adherents to the promises of immortality and reward in a future life held out by Christianity. Another consequence of high mortality among small farmers was the acceleration of the concentrating of land in large latifundia used for grazing rather than agriculture, a process which for economic reasons had been going on for some centuries. From the loss of manpower there followed a drop in the grain supply, since agriculture, in those days as today over much of the world, was tied directly to the availability of human labor. Farm machinery and modern agronomy alone could make up the loss by increasing the yield per acre per hour of man labor. These, the ancient world did not know.

Not only in the East, but also along the Danube frontier, the Empire was beset by vigorous and persistent enemies. The Emperor found much time for philosophic thought while living for years in a tent, campaigning against the Quadi and the Marcomanni, who in repeated offensives were attempting to break the Danube frontier. By great efforts Marcus Aurelius managed to defeat them again and again, and was in sight of total victory when he died in the field, in 180 A.D., a scholarly, melancholy, and reluctant warrior.

Nevertheless, a great society, like a strong body, may not for years show the ravages of a disease surely fatal in time. The Empire Marcus Aurelius bequeathed to his athletic and extrovert son, Commodus, showed every outward sign of majesty, strength, and permanence.

8

IT IS wholly a tribute to the tight organization of both military and civil aspects of the imperial government that sound policies could continue to be executed and routine administration satisfactorily carried on, even though the young Emperor, a boy of nineteen on his accession, flouted the responsibilities, as he concentrated on the license, of autocratic authority.

Before embarking on his enjoyment of Rome, Commodus made peace with the nearly conquered and absorbed Marcomanni and Quadi. Having felt at first hand the strength of Rome, these tribes were probably relieved to find their independence acknowledged even at the cost of the treaty, one of the terms of which was a requirement for thirteen thousand draftees to be incorporated in the auxiliary forces of the Empire. We may presume a proportion of these sturdy barbarians were eventually shipped as replacements to Britain without having wholly absorbed Roman discipline.

With the cessation of hostilities on the Danube, Commodus returned to Rome, where his frenetic activities earned ridicule among the plebs, contempt in the aristocracy, fear among businessmen, and gossip everywhere. Out of all these reactions the history of his reign has come down largely in outrageous anecdote, perhaps with some exaggeration.

Yet the realities were bad enough. To find time for his athletic exhibitions and private pleasures, Commodus delegated the conduct of imperial affairs to his underling, the Praetorian prefect, the sycophant Perennis. When that worthy's excesses were rewarded with murder, he was succeeded by a freedman, the avaricious and insatiable Cleander. The greed and favoritism of these two were merciless on Rome and hard on Italy. If the provinces escaped relatively unscathed, it was on the grounds of distance and inconvenience coupled with the superfluity of opportunity near at hand. Yet, since provincial appointments among others were freely on sale in Rome, some governorships at least went by sale to incompetents rather than by merit to the worthy.

Commodus had been Emperor for a mere two years when trouble

again broke out in the north of Britain. The known facts are few. The historian Dion Cassius lets us know only that the northern tribes crossed the wall that divided them from the Romans, met and soundly defeated a Roman army, killing the commander, who Dion suggests might have been the governor, then were stopped and themselves heavily defeated by another force under the governor Ulpius Marcellus, the whole campaign being rated as the most serious of all the wars of Commodus.

There can be no doubt that the wall referred to was the Antonine Wall for archeology shows no trace of disturbance at the Hadrianic Wall during this period. It has been already noted that Calpurnius Agricola, in moving north to reoccupy the Lowlands and the Antonine Wall, had been forced to spread his garrisons rather thin by the need to reactivate the Hadrianic Wall forts. It may well have happened that Calpurnius Agricola's successors, in the years of peace following his consolidation of the territory, relied on the common interest of the Lowland tribes in the preservation of peace to charge them with much of the defense of their own territory—naturally, under Roman guidance—and as a result the manpower problem resulted in the Antonine Wall's being held by extremely weakened, if not purely housekeeping, detachments.

In any event, the northern tribes, presumably the newly aggressive Caledonii or Maeatae, or both, did cross the Antonine Wall and defeat a Roman army somewhere in the Lowlands. If, as Dion Cassius suggests, it was the governor himself who was lost in the encounter, it seems unlikely that the news of the loss could have gotten back to Rome, and the new governor, Ulpius Marcellus, been sent out in time to meet and soundly defeat the northern invaders before they could have done more damage, down to Hadrian's Wall itself.

Ulpius Marcellus, the victorious governor, may have been the famous jurist of the time, or less likely his son. If in fact the governor was killed in the first defeat, perhaps Ulpius Marcellus the elderly jurist was in Britain as the *legatus iuridicus,* a deputy assigned to the Province to relieve the governor of the burden of legal work. As the next senior official in Britain, perhaps he took command in the field and by his victory won confirmation in the post of the fallen general. On the other hand, the general killed may have been of lesser rank, perhaps a legion commander, and if so, probably of the Sixth brought hastily north from York to stop the invasion. In any case, the victory seems to have been impressive enough to allow Commodus, happily irresponsible in Rome, to accept the honorary cognomen of "Britannicus," which he then appears to have added to the honors of the Sixth Legion, which thenceforward was able to emblazon its full name as *"Legio VI Victrix Britannica Pia Fidelis."*

When it came time to recall Ulpius Marcellus in honor, Commodus appears to have written a personal letter to Helvius Pertinax, asking him to accept the governorship. The young Emperor's reasons for seeking the service of this seasoned soldier-administrator and austere Roman patriot at a relatively advanced age are obscure, but may have rested on personal acquaintance and the added fact that Pertinax, earlier in his career, had served in Britain as praefectus of an auxiliary cohort, and so could be presumed to have some first-hand acquaintance with the defense problems of the Province. And certainly, after the dangerous nature of the northern invasion, a degree of unrest was sure to effect the population, calling for a governor of high repute and unquestioned qualifications.

Perhaps because his later and all-too-brief elevation to the Principate attracted the attention of contemporary writers, a good deal is known of Helvius Pertinax. His record, as Gibbon observed, "deserved well to be set down as expressive of the form of government and manners of the age."

Pertinax was born in Liguria, in northern Italy, in 126 A.D. in the halcyon days of Hadrian. His father, Helvius Successus, was the son of a slave who had obtained his freedom. The father was in relatively humble circumstances, a dealer in lumber and charcoal. But thanks to the flourishing state of public education in Italy, and indeed throughout the provinces at this time, the poverty of his parents did not prevent Pertinax from receiving enough schooling to become in his turn a teacher.

From this humdrum duty—perhaps students were then as much a trial to their preceptors as now—he went into the Army, earning or receiving the rank of centurion. Apparently showing high aptitude, he was promoted to the rank of praefectus or commander of an auxiliary cohort which he led with great distinction in the Parthian War of 162–165 under Verus, the co-Emperor, and his generals Statius Priscus and Avidius Cassius. The dates make it clear that at this stage of his career he was a mature man of thirty-six, who, had he been a participant in the senatorial career pattern instead of merely an equestrian, would already be in command of a legion.

From the East he was transferred to Britain, thus escaping the plague. He appears to have won the favorable attention of his superiors in Britain and promotion, for he next went to serve in Moesia, commanding an ala of auxiliary cavalry. From this troop command he was brought back to Italy to the relative sinecure of supervising the movement of military supplies along the Aemilian Way—the ancient road of the Republic which extended the Flaminian Way north from Ariminum (Rimini) on the Adriatic through the Po valley. This assignment may well have been, as Professor Birley points out, a sort of "home leave," carrying few duties and allowing much time for rest and private business. (Cf. E. Birley, "Senators in the Emperor's Service," *Proceedings of the British Academy,* xxxix [1954].)

His next frontier duty was command of the *Classis Germanica,* the fleet which patrolled the Rhine and its tributaries, performing on that river barrier much the same control functions as the numeri on Hadrian's Wall. From this assignment Pertinax passed to the predominantly civil task of collector of imperial revenues in the province of Dacia, north of the Danube.

Here he ran into the first check in his career, being dismissed by Marcus Aurelius on the basis of adverse reports. It is easy to understand this happening, for a collector of revenue, if honest, could not avoid irritating, if not insulting, by failure of conniving accommodation, the various types of greedy and influential Roman businessmen whose eagerness for quick profit was not always distinguishable from fraud. But Pertinax had friends, too, not afraid to present his side of the affair to the Emperor. His performance of duty vindicated, he was reinstated with honor and given command of a vexillatio, a major detachment of a legion, and carried out this duty with such noticeable efficiency that Marcus Aurelius, in handsome amends, nominated him for the Senate—a sure promise of higher responsibilities to come. Quickly he served as praetor and then went to command a legion, I Minerva, stationed in Rhaetia and Noricum, provinces corresponding roughly to modern Switzerland and Austria.

In this capacity and sometime after 172 A.D., at the approximate age of forty-six, Pertinax attacked and threw back some tribes which had attempted to invade the provinces.

His generalship in battle thus proved, his future career, barring political canard or an Emperor's dislike, was assured. He was soon elected consul—an office which, however honorary, was a necessary precursor to provincial governorship. When Marcus Aurelius died in 180 A.D., Pertinax had already served as governor of Upper Moesia, and then of Dacia, and was currently holding the plum of overseas appointments—the governorship of Syria. The confidence he had earned from Marcus Aurelius is proved by the latter's naming Pertinax in his will as one of the guardians of the new Emperor, Commodus, thus elevating him to a position of supreme influence. From the most humble of beginnings this soldier and administrator had reached the summit of a long career of honor and distinction, of dedicated service in many lands, on many frontiers, in frequent battles, maintaining and exalting the greatness, the invincibility of Rome.

Perhaps finding the guardianship of the willful Commodus distasteful if not dangerous, Pertinax soon retired gracefully to his old home in Liguria. There he lived for some years in peace and anonymity until recalled in 185 A.D. to assume command in Britain.

Historians labor his integrity, his honesty, his devotion to duty, his military prowess. Reading between their lines, it is possible to discern also a certain self-assurance, natural enough in a man who had carried so many diverse responsibilities so well but approaching arrogance in the methods he employed. Apparently Pertinax, sure of himself and of his motives, did not greatly care if he made enemies in performing his duty. And when he found himself in command of troops undisciplined or lacking in combat effectiveness, he seems to have driven them unmercifully until they attained his high standards.

It may be that these intransigent qualities in Pertinax's make-up contributed to the difficulties he met with in Britain.

All that is known is that there was a mutiny of some part of the garrison. It is unlikely that the mutineers were from any of the three regular legions stationed in Britain. Of these, II Augusta and XX Valeria Victrix had been serving in Britain since the conquest—142 years earlier. Legio VI Victrix Britannica Pia Fidelis had been stationed at Eburacum (York) since 122 A.D. or for 63 years. Further, that legion, and undoubtedly detachments at least of the other two, had shared in the great victory won by Ulpius Marcellus only a few years back. Troop units which share the memory of a recent major victory seldom rebel. All three, barring drafts of replacements sent from the Rhineland during the Brigantian revolt of 155–158 A.D., were made up of locally recruited personnel in the main; all Roman citizens and many sons of retired veterans of both the legions and the auxiliaries. While these soldiers may well have formed attachments and relationships in the vici, or towns, growing up adjacent to their permanent stations, causing them to indulge in vociferous grumbling when suddenly ordered to distant fields of trouble, it is unlikely to have taken any more serious form than the similar reaction even today associated with such demands on soldiers.

On the whole, there is more reason to look for the source of the difficulty in the auxiliaries and perhaps uniquely in the newly-en-rolled Marcomanni and Quadi sent from the Danube frontier under the terms of Commodus' peace treaty. These draftees, lamenting the wild freedom of their tribal days, may well have been not yet recon-ciled to the realities of Roman discipline.

The mutiny seems to have involved Pertinax personally for he himself was attacked and roughly handled. So unheard-of a sacrilege (in that day) as assault on the person of the Divine Augustus' deputy evokes the picture of a commander so self-assured as to be incapable of believing he is not safe among his own troops no matter what harshness of discipline he has inflicted on them. The episode indicates courage, even arrogance, unbounded either by discretion or the abil-ity to weigh beforehand the temper of his men. The personal attack must have come as quite a shock, for Pertinax, after he recovered, appears to have written the Emperor, requesting relief and replace-ment on the grounds that his effectiveness as governor had been de-stroyed. Curiously for a man of such extended and diversified ex-perience, he seems to have learned nothing from the incident, as he was soon to demonstrate.

By the end of 191 A.D. Pertinax was back in Rome, holding the important office of *Praefectus Urbis,* after a short tour in the prestig-ious proconsulship of Africa. He had opportunity to observe, per-haps in sadness mixed with contempt, the murderous proclivities of his whilom ward, the Emperor, before reaction brought about the latter's death. Just over thirty years of age, with rather a record in public crime and private debauchery behind him, Commodus was murdered by his mistress, Marcia, and her gladiator accomplice on New Year's Day, 192 A.D.

The Senate, hearing the welcome news, reacted hysterically in ordering the corpse dragged through the streets by a hook under its chin and thrown into the Tiber. Then, recovering some vestige of dignity, it rallied, and sensing the need for quick action, prevailed upon the reluctant, if not prescient, Pertinax to accept the Principate. It was obviously a choice made with the best of intentions. A former governor of Syria and of Britain, a soldier of proved ability, an experienced pro-consul, a man of rock-ribbed integrity and firm purpose already in control of the city—the Senate may also have noted that at the age of sixty-five, Pertinax was unlikely to indulge in the vices that had so distinguished Commodus.

Once installed, Pertinax acted—as his prior career had promised —with stiff decision and disregard of injured feelings or invaded interests. Herodian is authority for saying he carried himself as an ordinary man, but his actions were those of an uncompromising, honest, and none too tactful general. Dion Cassius says; "He did everything that a good Emperor should do," but his way of doing it was here as fatal as it had nearly been in Britain. He might have succeeded in his measures to reduce taxes, and in his auctioning off of the gold and silver vessels, the silk hangings, and the slave girls he found in Commodus' palace, but when he severely cut the perquisites of the secretariat and combined with this incautious act an order for rigid economies and the re-establishment of iron discipline in the Praetorian Guard, he tried to do too much too soon. When three hundred Praetorians forced their way into the palace, possibly only to clamor for restoration of their lost privileges, he faced them as courageously and as rashly as he had the mutineers in Britain, and was struck down. The Praetorians stuck his head on a pole and carried it back to their camp. Pertinax had been Emperor less than three months.

The news of the slaughter of Pertinax spread swiftly through the Empire, evoking in thoughtful men the foreboding that the horrible anarchy and destruction that had followed the death of Nero over one hundred years earlier were again to be suffered.

Around the rim of the Roman world, the officers and men of the guardian legions, many of whom had served under his command, remembered Pertinax with tardy affection and posthumous respect. Their indignation soon turned to jealous anger when they heard the sequel—how the insolent Praetorians from the security of their camp, had coolly put the Principate up for auction to the highest bidder, and how it had been sold to the miserably ambitious Didius Severus Julianus who topped equally miserable but less solvent competitors with a bid of 6,250 denarii per Praetorian.‡‡ The frontier legions, moved perhaps as much by envy of this unexampled bribe as by indignation at the degrading transaction, reacted in fury.

To the provincial governors, all of whom were men of senatorial rank, and those stationed on the frontiers, experienced and dedicated soldiers, the story of the brutal murder and callous aftermath must have come as a shock. After experiencing and surviving with honor the vagaries of Commodus, the selection of Pertinax for the Principate must have seemed to them the dawn of a new era of probity and responsibility in the autocracy, a presage of a restoration of the felicity known through the reigns of Trajan, Hadrian, Antoninus Pius, and Marcus Aurelius. To have this high promise cut short, with anarchy the certain substitute, must have been a bitter disappointment.

Some of the governors certainly were horrified and filled with shame. Was this the Empire, the custodian of civilization, they had served over years of arduous duty, rising slowly through the different grades, proving themselves in battle and in governing? Was Rome an Empire so weak and yet so wealthy that a spoiled corps of armed irresponsibles could murder and sell with impunity that for which they had so interminably toiled and risked their lives?

There were others no doubt who, always expecting the worst, merely shook their heads in dismay before coolly assessing the possible effects upon their own careers.

But both groups, the horrified and the cynics, being at the same time Senators, had to consider the dangers, personal and imperial, inherent in the whims of Julianus, once their insignificant colleague, now by contemptible bribery their unchallengeable superior.

But was he unchallengeable? The principal frontier governors could not have been unaware of the fierce resentment of their legionaries. Perhaps to refrain from action was to court mutiny; but to challenge Julianus, apparently secure in Rome under the protection of the Praetorian Guard, could have but one of two outcomes—the uneasy Principate itself, or a traitor's death.

About this time, another message may have reached the frontier

‡‡ Equivalent to about five years' pay; a Praetorian normally received double the compensation of a legionary.

garrisons, lending at least encouragement if not legal sanction to armed protest—how the volatile population of Rome, generally amused at debauchery and corruption in the Principate, had risen in outrage against the purchasing usurper and asked, even pleaded, with the legions to come to the rescue.

Three among the most powerful provincial governors—Caius Pescennius Niger, commanding in Syria; Lucius Septimius Severus, legate of Pannonia; and in far-off Britain, Decimus Clodius Albinus —listened to the rising murmurs of their troops and considered each his dilemma.

With what encouragement, connivance, or even reluctant resignation of the three governors we do not know, the legions in Britain, Pannonia, and Syria saluted their respective commanders as Augustus. Thenceforward the three were in the hands of fate, a fate determined by individual temperament, by factors of time and distance, by swift decision or the lack of it, by leadership in battle, and the simple personal loyalty of angry soldiers willing to gamble their own lives rather than let the Praetorians go scatheless to enjoy their rich reward for murder.

IX

THE DISMAL CENTURY
196-287 A.D.

. . . occidit, occidit,
Spes omnes et fortuna nostri
—HORACE, *Odes*

1

OVER THE GAP OF SEVENTEEN HUNDRED years we can find, if not sympathy, at least understanding for these three frontier commanders—Niger, Severus, and Albinus—in the dilemma they faced. We cannot judge these men in the light of our own constitutional traditions, but must consider them in relation to their time, subject to its stresses, prisoners and in part victims of an era in which military power was the ultimate court of appeal in internal affairs. cf. Latin America

Each of these three governors had grown to manhood in the peaceful, orderly reign of Antoninus Pius. Each had loyally served his successor, Marcus Aurelius, gaining distinction and successive promotions under that Emperor's wisdom, probity, and patriotism. Each had accepted, without recorded cavil or protest, the succession of the youthful and unpredictable Commodus. Each in his various assignments had patiently and loyally served Rome while that irresponsible adolescent wasted the resources of the Empire in extravagant misgovernment. During his reign of twelve years, no one of the three could have felt wholly safe from his suspicion, caprice, or insensate cruelties.

Perhaps they regretted the implication of anarchy in Commodus' murder more than the fact itself. But when the relief which followed the selection of their respected colleague Pertinax was dissipated after a mere three months in office by his murder, and the subsequent crassly commercial usurpation of Julianus, the reborn specter of anarchy may have made each in his way despair of the Empire.

In retrospect it is clear that the proper course for these governors was to get together, agree on a candidate to supplant Julianus, and by the sheer superiority of their joined power, force the issue without bloodshed. Perhaps they tried to get together. Certainly, correspondence passed among them, and undoubtedly the other, less powerful commanders along the Rhine-Danube frontier were sounded out. But the necessarily long delays in communication over the distances involved could not only breed mutual suspicion, but also give Julianus time to consolidate his position. Time therefore was of the essence, with the urgency multiplied by the temper of the legions and the appeals from Rome. Where time was so important, the vital and perhaps decisive factor in the complex situation was that Severus, in Pannonia, was closest to Rome.

Lucius Septimius Pertinax * Severus, legate of Pannonia and Illyria, was an African, born at Leptis Magna on the Gulf of Sirte in modern Tripolitania. His ancestors were Punic-speaking Phoenicians absorbed in Rome since the sack of Carthage 340-odd years before. It is said he spoke Latin with a Punic accent, whatever that might mean. He had been well educated at Carthage and at Athens, liked the company of philosophers, and was a trained jurist. He had no particular military reputation, served only intermittently in government appointments, and in the intervals practiced law in Rome. Marcus Aurelius, sensing merit, had made him a praetor at the age of thirty-two, later gave him command of a legion, IV Flavia Firma. It seems likely that he displayed no great military competence while on that duty, since his next appointments were as governor successively of the senatorial provinces of Gallia Lugdunensis and Sicilia. These appointments, involving no military command or duties, seem to have been largely civil in character and held in general by Senators not considered wholly competent to handle a frontier province. But this selection system appears to have broken down to some ex-

---

* This cognomen Severus apparently took after his success, to mark his having avenged Helvius Pertinax, and to establish in the public mind the legitimacy of his succession.

tent during the reign of Antoninus Pius—who himself never left Italy during his reign—and must have been largely thrown overboard during the reign of Commodus by the cupidities of Perennis and Cleander. It is not unlikely that to obtain command of such an important frontier province as Pannonia, Severus had been obliged to purchase the honor from Cleander. Yet when the issue was joined, Severus proved himself an extremely competent general.

As governor of Pannonia he had under his command four legions, two of which we have already encountered—XIV Gemina, whose service in Britain from the invasion of 43 A.D. to 66 A.D. and its valorous part in putting down Boudicca's revolt had earned it the honorific "Martia Victrix"; and II Adiutrix, which had served in Britain in the days of Cerealis and Agricola. The other two were I Adiutrix and X Gemina. These four legions, with the auxiliaries of the frontier posts, gave Severus an approximate ready strength of about forty thousand men. These troops, both legions and auxiliaries, had been constantly exercised in border wars along the Danube and were hardened and combat ready, eager above all things to take on the supercilious Praetorians.

Accepting with real or feigned reluctance the acclamation of his legions as Augustus and Imperator, Severus called on them to march on Rome to rescue the fatherland. The enthusiasm of the legionaries for this adventure into Italy, which most of them in all likelihood had never yet seen, was fortified by Severus' promise of a donative to each man of 12,000 drachmas †—nearly twice as much as Julianus had paid the Praetorians, a bribe that so shocked Severus at the time. Having conceded so much to reinforce loyalty by expectation, Severus became again the strict disciplinarian and inspiring commander. Leaving the auxiliaries under a deputy to maintain a weakened and probably desultory watch on the frontier, he marshaled his legions and started for Rome.

From his two major border fortresses—Carnuntum on the Danube, near modern Bratislava, and Aquincum, now Budapest—by road to Rome was something over six hundred miles. By forced march, Severus made it in thirty days, pausing at Interamnia, some seventy miles from the city.

News of his nearness brought consternation to Julianus, mixed

† The drachma seems to have been roughly equivalent to the denarius of the time.

Hadrian's Wall: Granaries at the Fort at Borcovicum

The Province about 150 A.D.

Cantonal Capitals

1. Durovernum Cantiacorum (Canterbury)
2. Noviomagus Regnensium (Chichester)
3. Venta Belgarum (Winchester)
4. Calleva Atrebatum (Silchester)
5. Durnovaria (Dorchester)
6. Isca Dumnoniorum (Exeter)
7. Corinium Dobunnorum (Cirencester)
8. Venta Silurum (Caerwent)
9. Viroconium Cornoviorum (Wroxeter)
10. Ratae Coritanorum (Leicester)
11. Isurium Brigantum (Aldborough)
12. Petuaria Parisiorum (Brough, Yorkshire)
13. Venta Icenorum (Caistor St. Edmunds, Norfolk)
14. Verulamium Catevellaunorum (St. Albans, Herts)

Legionary Fortresses

Isca Silurum (Caerleon-on-Usk)
Deva (Chester)
Eburacum (York)

Colonies

Camulodunum (Colchester)
Lindum Colonia (Lincoln)
Glevum (Gloucester)
Eburacum
Deva ?

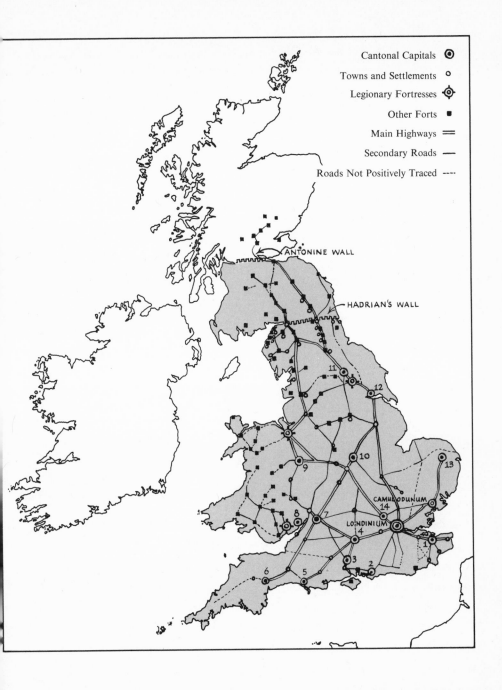

Temple of Mithras at Bucklebury

feelings to the Senate, and unease to the Praetorians whose fondness for dress uniforms and double pay was combined with a marked distaste for campaigning. Content to lord it over the Senate and the Palace, they viewed with considerable reluctance the prospect of an armed encounter with the crack Pannonian legions. Severus quickly took care of them.

He first sent emissaries to the Praetorian camp where promises of leniency to the corps as a whole speedily produced the surrender, for execution, of those directly responsible for the murder of Pertinax. Then he ordered the corps to assemble without arms outside the city to hear an address. Once formed, the Praetorians—who may have expected to be pleaded with for their co-operation and perhaps even offered another bribe—found themselves surrounded by the threatening spears of highly unfriendly legionaries.

While this was going on, Severus sent a detachment to seize the Guard barracks and arms. The take-over accomplished, he mounted the rostrum before the stunned Praetorians and in the sternest terms expressed his disapprobation of their conduct and general character. He ended by ordering the Corps disbanded, and commanding that each soldier, under pain of death, depart the city and thereafter never again approach within one hundred miles of Rome.

The Praetorians eliminated, a quick search found Julianus cowering in the Palace. The tribune in charge of the search party, with a nice appreciation of neatness, led the once-able senator, who from greed for power or the tongue-lashing of an ambitious wife had presumed to buy an empire, into a bathroom, and there beheaded him.

The Senate, which under Julianus' urging and the Praetorians' threats had declared Severus a public enemy, quickly recanted, naming him Augustus and Deliverer. Their haste in the matter is amply explained by the fact that Severus marched his tough legions, in full combat gear, directly into the city, although he himself, possibly in sardonic gesture, delayed long enough to honor tradition by changing from armor to the *toga laticlavia*.‡

With Julianus dead, the Praetorians disbanded, Pertinax avenged, and Severus confirmed by the Senate, the proper course for both Pescennius Niger in Syria and Clodius Albinus in Britain was to accept a *fait accompli* and announce their adherence to the new Emperor. These adherences seem not to have arrived, at least in time

‡ Toga with the broad purple stripe worn by persons of senatorial rank.

to satisfy the impatient and perhaps uneasy Severus, as unwilling to allow his rivals to combine against him as he had been to grant time to Julianus. We do not know if Albinus in Britain and Niger in Syria were restrained from accepting the new Emperor by personal pique, thwarted ambition, or merely the renewed demands of their troops, as word of Severus' donative, equal to ten years' pay or half a twenty-year enlistment, spread among them.

The canny Severus announced to the Senate his intention of naming Albinus as Caesar and his colleague in governing the Empire. Undoubtedly notice of the action was quickly passed to Albinus, either to obtain his acceptance or to forestall any offensive steps he might be contemplating. So much done, Severus marched his legions out of the capital within thirty days of his arrival and set off eastward to meet the army of Niger.

Severus' three years of successful campaigning against Niger, including the destruction of Byzantium (later Constantinople, now Istanbul) are of import in the story of Britain only as they witnessed the formation of the hopelessly tardy decision of Albinus to embark his army, and by its help—or at its demand—with the apparent support of units from the Rhine frontier, challenge what had become in his mind a usurpation of imperial power as illegal and detestable as that of Julianus. There is a tale to the effect that any reluctance on the part of Albinus to force the issue was rudely terminated when emissaries of Severus, under the pretext of delivering an important letter, attempted his assassination.

Britain was stripped of garrison for the effort. The three legions, and surely the best of the auxiliary units, were put on ships to cross the Channel. It seems clear that the Antonine Wall and the Lowlands were emptied of defenders, and, at best, but small detachments of care-taking troops left on Hadrian's Wall.

The armies of Albinus and Severus, each reported with usual exaggeration at 150,000 men, met in civil and needless conflict near Lugdunum (Lyon), on the Rhone, on the 19th of February, 197 A.D. After heavy fighting and severe casualties on both sides, Severus rallied from near defeat and won the day. Albinus, fleeing the battlefield, took his own life. Severus ordered his head cut off and sent to Rome, perhaps as an earnest to the Senate of the fate awaiting others intemperate enough to challenge his imperial authority.

The British legions had suffered heavily in the battle. It took many months for Severus to fill the ranks with replacements and send them back to their old stations under his own appointee as governor, Virus Lupus.

The news of Albinus' defeat in distant Gaul was not long in reaching Britain, to drive newly made widows and orphans into mourning, to create consternation among the nearly defenseless civil population, and, as it passed by the normal processes of gossip and wilderness telegraph to the eager ears of the Caledonii and Maeatae, to whisper opportunity.

Scouting the Antonine Wall denuded of garrisons, listening to words from friends to the south, the northern tribes saw no need to hurry. Roman Britain—the whole Province, with its rich cities, its luxurious country villas and farmsteads; its miscellany of useful household goods, its cattle and sheep in pasture; its helpless population ripe for slaughter, rapine, or the slave market—all, all lay spread before them, there for the taking. This time, let there be no hurry. Let it be done properly, soundly, with no half measures.

2

WHEN THE attack came, it came in great strength, indicating a heretofore unknown co-ordination of effort and leadership. After months of preparation the claymore-swinging Caledonii and the fierce Maeatae broke through the Antonine Wall, massacred the few caretaker troops, and exhibited their long-pent-up resentment by destroying much of the turf embankment along with its empty supporting forts.

Moving south in strength, they were joined by hopefuls from the Lowland clans, sources of sound intelligence on areas and installations worth plundering. So guided, as we know from archeological studies, they systematically wrecked the interlocking network of forts and traffic control posts north of Hadrian's Wall. In this and subsequent operations there is little reason to believe the Highlanders less ferocious in victory than were the Trinovantes and Iceni under Boudicca 140 years earlier.

Already loaded down with booty and exhilarated by their unimpeded progress, the tribal horde came at last within sight of Hadrian's Wall. One would like to think that the Caledonian tribesmen, lately burst from the fastnesses and fogbound lochs of the Grampians, might have paused in astonishment and awe, even in fear, before the majestic barrier stretching interminably to the horizon on east and west. At last the mighty, impenetrable Wall of which they had heard in travelers' tales, but which the vast majority could never have seen before, was there in front of them—more than fitted stone and mortar, more than rounded turret and supporting fortress, but the outstretched hand of mighty and eternal Rome saying without words, but by the mere fact of its presence, "Thus far, and no farther, on your peril."

But the mere presence was not enough. A few exploratory attacks proved the absence of those defending forces which alone could have brought the Wall to life. At many points the wild Highlanders streamed across, tearing at the masonry, destroying milecastles and fortresses. South like a plague of locusts the tribesmen swarmed, killing, looting, burning. Even the empty fortress of the Sixth Legion at Eburacum was heavily damaged and taken. Perhaps some few auxiliary cohorts, retreating before the onslaught, fled to Deva, and there in some desperate fashion manned the stone ramparts of the Twentieth's fortress. At least archeology tells us Deva escaped destruction, or even identifiable damage, in this unpredictable whirlwind. Bypassed, for good or ill, it remained intact while the storm of devastation moved on to Viroconium by the Severn, the pleasant white city under the Wrekin which less than seventy years earlier (130 A.D.) had raised a magnificent forum and basilica with a dedicatory inscription to Hadrian. There the raiders wreaked heavy damage.

Beyond Viroconium on the west, and Lindum on the east, the tribal offensive appears to have come to a slow reluctant halt, either because the movement had lost its momentum or because Lupus, the governor, had been able to take some minor measures for the defense of the old Trent-Severn line of the Fosse Way.

Probably the halt short of the richest and most settled part of the Province was a consequence of both factors. It is easy to believe that the Highland chieftains, once things got moving, were helpless to halt defection or to maintain that modicum of discipline needed to keep their forces in co-ordinated movement. We can imagine that all the way south from the Antonine Wall surfeited tribesmen, leading a stolen oxcart laden with plunder that would mean wealth and unknown comfort in their Highland crofts, driving ahead herds of sequestered cattle and sheep, had turned aside from the continuing advance and, content with their booty, started back home. This process would be cumulative as the raiders moved farther south, until finally the tribes would have broken up into small bands likely to be stopped by any show of Roman resistance. It is probable that this condition was reached before the Fosse Way, and that a few Roman patrols, aided by the roused citizenry, were able to bring the scattered horde to a stop. The process was accelerated by judicious bribery. The governor, Virus Lupus, found ignominy profitable and a retreat bought with money handouts to the Highland chiefs preferable to suffering their continued and obnoxious presence.

Severus himself, who if unoccupied might have brought adequate forces quickly to Britain, was wholly absorbed in affairs of greater immediacy in the east. Left to himself, Lupus, once the satiated Highlanders had departed north, began with inadequate resources the work of reconstruction. Not only the legionary fortress at Eburacum but about thirty forts of the Hadrianic Wall complex and its southern supporting installations had been heavily damaged. Reconstruction was started on Eburacum and the supporting forts at once, but even ten years later work was still continuing in the counties immediately south of the Wall, although the Wall forts and their outposts in Dumfries and Northumberland had been rebuilt and even extended, particularly in the east.

We must believe that the destruction to the embryonic civil settlements growing up south of the Wall as a result of Hadrian's frontier policy was equally severe, if difficult to trace.

North of the Wall, in the Scots Lowlands, the new and aggressive governor, Alfenius Senecio, was fighting and winning victories, indicating perhaps that the purchased retreat did not, in the minds of the Caledonian and Maeatean chieftains, include relinquishing that area. But in the East, Severus the Emperor had been victorious, and by 207, in answer to the request of Senecio "either for more troops to reinforce the frontier, or an Imperial Expedition," was ready to give Scotland his personal and unfriendly attention.

The Emperor appears to have sent ahead to Britain his elder son, the Bassianus we know as Caracalla, so-named from the Gallic cloak he introduced to Roman fashion. Severus himself followed in 208 A.D., accompanied by the Empress, Julia Domna, and their second son, Geta. Heavy drafts of reinforcements followed.

Severus, exhibiting the long Roman memory for injury, set up his headquarters in the restored fortress at Eburacum and immediately put in train elaborate plans for inflicting on the Caledonii and Maeatae such a lesson that the survivors might later think twice before engaging so cheerfully in a freebooting expedition against Rome.

Severus was nothing if not thorough. Both his governors, Lupus and Senecio, had done work on the rebuilding of Corstopitum (Corbridge), the Wall supply depot at the crossing of the Stanegate and Dere Street. Major construction of granaries and storehouses was started by Severus, as well as other work indicating that he may have meant to establish on the site a legionary fortress for closer support of the whole northern frontier. Arrangements were made for the supply of his forces by sea, to the Firths of Forth and Tay. Then in 209 A.D. he moved into Scotland on what inscriptions and contemporary historians called "the most fortunate British Expedition."

Details of the expedition are lacking, although it seems to have resulted, perhaps from its very size and portentousness, in a quick submission of the Highland clans.

As this text is being written, the discovery, by British schoolboys, of a hitherto unknown Roman fort at Carpow, on the Tay estuary, has been announced. Preliminary examination indicates it was a major installation of about thirty acres—big enough for a legion plus extensive warehouses—with a massive headquarters building of such solid foundations that its intended permanence must be presumed. Recovered roof tiles bear the stamp of the Sixth Legion: "VI V B P F," or (Legio) "VI Victrix Britannica Pia Fidelis." The dates of its building and occupation are yet to be determined. But in view of the dearth of evidence for any earlier extensive occupation of Perthshire after Agricola,§ and the known thoroughness of Serverus' preparations, it seems, at this writing, likely to have been constructed by him as a forward fortress and supply depot, capable of receiving, storing, and reissuing to the troops supplies brought by ship up the Tay estuary. The existence of such a formidable fort and supply base so far north might, if it be established as of Severan construction, also identify as his the already located marching camps in Angus and Kincardine and as far north as Glenmailen in Aberdeen. But this is

§ Remains of a smaller coastal installation, identified as "Horrea Classis" (fleet base) near Carpow, were already known.

guesswork only. When detailed excavations, (undertaken in August, 1962, under the supervision of Professor E. Birley), finally establish the facts of this remarkable and significant discovery, the explanation may well be quite different.

Whatever the course and extent of the "most fortunate British Expedition," Severus appears to have been satisfied with its results. After obtaining the submission of the clans and inflicting condign punishment for their crimes, he returned with his army, less garrison detachments, to Eburacum for the winter.

While at Eburacum he learned that the Maeatae, in spite of their submission and the lesson presumably taught them, had again broken out in revolt. Whether it was a major tribal uprising or merely an isolated attack on an exposed Roman garrison is not recorded, nor has archeology so far shed any light. But it was enough for the thoroughly exasperated and never-too-patient Severus to set aside plans for a return to the continent and instead to initiate operations for the following summer designed to effect the total extermination of the Maeatae.

From this fate the Scots tribes were saved by the death of Severus at Eburacum on February 4, 211 A.D., at the age of sixty-five, after a reign of eighteen years. In accordance with his will, he was succeeded by his sons, Caracalla and Geta, who became co-Emperors. This untenable arrangement could last only long enough for one to be successful in murdering the other. Caracalla struck first, a year later, in Rome, killing Geta even while their mother, Julia Domna, sought to protect her younger son.

But before that fraternal gesture, and even before following his father's ashes in filial reverence to Rome, Caracalla appears to have conducted another Scottish campaign, with unrecorded results. Yet peace terms were agreed upon. The clan chieftains appear to have been hard bargainers, for as a result Caracalla withdrew all garrisons back to Hadrian's Wall, abandoning the remains of the Antonine Wall, but maintaining patrols—probably from the retained fort of Trimontium—through the Cheviot Hills and the Lothians, and, in the west, through Galloway and Dumfries. Further surveillance and support of the Lowlands was supplied by forts at Habitancum (Risingham) and Bremenium (High Rochester) in Northumberland along Dere Street, and in the west by the Hadrianic outpost forts of Fanum

Cocidi (Bewcastle) and Castra Exploratorum (Netherby) in Cumberland. In these installations a new kind of military specialist appears in the Roman Army—the *exploratores,* units specially trained and equipped for patrolling frontiers.

But the most subtle of Caracalla's arrangements was his achievement in enlisting in their own as well as in the frontier defense the Lowland tribes who, of course, to some extent, had suffered from their Highland neighbors. He managed this by conferring on them a new and free status as *foederati,* client kingdoms, with a relationship to Rome similar to that of Cogidumnus and the Regnenses of earlier times. He doubtless assured them of assistance from the Roman frontier forces in the event of aggression, and to make sure their new liberty did not turn against Rome, limited them to certain areas of assembly, locations later listed in the *Ravenna Cosmography.*

These arrangements of Caracalla had been generally underrated by historians until Dr. I. A. Richmond called attention to them in his book *Roman Britain* (London, Penguin Books, 1955). In his words, "They guaranteed peace in northern Britain for longer than the action of any other Roman general had ever enforced it; and they seem to have achieved this despite the serious worsening of political and economic conditions that afflicted the Empire during the frequent collapses of central authority in the middle and later years of the third century A.D."

Granting that these arrangements represented a marked retreat from his father's policy of extermination of the Highland tribes, they seem to have been negotiated in good faith and scrupulously kept by all parties. The result was to preserve the peace for over one hundred years—an achievement modern Britain might envy.

Hadrian's Wall, reconstructed and strengthened under Severus (the western portion, originally of turf, had been rebuilt of stone and concrete, much of it on a line north of the earlier barrier, probably by Calpurnius Agricola, around 162 A.D.), settled down with its garrisons to year after year of peaceful, routine existence. Soldiers enlisted, served out their terms, acquired Roman citizenship, and settled in retirement near the Wall, there to raise sons and daughters. The civil communities south of the Wall prospered, grew in area and population, proliferated, and became centers of a not inconsiderable traffic and commerce with the north. The seasons came and went, the years passed, generations of Roman Britons were born and gathered to their fathers, while the great barrier stood, the northern edge of the Roman world, silent witness to the persistent vitality of the Empire.

3

Two DECISIONS, one by Severus, one by Caracalla, had their effects in Britain.

Serverus, holding to the memory of the power Albinus had been able to marshal against him on the continent, determined to eliminate the power of future British governors to repeat the performance. To achieve this end, he divided the Province into two: Britannia Superior, with capital at Londinium, and Britannia Inferior, with headquarters at Eburacum. Apparently control of one legion, II Augusta, in Wales, went to the governor at Londinium, while the governor at York, charged with the frontier, commanded both the Sixth at York and the Twentieth at Deva, along with the auxiliaries, numeri, and exploratores of the border and the Wall. Thenceforward two governors, independent of each other and both answerable directly to the Emperor, ruled in Britain with the consequent multiplication of staffs, bureaucracy, and inertia inseparable from proliferating government.

In 212 A.D. Caracalla, finding himself pressed for funds, raised the inheritance tax from five to ten per cent. On being told the additional revenue would be modest, since the tax applied to Roman citizens only, he published the famed "Antonine Constitution" which gave full Roman citizenship to every free-born male within the Empire (with the exception of Egypt, which remained as it had been since the days of Augustus the personal estate of the Emperor).

Thus at a stroke of the stylus the citizenship, theretofore a privilege so treasured and sparingly granted, received a vast accretion. But it came at a time when the burdens were beginning to outweigh the benefits. It is interesting, if useless, to consider what an exhilarating effect such a measure might have had on the Empire if initiated one hundred years earlier, say in the time of Trajan, and what changes in history, carrying their consequences into modern times, might have resulted.

4

FOR NEARLY the balance of the third century A.D. the two provinces
of Britain appear to have been permitted to go their quiet ways with
little interference, or even interest, at the center of Empire. The island
peoples could consider themselves blessed, for on the continent and
throughout the balance of the Empire at large, the period was one of
undiluted anarchy, chaos, and trouble.

External pressures on the frontiers could have been better handled
had the central authority possessed the stability and approached the
standards of Vespasian, Trajan, Hadrian, the Antonines, and Severus.
But with no sound precedent accepted for a peaceful and legal succession, the death of an Emperor invited widespread competition to
fill the vacancy. What had occurred only twice in two hundred years,
first after the death of Nero in 68 and then at the murder of Pertinax
in 193, became endemic.

In this murderous competition the frontier legions were com-
pletely out of hand. The memory of how the Pannonian legions had
humbled the Praetorian Guard and put its own general on the throne
with resulting financial gain was a lethal precedent. No matter how
disciplined and able in their routine duties of guarding the frontier,
when word of an Emperor's death reached the barracks and camps,
the hope and expectation of an immense money gift prompted one
or more provincial armies to acclaim their general "Augustus et
Imperator," often enough with that ambitious individual's connivance,
perhaps at least as often to his despair.

The process was accelerated by the indisposition of the troops
long to endure an Emperor who failed in any way to meet their
turbulent demands. The record, over the near sixty-five years that followed, speaks for itself. Caracalla was murdered in 217; Macrinus in
219; Elagabalus in 222; Alexander Severus, a nice boy who meant
well and tried hard, in 235; Maximinus, the Thracian peasant and
giant, in 238; Pupienus Maximus and Balbinus, after three months
of joint rule, in the same year; Gordian III by his troops while fighting the Persians in 244. Philip the Arab was killed in battle by
Decius in 249; Decius himself fell in a disastrous defeat of Roman
arms by the Goths in 251; Gallus, who followed Decius, was mur-

dered by his troops in 253; and Aemilianus, his successor, met the same fate within months.

These were merely temporarily successful candidates. A whole succession of others, governors of different provinces pushed by ambition or the frenzy of their troops, received only local recognition until fate, in one gruesome shape or another, caught up with them.

Gordian I was proclaimed Emperor by his troops in Africa in 237, along with his son, Gordian II. Within two months the latter was killed in battle by troops loyal to Maximinus, ending at the age of forty-five a life both licentious and scholarly, if we are to believe a tale that credits him with twenty-two concubines and a library of 62,000 volumes. His father, Gordian I, learning of his death, anticipated the inevitable by committing suicide.

Marinus, a legion commander of Moesia, named himself Augustus and in a reversal of form was killed by his outraged troops in 249; Marcus Fulvius Rufus Jotopianus, governor of Syria, essayed the purple with the same fate within the year. His troops, perhaps judging his chances of success bad and theirs therefore inexorably worse, cut off his head and sent it as a mark of their loyalty to Decius.

Pacatianus, one of Philip the Arab's generals, revolted, claimed the title of Augustus, and was slain, probably in 245; Sponsiamus in Dacia, a usurper, was killed in 249; and Hostilianus, son of Decius, and adopted as son and colleague by Gallus, died of a pestilence in 251 before fate caught up with him.

It could hardly be expected that Rome's many and aggressive border enemies would fail to exploit the opportunity offered by this internal hemorrhage. Along the Rhine and the Danube, on the Asian frontiers, and in the Mauretanias the once stoutly defended boundaries of the Empire suffered assault, infiltration, and pillage while the legions and auxiliaries battled among themselves on the side of one candidate or another.

And there was worse to come. Valerian succeeded Aemilianus in 253 A.D. He was fortunate only in his son, Gallienus, a Roman of the old stamp, cultured, courageous, indomitable, and an able general. Valerian, facing war on both the Rhine-Danube frontier and in the East, gave his son the task of maintaining the European frontier while he went off to Asia after the newly established and aggressive empire of the Persians. In 260 he was overwhelmed in battle by Shapur I and taken prisoner. He died an ignominious death in captivity, the first Emperor of Rome ever to fall alive into the hands of the enemy.

Gallienus, succeeding his father as sole Emperor, in a series of swift campaigns against the Franks and the Alemanni threatening the Rhine, the newly aggressive Marcomanni, the Goths, and the Scythians probing the Danube, did his mighty best, winning victory after victory, and discouraging if not ending the barbarian attempts to penetrate the frontiers. But the pressure was too heavy, the forces affecting the integrity of the troops too perverse. He too was murdered by his men, in 268.

Throughout all this continental uproar, little is heard of Britain. Perhaps the lesson of Albinus remained a firm restraining hand on the memory of the legions; perhaps the action of Severus in dividing the Province divorced from both governors the means to enter the continental cockpit. The northern frontier remained quiet, and so far as we can tell the island people enjoyed a reasonable degree of prosperity and happiness.

Another, and important factor in the peace of Britain during part of this anarchic turmoil was the action of Postumus, Governor of Gaul, in 258. That able Roman, perhaps heartily sick of the turmoil, and aware of the waiting vengeance of Gallienus for the killing of the latter's son, Saloninus, by troops of the Rhine army, when declared Augustus by that army, accepted it, only for a new entity, the *Imperium Galliarum,* in what was perhaps the first "Free French" movement. Spain and Britain, under what diplomatic or military pressures we do not know, joined with him, giving the new "Imperium" a power strong enough to dissuade Gallienus, fully occupied elsewhere, from interference.

Apparently Postumus set up the complete governmental panoply of the Empire from which he had seceded, with its consuls and other officials. Over this new polity he reigned for ten years, was followed by Victorinus in 269 and 270, then by Tetricus, who reigned until the vigorous Aurelian, Emperor in Rome, having both stamped out internal rivals and dealt with the highly publicized adventures of Zenobia, Queen of Palmyra, turned his attention to the Western schism. Tetricus, last emperor of the Imperium Galliarum, was defeated by Aurelian at Châlons in 273 A.D., with the result that Gaul, Britain, and Spain were restored to the central government.

There is no record of the process or reasoning that brought the two British governors and the garrison to adhere to the Imperium Galliarum. Perhaps the realities of geography, with Gaul separating them from Rome so long as its secession lasted, were enough. But there is ample evidence, in the form of altars, inscriptions, and milestones uncovered in Britain, to prove that the adherence was complete through most of the life of the Gallic Empire.

There is, for example, an altar from Camboglanna (Birdoswald) on Hadrian's Wall, raised to Jupiter, Greatest and Best, by Cohors I Aelia Dacorum Postumiana, under the command of Marcius Gallicus; and another, also from Birdoswald, by the same cohort when commanded by Probius Augendus. A milestone in Cornwall and another in Wales record loyalty to "the Imperator and Caesar, our lord Marcus Cassianus Latinus Postumus, loyal and faithful, Augustus."

Other milestones scattered around the country record the reigns of Victorinus and Tetricus, while again at Birdoswald, that altar-raising first cohort of Dacians activated by Hadrian had changed its honorific from "Postumiana" to "Tetricianorum" to proclaim its loyalty to the last Emperor of the Gauls.

Then there is the altar found at a milecastle two miles west of Birdoswald put up by soldiers of the Twentieth Legion ¶ to the god Cocidius, and giving the names of two consuls of the Imperium Galliarum theretofore unknown, but established by Professor Birley as serving between 262 and 266.

As the island provinces appear to have adhered to Postumus as a recognition of the realities of the time, the change back to the central government under Aurelian seems also to have passed without recorded difficulty or incident. It is not unreasonable to suppose that its only effect, lost on the mass of the population, was the replacement of the two governors and other high officials by new men, sent to take charge by Aurelian.

We today find it hard to understand how any government could survive the sixty-odd years of internal strife, barbarian invasion, and corrupted character which the Roman Empire suffered between the death of Caracalla and the accession of Aurelian.

Yet a persistent vitality, capable of rising to heights when properly channeled, seemed still to exist in the tortured body of the State.

¶ The presence of a detachment of the Twentieth Legion in a Wall milecastle is unexplained. Probably they were there to perform repairs or maintenance beyond the skills of the members of the normal garrison.

In three years of military and political effort the astute Aurelian succeeded in uniting once again an Empire seemingly fragmented beyond succor. His effort however was only a promising start on a gigantic task and was cut short by his assassination in Asia in 275.

His successor, Tacitus, said to be a descendant of the historian, already an old man of seventy-five when named to the Principate by the Senate, lasted but six months before dying of exhaustion. The Eastern army, reverting to type, named as "Augustus" their general Probus.

Probus carried on the work of Aurelian, vigorously defended the borders, restored and strengthened the limes along the Rhine-Danube frontier, and, to develop a reliable instrument of policy, sought to reinculcate in the Army the loyalty, discipline, and combat efficiency of old. We hear of him in connection with Britain only because he sent there, for settlement, several thousand Frankish prisoners of war.

Probus' efforts to reform the Army succeeded well enough to allow him hope of full success. But when he turned his troops from war and garrison life to arduous public works—probably the repair of roads, frontier forts, aqueducts, and similar works sadly deteriorated in the neglect of sixty years—they gave vent to their resentment of this unwelcome labor by murdering him in 282.

Then the Army accepted Carus, who had commanded the Praetorian Guard under Probus. Carus reigned for sixteen months before dying at Ctesiphon, in Mesopotamia, struck, according to report, by lightning.

Carus was succeeded by his two sons, Numerianus and Carinus. Numerianus died in the East after nine months of office. Carinus, ably defending the Western frontier, lasted another year before falling at the hands of an angry husband.

Then, in 284, without knowing they had selected a man they could neither control nor destroy, the Army settled on an Illyrian commoner who had risen through the ranks to high command, Caius Valerianus Diocletianus.

The reforms—if that is a proper description—of Diocletian and his reorganization of the Empire are too well known to require repetition in this story of Britannia. It is enough to note that they represented, in sum, an earnest effort in both politics and economics to save the State from external pressures and internal decay. That the once respected freedoms of the citizens, steadily whittled away since the days of the Antonines, were now largely lost in a welter of regulations, heavy taxation, price-fixing,|| and restriction of movement and employment indistinguishable from peonage seems to have been considered by Diocletian and his successors as the necessary price for another two hundred years of corporate survival.

In his reorganization, Diocletian not only severely separated the military from the civil functions but divided control of the Empire into two parts, taking for himself the East and setting up as co-Augustus in the West a tough, uneducated soldier, Maximianus Hercules.# Maximianus set up his headquarters at Mediolanum (Milan), both closer to the frontiers he must defend and reasonably removed from the intrigues of Rome.

Hardly was Maximianus settled in his new praetorium, barely had he had time to gather in his hands the reins of power in the West, when to the myriad administrative problems of his provinces, and to the urgent measures needed for the defense of his long frontiers, was added a new and perplexing irritation—the growth of piracy in the North Sea and Channel, taking the form of hit-and-run raids on the coastal settlements of Gaul and Britain.

5

In the *Geographical Outline* of Claudius Ptolemaeus, compiled in Alexandria during the reign of Antoninus Pius, occurs the first mention in history of an obscure and remote Germanic tribe, the Saxons.

They were believed to inhabit what are now the Frisian Islands,

---

|| An extant example is an edict published in 301 A.D. in the names of Diocletian, Maximianus, Galerius, and Constantinus, thus encompassing the entire Empire in its jurisdiction. It expresses official contempt for extortionary practices of merchants and shopkeepers and sets maximum prices for such commodities as oil, salt, honey, meat, poultry, fish, vegetables, fruit, grain, wine, beer, clothing, hides, boots, and shoes; as well as maximum pay scales for laborers, artisans, schoolmasters, and other occupational workers.

This irascible and often vacillating gentleman has left a hunting lodge near the present-day town of Piazza Armerina, Sicily. However modest by his standards, the remains excavated and partially restored by Italian archeologists permit the re-creation of the conditions under which such exalted personages took to "roughing it"; the mosaics, in a remarkable state of preservation, are world famous.

the coast of Schleswig, and the lowlands of the Elbe, Weser, and Ems estuaries. Beyond the fringe of Roman conquest, beyond even the farthest range and penetration of Roman punitive expeditions across the Rhine, these hardy folk took naturally to the sea; first, perhaps, as fishermen; then, as itinerant traders spread word of rich and complacent civilizations to the southwest, as raiders, a way of life both more remunerative and more exciting than their gaunt marshlands had so far afforded.

Somehow in their prehistory, they had learned the art of constructing swift, manageable, and seaworthy craft of extremely shallow draft. They had also picked up as much of the lore of sailing as their single square sails would permit, and by the time they attracted unfavorable notice, were able to find their way, on short voyages, out of sight of land.

Contemporary writers after Ptolemaeus deemed them brave, reckless, merciless, foolhardy, savage beyond civilized comprehension—which, for the day, was saying a good deal—eager to fight, and unafraid to die. Their name excited loathing and terror in the ancient world. Later the historians of England up to Victorian times, glorying in their Saxon heritage,** assigned high virile qualities to these murderous freebooters.

Whatever the truth of their nature, the Saxons, in the years around the accession of Diocletian, began to venture from their marshy havens and river mouths south along the European coast. They investigated with predatory interest the wealth and prosperity, the long-settled peace and careless security of the Romanized countryside beyond the Rhine River mouths. By degrees they ventured farther, down the coast of what is now Belgium, poked into the estuary of the Scheldt, and reconnoitered the coastline at least as far as the sea reaches of the Seine. Rounding Cape Gris-Nez, on any half-clear day, the white cliffs of Britain were easily visible to starboard, stirring curiosity while whetting greed.

The North Sea coast of Britain, with its many rivers and tidal estuaries permitting navigation well inland, proved an irresistible lure to these pitiless adventurers. Standing offshore until dusk, a couple of

---

** J. R. Green, in *A Short History of the English People* (New York, Harper, 1891), writes: "It is with the landing of Hengist and his war band at Ebbsfleet on the shores of the Isle of Thanet that English history begins. No spot in Britain can be so sacred to Englishmen as that which first felt the tread of English feet."

hours' vigorous rowing brought their keels softly grating on sandy beach or river flat. Their raids on unsuspecting farms and isolated villages were swift and merciless. Men, resisting or not, were butchered, the livestock within reach slaughtered, children and old women left to die in flaming homesteads. Gathering what valuables they could find—tools, weapons, jewelry, and the comelier of the female sex—they were off as quietly as they had come, and out of sight of land by dawn.

An understandable roar of protest arose, compounded by the novel nature of the attacks and the terror they produced. Danger from the sea was something new to provincial inhabitants long accustomed to the Roman peace behind defended land frontiers. The open farms and villages of Britain's east coast knew from folklore of the wild Highlanders restive and menacing beyond the Wall. But seaborne raids, conducted with the utmost savagery and on unpredictable target areas, were another matter. The government must do something.

Maximianus, reading the reports in Milan, ordered energetic countermeasures, including the construction of signal towers along the threatened coasts and, offensively, major augmentation of the Classis Britannica, the Roman fleet which had patrolled the Channel since the first century A.D.

This last action could not have been simple. For over two hundred years the chief functions of the Channel fleet had been those we associate with the Coast Guard rather than with the Navy. Keeping track of merchant vessels, maintaining lighthouses, chasing smugglers, and assisting in the collection of customs were necessary duties but hardly sound preparation for offensive action at sea.

But the task was undertaken with typical Roman thoroughness. While the new fighting galleys were being built, bases for the greater fleet to come were expanded and filled with naval stores at Gesoriacum (Boulogne), in Belgica; and in Britain, at Lemanis (Lympne), Dubrae (Dover), and Rutupiae (Richborough). Farther west along the Channel coast of Britain, Anderida (Pevensey), Clausentum (Bitterne), and Portus Adurni (Portchester) provided shelter and resupply for vessels driven down-Channel by wind, weather, or duty.

The enlistment and training of seamen, marines, and even ship captains for aggressive naval warfare was an essential prerequisite to offensive operations. Casting about for a commander capable of preparing, and then of leading, the fleet against the marauding Saxons, Maximianus selected a Belgic Gaul, a soldier and seaman in the service of Rome—one Carausius,†† a native of Menapia, a lowland district between the Scheldt and the Meuse.

It was, on the whole, an unfortunate selection.

†† His other names, Marcus Aurelius Valerius, were doubtless assumed after he had seized control of Britain and unilaterally elevated himself to equality and condominium with Diocletian and Maximianus.

X

DISSOLUTION
287 A.D. AND AFTERWARD

You had nothing but an arch, a road, an army and
a law. And yet a man might walk from the east to the
west because of it—yes, and speak the same tongue
all the way. I do not admire you, but you were a great
people.

—STEPHEN VINCENT BENÉT,
"The Last of the Legions"

1

CARAUSIUS, ADMIRAL OF THE CHANNEL AND
North Sea littoral, has come down to us as able, energetic, enterprising, ambitious, and unscrupulous. To
Eutropius, who made some unflattering remarks about
him (probably obtained from government sources), he
must have appeared an unmitigated scoundrel. But then,
we must judge him against his times. In any case, there seems to have
been nothing petty about Carausius. What he did, for good or ill, he
did in a big way.

His earlier record, or what we know of it, explains in some degree his selection for the important naval command. Carausius appears to have been a pilot or shipmaster, familiar through his work
with the coastal waters and many estuaries of Belgica and the Rhine
mouths. In the course of his work it may be believed he crossed many
times to Britain, and knew intimately those harbors and ports through
which trans-Channel sea traffic was handled. Additionally, as a
soldier, he had earned distinction in the desperate fighting involved

in putting down the revolt of some Gallic peasants known as the Bagaudae.

It seems probable that in recruiting new personnel for the ships in construction Carausius had to draw mainly on the maritime population of the Low Countries, kin to himself and racially, if distantly, connected with the Saxons to the northeast. His methods of recruitment, officer selection, and training seem to have won for him, from his new crews, a large measure of personal loyalty.

Like others before him and after in those troubled times, ambition and a sense of self-preservation may have bade him look to himself lest he be uselessly sacrificed to a dying Empire. Possibly his youth, spent in the autonomy of the Imperium Galliarum, had taught him that while order, law, peace, and opportunity for constructive civil development might have been established in the first instance by Rome, these desirable conditions could be locally maintained without being involved in the worldwide problems and murderous rivalries of the Imperial Government.

For an ambitious man thus oriented, the first task was to build personal wealth and influence to furnish a base of power or, if Fortuna failed to smile, the means of livelihood in flight. Thus, while energetically embarked with his now ready fleet on the task of suppressing Saxon piracy, it was not too long, if the later charges against him had substance, before it occurred to Carausius that his personal wealth would benefit if his ships ignored the raiders on their outward voyages, waited until their raid was successful, then pounced upon them, spoil-laden, on their way home.

This procedure of course involved interception, fighting, and losses. A safer method was to come to terms with the Saxon pirates, allow their ships to pass outward bound, then to rendezvous with them on the way home, exacting a reasonable percentage of the booty for the official, if clandestine, protection. In its principles if not in its precise application, this technique too we have inherited from antiquity.

There was naturally one flaw in an arrangement otherwise so mutually satisfactory to fleet and pirates—the unmanageable inclination of the victims in Belgica and Britain to protest. Suspicion in high places was inevitably aroused, and evidence of collusion could not be wholly suppressed. But communications were slow and Maximianus in Milan was far away.

If we are to believe the contemporary historians, before Maximianus was forced by a formidable assembly of evidence to the conclusion that his Channel admiral was engaged in traitorous malfeasance, Carausius is supposed to have accumulated a large personal fortune and to have shared enough of it with the officers and men of the fleet to reinforce both their personal loyalty to him and their complicity in his punishable activities.

So foresighted an operator was therefore fully informed, by methods he would have taken pains to establish beforehand, of the progress of complaints against him. When he learned, perhaps in 286, that orders were on the way from Milan that he be seized and executed, he was fully prepared with an audacious response.

Boldly assembling the fleet, and leaving behind a garrison to hold fortified Gesoriacum against the Empire, he sailed for Britain. By bribery, or a donative as it was then respectably known; by oratory, meaning a gross misrepresentation of his authority and intentions; by surprise backed by immediately available power; or by a judicious mixture of all three; he obtained the adherence of the Roman British authorities and the submission of the garrisons. This seizure of power accomplished, he proclaimed himself Augustus, adopted the honorific names of Marcus Aurelius Valerius, and settled down to control the two provinces of Britain and the country around his base of Gesoriacum in Belgica as the self-appointed equal of Maximianus in Milan and of the august Diocletian, already transforming himself from Roman Emperor into oriental potentate in Nicomedia.

It remains, because unrecorded, a mystery as to how this magistral effrontery could have succeeded. Carausius certainly could not have had, in his fleet, any force capable of meeting even one of the legions stationed in Britain. Yet, if he sailed up the Thames to the walls of Londinium, his fleet marine force probably could have won the city easily before Legio II Augusta could be summoned from the west. Additionally, he had control of the Channel, across which all communication with Maximianus had to pass.

Londinium at this time was a thriving port and diocesan capital, the largest Roman city north of the Alps. It covered an area of about 330 acres on the left bank of the Thames, with a population probably in the neighborhood of 40,000. Its great battlemented and bastioned walls ran in an arc from the river at the Tower of London for two miles, to reach the river again at about Blackfriars. The various openings through the Wall are remembered by the familiar names (running west to east) of Ludgate, Newgate, Aldersgate, Cripplegate (the northwest bastion), Moorgate, Bishopsgate, and Aldgate. The Walbrook ran through the center of the city underneath where the Bank of England now stands. The Basilica was in the area between Leadenhall Street and Fenchurch, and the imposing baths near the river between Eastcheap and Lower Thames Street. Many sections of the Wall survive.

We may assume squadrons of Carausius' fleet, in their assigned task of patrolling for Saxon pirates, to have been familiar sights in the Thames estuary, and even at Londinium dockside. Carausius himself, as admiral, must surely have had close official contact with the British. It seems likely he was able to achieve substantial surprise and, with a relatively small force, seize control of the capital, the official records, the signal system, and the diocesan treasury, presenting the authorities with a *fait accompli*.

It becomes more understandable if we try to reconstruct the probable attitudes of the two governors, the garrisons, and the populace. The governors, appointees of Diocletian, in their earlier careers had almost certainly played roles in the bloody struggles for the throne. Their assignments to Britain, remote and untouched by the convulsions on the continent, may well have seemed salubrious refuge, carrying the promise of life prolonged by their absence from the risky drama being played out in blood at the center of Empire. That the struggle for imperial honors had at last reached Britain, so long immune from such disturbances, was a fact that had to be accepted. Where there had been two Augusti, there were now three. One of them had honored the island provinces by taking up residence, and establishing an imperial capital at Londinium. What was there to question?

Perhaps, in the way rumors get around, the governors later learned the whole episode was an audacious usurpation. By that time it was too late. Carausius was proving himself an able and forceful ruler, taking sound measures for the government and defense of the island provinces, including a vigorous campaign at sea against his erstwhile allies, the Saxon pirates.

The legions and auxiliaries of the Wall, soldiers and officers who remembered the fifteen-year rule of the Imperium Galliarum in Britain, could hardly have considered the presence of Carausius, holding imperial honors, as cause for rebellion. And the populace, regaled for two generations with tales of the horrors going on in the continental Empire while they had been blessed with peace, could only rejoice in the presence of an Augustus who was also a formidable naval commander, capable of stopping the Saxon depredations.

The audacious insolence of Carausius in declaring himself coequal with Maximianus in Milan and Diocletian in Nicomedia seems to have met with scorn in both plus anger in Maximianus. The latter brusquely ordered the building of another fleet and the training of a new, presumably loyal, complement of officers and seamen. But Maximianus seems to have moved too soon. His raw fleet met that of Carausius and was ignominiously defeated, thus demonstrating, to Maximianus' humiliation and Carausius' satisfaction, that naval tactics have to be learned by arduous training, and that the organization and handling of a fighting fleet is no task for landlubbers.

There was nothing left for Maximianus to do save play for time. Diocletian, who had an odd sense of humor anyway, along with subtlety, probably not only counseled patience, but persuaded Maximianus they should jointly recognize Carausius as their coequal colleague. So, unlike the secession of the Imperium Galliarum, the British provinces remained, if only officially, part of the Empire.

For six years Carausius was left in undisturbed control of Britain and coastal Belgica, protected by the only effective fleet north of Gibraltar. One great advantage he possessed in carrying out the task of giving the island strong yet beneficent government was that the revenues were retained, rather than paid to the central government, giving him relatively ample financial resources. At least he was able to issue his own coins, which could hardly be expected to pass as legal tender elsewhere in the Empire. The reverse inscription on one of his issues, "By Public Demand," perhaps allows us to grant Carausius, too, a sardonic sense of humor. On the other hand, it may well express the real enthusiasm of the populace for his rule, since later generations of Roman Britons looked back with nostalgia on his time, an indication perhaps that taxes and other burdens, if not reduced, at least were not increased. The northern frontier remained quiet, the Scoti of Ireland were as yet only talking among themselves of the rich booty which might repay a descent on the west coast, and the Saxon piracies were reduced to near nothing by successive defeats at sea.

Since Carausius is the only major Roman commander in some centuries who appears to have had a sound grasp of naval matters, it is possible he originated the scout ships which Vegetius, writing some ninety years later in the reign of Valentinian II, described as an important part of the sea defenses of Britain. They were small craft and lean, very swift under oars, and highly maneuverable. They carried twenty oarsmen and, to lessen their visibility in the haze and fog so frequent in the North Sea and the Channel, were painted sea green throughout—hull, masts, oars, rigging, and sails. Even the crews were uniformed in the same color. They were intended, not for fighting but for use as scouts, able to detect enemy vessels at distances from which they themselves could not be observed and to give the alarm for interception.

Carausius further extended the system of signal towers ordered by Maximianus, an example of which was the transformation of the great four-way arch at Rutupiae, the formal gateway to Britain, into a watchtower. He also began the construction of a system of coastal fortifications, all the way from the Wash around to the Isle of Wight, garrisoned by combined forces of soldiers and sailors, forming a co-ordinated group of bases for sea patrols and efficient interception. With formidable later additions this system was to become in the time of Constantine a separate military command under a new officer, the Count of the Saxon Shore—*Comes Littoris Saxonici.*

During the rule of Carausius there was quiet in the north. This security and peace followed less from any lack of enterprise on the part of the Highland clans—now becoming known en masse to the Roman Britons as the *Populi Picti* "Painted Peoples" (whence the later generic term "the Picts")—than from the co-operation of the foederati of the Lowlands backed up by the Wall garrison and the exploratores of the forward posts. These mobile columns, working in unison with the foederati certainly as far north as the dismantled Antonine Wall, may be expected to have taken a profoundly skeptical attitude toward any gatherings of tribesmen large enough to become an aggressive formation.

But both the Highland clans and the foederati must have been aware that the Wall garrison and its forward elements alone provided the excess strength to discourage attack. Without those garrisons, without the ever-watchful sentries on their nightly rounds, without the interlocking signal stations flashing their messages of well-being or of alarm across the Wall's seventy miles of length and down the extent of its flanking supports, without the trumpet calls hastily summoning detachments to points of danger, the mighty bastion of Rome Eternal was but a static obstacle, easy to cross.

As the years of Carausius' pre-empted majesty rolled on, another threat appeared, this time from the west. The Scoti, as the Celtic tribes of Ireland were collectively known to the Roman British, moved by what mutual dares, avarice, and exhortation we can never know, emerged as sea-raiders in their own right, operating against the Galloway peninsula, the coasts of Cumberland, Westmoreland, Lancashire, and North Wales. Finding empty land in Galloway— perhaps the result of depopulation following Roman punitive expeditions into this area of persistent hostility—some of the Ulster tribesmen emigrated en masse and settled, curious, excitable, and grandiloquent foreigners in a land of kinsmen.

To meet this threat, minor in its beginnings by contrast to what was to develop later, Carausius appears to have established a naval base at Cardiff, Wales, and to have built watchtowers and signal stations along the coast. Other bases were doubtless established farther north than Cardiff, one of which appears to have been at Segontium (Caernarvon) on the northwest tip of Wales. In effect, Carausius found it necessary to duplicate on the west coast the system of defense against seaborne raids already established on the east.

So, for six years from 287 to 293 A.D., went matters in Britain under Carausius, onetime Praefectus Classis Britannicae, self-styled Augustus, temporarily coequal ruler of the Empire along with two rough soldier-emperors who waited only on the availability of adequate force to cut his throat.

2

IN 292 A.D. Diocletian and Maximianus, in an attempt to legitimize the succession and thereby eliminate the civil wars which had all too often followed the death of incumbents, decided to add to the imperial structure two deputies and heirs, to be called "Caesar." In the East, Diocletian selected the able, if impulsive, Galerius. For his deputy in the West, Maximianus, with Diocletian's approval, chose the equally able but far from impulsive Constantius, surnamed "Chlorus"—people said because of his excessively pale complexion, but in retrospect more probably a reflection of his personality.

Constantius, at the time of his elevation, was about forty-three years old. He came from a distinguished family of Dardania in upper Moesia, and was related through his mother to Claudius Gothicus, who in 268 had been temporarily acclaimed Augustus by his army and had died of the plague in 270. Constantius had proved high military and administrative ability by service in the Army and as governor of Dalmatia (southern Illyricum, now southern Yugoslavia and Albania).

To his new deputy Maximianus Hercules assigned responsibility for the newly organized praefecture of the Gauls, which included not only the Rhine frontier, the Gallic provinces, Spain, and western Tingitana in Africa, but also temporarily seceded Gesoriacum and Britain. In view of subsequent events, it is difficult not to believe that Maximianus, in outlining Constantius' duties, put a high priority on the humbling of Carausius.

Constantius established his civil and military headquarters at Colonia Augusta Treverorum (today Trier, on the Moselle), a city which for centuries had been the command headquarters of the Rhine frontier. Once routine business was out of the way, and Constantius satisfied that no imminent threat from beyond the Rhine would interfere, he set about the long and complex task of bringing to Carausius a clear if short-lived insight into the error of his ways. The first objective, naturally enough, was northwest Belgica surrounding the fortified port of Gesoriacum (Boulogne), the continental territory held and ruled by Carausius.

For all his provincial origin, or perhaps because of it, Constantius possessed more than a fair share of old-fashioned Roman pertinacity. The siege of the port city was carefully organized and inexorably pressed, including the formidable task of building a long mole which closed up the harbor, denying access to help from Britain and bottling up the portion of Carausius' fleet that failed to escape. This work alone took months.

Slowly the resources and supplies of the stubbornly defending garrison were exhausted. The tenacity of the defense, in times when allegiance to one or the other imperial authority might well have been governed by expediency rather than sentiment, is eloquent testimony to the loyalty Carausius could inspire. But loyalty cannot outlive starvation. A final assault by Constantius' forces took the city, the port area, and the impounded fleet.

With coastal Belgica once more brought to fealty, Constantius started on the next step, the building, equipping, and training of a fleet capable, not only of successfully challenging the crack navy of Carausius, but also of transporting the army he intended to land in Britain.

Having less confidence in his own knowledge of seafaring matters than Maximianus had had, Constantius sought and found an expert admiral in the person of a Greek, one Asclepiodotus. His identity is uncertain. He may be the man mentioned by Vopiscus (one of the six authors of the remarkably unreliable Augustan Histories) as a general under Probus, and an author in his own right who later pro- duced a life of Diocletian. His name and probable origin suggest that he obtained his naval experience in the *Classis Euxina,* Rome's Black Sea Fleet, long a training duty for sailors.

Carausius, helpless to aid or to rescue his loyal adherents in Gesoriacum, fully aware of the payment his imperial colleagues were about to exact for his self-elevation to their Augustan level, worked feverishly to strengthen his fleet and army. Between his proved naval competence and the military pertinacity of Constantius, the eventual issue might have been in doubt. But in 293 A.D., about the time Gesoriacum fell, a violent quarrel broke out between Carausius and his deputy Allectus, perhaps over the strategy to be adopted in meeting the implacable Constantius, and Allectus succeeded in having Carausius killed. The murderer assumed the titles and the authority of the slain admiral. Apparently the fleet and army of Britain accepted the regicide as beyond their sphere of competence. Constantius, learning of the deed, merely went ahead with his methodical and thorough preparations for another three years.

In the time left him, Allectus, possibly regretting the injudicious haste with which he had eliminated a competent admiral, his late superior, took what measures were possible. He held the fleet in con- stant patrol along the Channel coast and the North Sea approaches —quite possibly in his ignorance depleting shipboard supplies and wearing down his crews in the process—ordered the legions in from their fortresses to a concentration point near Londinium, and ruth- lessly stripped the Wall of its auxiliary garrisons to bolster his land forces. This last and inviting act quickly became known among the Highland tribes.

In 296 A.D. Constantius was ready. His first move was to send his admiral, Asclepiodotus, with a major portion of the fighting ships and part of the land army to sail down-Channel, neutralize the naval base at Clausentum (Bitterne), in the Solent, and so occupy the fleet of Allectus that the passage would be cleared for his own transports and their escort to reach Britain and disembark his army. As it turned out, this western flanking attack was all that was necessary.

Asclepiodotus proved himself a Greek worthy of the traditions of Themistocles, with perhaps a dash of Macedonian Alexander. Sailing on a stormy day from Gesoriacum, and thanks either to the weather or to his own skill, he was able to land his forces before Constantius, apparently delayed, could get started. Once landed, Asclepiodotus with admirable dispatch started north for Londinium and Allectus. The latter, hearing of the approaching imperial forces, moved hastily south to meet him.

Information on Allectus is sparse. What little exists indicates that he rose to high position on the civil side of Roman governmental affairs, at this period largely if not entirely divorced from military matters at levels below the two Caesars. How he became Carausius' deputy is uncertain. If his assumed civil background is fact, it goes far to explain his mistakes, for they were those a centurion of only a few years' service would be unlikely to make. All he forgot in his determination to meet and defeat Asclepiodotus before Constantius could land and join him was a little common sense about marching men too fast and for too long periods; about overly heavy packs; about how to keep stragglers up with the column; and how to move quickly and effectively from line of march to line of battle. These fundamentals were learned early in the education of every Roman who rose to high command. Had Allectus not escaped their impact, things might have turned out differently.

As it was, he drove his column mercilessly, oblivious both to increasing fatigue and to the natural reluctance of his men to meet other Roman troops in battle. By the time he made contact with Asclepiodotus' relatively rested forces on the Chichester-Silchester road, not far from the Roman walled town of Calleva Atrebatum, Allectus appears to have retained command over but a fraction of his force. In the ensuing rout, he himself was killed.

In the aftermath of battle, Calleva Atrebatum was sacked, either by the victorious troops of Asclepiodotus, or by the disorganized rabble that was the fleeing remnant of Allectus' army.

Constantius, a short while later, landed without opposition and was enthusiastically greeted by the townsfolk of Londinium, many of them no doubt hardly aware that anything more serious than a palace revolution had taken place. On the other hand, the reported enthusiasm could well have rested on the presence in Britain of an imperial Caesar with a powerful army able to meet dangers which had developed in the north and west.

3

EVEN BEFORE Allectus moved south from Londinium to defeat and death, the Highland clans had verified that the Wall garrison, amounting to perhaps about twenty-five thousand men in all, had been moved south. Brushing aside the foederati of the Lowlands, the Caledonii and Maeatae swarmed down on Hadrian's barrier, crossed it without hindrance, and swept south. At the same time, more perhaps from chance than by collusion, the Irish sea-raiders descended in force on the west coast. The great legionary fortresses at Chester and York were both taken with as much destruction as stone walls and buildings permitted. All through the north as far as York, and in the west through Cumberland, Westmoreland, Lancashire, Cheshire, and North Wales, farms, villages, and small forts were ravaged and destroyed with heavy loss of life and property. It was a major disaster to Roman Britain, yet once again the southeastern portion of the island, the long-settled, most civilized region, remained relatively unscathed.

Constantius reacted to the challenge with the same steadiness and methodical preparation he had exhibited in handling his cross-Channel expedition. He reorganized the defeated British legions and auxiliaries and incorporated them in his own army. He then moved north against the raiders who undoubtedly had already displayed the same tendency to scatter after plunder which had limited earlier forays.

With what patrolling and searches, with what minor actions and larger battles we know not, Constantius rounded up the raider bands and drove those who managed to survive back across the Wall, left their further fate to the waiting foederati of the Lowlands, and started patiently to repair the damage done.

The breaches in the Wall were repaired, and its supporting forts and supply depots rebuilt. At Corstopitum (Corbridge) there is evidence of roads recovered at a higher level than formerly, of buildings repaired, some from the foundations up, and of two military compounds made into one. Apparently there was an increase in its garrison, or artisan, personnel. The Wall fortress of Vindolanda (Chesterholm) was entirely rebuilt, on a new plan, facing north, and covering about three and one-half acres. The north and west gateways each had a single arched-over passageway flanked by towers. Indicating that the garrison now might be required to fight from its walls are platforms for artillery at the northwest angle and along the east rampart. Other Wall forts received varying degrees of reconstruction.

South of the Wall, the legionary fortresses of York and Chester were rebuilt in a majestic and solid Roman architectural dignity more stately by far than their Trajanic predecessors. To give depth to the Wall defenses, Constantius not only restored the old supporting forts but built new ones throughout Yorkshire, Durham, and the west, generally designed for cavalry units mobile enough to round up any raiders who had been able to penetrate the Wall.

As a result of these efforts a new peaceful period was ensured in the north, marked by a new economic prosperity of the region and a growth of the population both on farms and in the towns. Particularly noticeable was the growth of vici, some of considerable extent and obvious well-being and prosperity, close to the Wall forts themselves. The vicus impinging on the Wall fort of Borcovicum (Housesteads) grew to include many stone buildings housing merchants in solid comfort. The vicus adjacent to the fort at Vindolanda (Chesterholm) seems to have been populated by civilians with enough communal spirit to set up an altar inscribed by the *vicani Vindolandesses*. Nearly every other Wall fort, as well as those to the south, appears to have had some rather substantial civil settlement close to it. Thus, nearly two hundred years after its initiation, Hadrian's frontier policy was bearing fruit.

With an eye to the steadily increasing activity of the Scoti, raiding from Ireland, Constantius found himself obliged to strengthen and extend the system of watchtowers and signal stations on the west coast started by Carausius. On the east, for defense against the Saxons, Constantius built a new series of coastal forts, from Humber around South Foreland to the Isle of Wight. These new constructions were twice as large as the earlier stations of Carausius, with masonry walls ten to fourteen feet thick, reinforced with bastions, and fifteen to sixteen feet high. This system of coast defense with its fleet, Constantius or his son organized into a separate military command, the *Littoris Saxonici.* The Wall garrison and the legions were placed under the command of a military officer with no civil duties, the *Dux Britanniae,* with headquarters at York.

The civil arm was headed by a new official, the *Vicarius Britanniae,* with his capital in Londinium, while the two provinces of Severus' establishment were newly divided into four, each headed by a *praeses.* Thus Constantius applied in Britain the general reorganization of the Empire devised by Diocletian.

These dispositions appear to have taken about two years to initiate and see started, for in 298 A.D. Constantius was back in Gaul, snatching victory from near-defeat in a ferocious battle fought near Langres against a swarm of invading Alemanni.

In 305 A.D. Diocletian and Maximianus Hercules retired, the latter with considerable reluctance. Constantius and his fellow Caesar, Galerius, in the East, assumed the titles of Augustus. But Constantius had less than a year to enjoy his elevation to supreme ruler of the West. Back in Britain, he died at York on July 25, 306. Constantinus, his son by his first wife, Helena—rumored to be a Briton, and later canonized for identifying some old lumber found in Jerusalem as the True Cross—was with him. The British army, in ignorance or disdain of the wishes of Galerius in the East, acclaimed the son as Augustus to take the place of his father. When word of the elevation reached Gaul, the Rhine garrisons unhesitatingly accepted the thirty-four-year-old son of the commander they had been taught to respect.

Even so, Constantinus had seven more years of hard fighting on the continent before the western portion of the Empire was firmly in his grasp. In the process he found himself under the necessity of putting to death, among others, the former Emperor Maximianus, who, in the boredom of retirement, had regretted relinquishing the suzerainty of the West and joined his son, Maxentius, in challenging the claim of Constantinus.

Professor Birley has shown that the success of the dispositions of Constantius Chlorus in restoring the Wall, and the peace of the Lowlands beyond, so lightened the work of the garrisons as to make them vulnerable to withdrawal by Constantinus in his continental wars. It is Professor Birley's opinion that the withdrawals were not by complete units but by detachments taken as needed, leaving the unit in position at drastically weakened strength. An example he gives is that of the Tungrian archers shown to be in Constantinus' field army, who probably were a detachment drawn from Cohors I Tungrorum of the Borcovicum (Housesteads) garrison.

These detachments seem never to have been returned to their parent units, nor was there any substitute reinforcing of Britain. For with the West securely under his control, Constantinus found himself at odds with the successor to Galerius in the East, the co-Augustus Licinius. More years of fighting followed, punctuated here and there with murders and treachery, and marked by the shrewd exploitation of a rising religious sect, until in 324 Constantinus could gather in his blood-soaked hands the unchallenged mastery of the whole Empire. The ruthless and cynical process earned him the praise of posterity and the name of Constantine the Great.

4

DURING THE seventy-odd years following the landing of Constantius Chlorus in 296 A.D., Britain enjoyed relative immunity from the crippling effects of the various economic measures initiated by Diocletian and enlarged by Constantine in an attempt to halt, among other woes, a galloping inflation.

The immunity was only relative. Agriculture remained the chief pursuit of the island inhabitants. Exports were still chiefly hides, wool, and metals; imports few save for the luxury items demanded by the wealthier class. Restrictions on changing employment, having the effect of binding the agricultural laborer to the soil and the artisan's son to his father's trade, although surely onerous, could have been patently painful only to a small percentage of the population. As

Professor Haywood remarks, "There are those who know to their sorrow that there is one thing worse than being frozen to one's occupation and that is to be frozen out of it." * Nevertheless, these measures did have the baneful effect of limiting the ability of a man possessing ambition and initiative to rise above his father's station.

From inflation, salaried officialdom probably suffered more than the bulk of a population able in large measure to resort to barter and to payments in kind. The large farming estates, comprising the villa system, seem to have survived and even prospered in this period. The towns, on the other hand, appear to have gone into decline and to have suffered enough population losses to become in many cases almost deserted.

Back on the continent Constantine the Great, after raising Christianity to respectability without himself taking its tenets and discipline too seriously, died in 337 A.D. He was succeeded, after some fraternal and bloody bickering, by the second of his three sons, Constantius II, who lasted until 361 A.D. He died while leading reluctant troops against his cousin Julian, Caesar of the West, who succeeded as sole Emperor.

Julian was a Roman of the old school, a rather pedantic author but an able soldier and administrator, who was also a pious believer in the old gods and in the stern ethics of the Stoics diluted by a considerable admixture of the rarefied Neoplatonism taught by Plotinus. To him the new religion raised to respectability by Constantine seemed a peculiarly repulsive mixture of superstition in belief and arrogance in promulgation. The doctrinal squabbles of the Church fathers and their ill-concealed interest in secular power struck him as, if not wholly hypocritical, at least lacking in verifiable divine endorsement. Christian authors named him "The Apostate" and did their best to insure him the execration of posterity.

Two items of interest connect him with Britain. While Caesar of the West, he alleviated the rigors of a major famine in Gaul by ordering shipped from Britain an amount of wheat estimated at 120,000 *medimni,* or about 180,000 bushels. If such a considerable amount represented the surplus of one year's harvest in Britain it is surely evidence of a flourishing agriculture on the island. However, it is possible that a portion at least was derived from grain stored for the

* R. M. Haywood, *The Myth of Rome's Fall* (New York, Thomas Y. Crowell Co. Inc., 1958), p. 112.

consumption of the troops and therefore represented an emergency requisition to be later repaid from Gallic harvests.

Also, during his tenure as Caesar of the West, new trouble, the details of which are lost, arose in North Britain, beyond the Wall. Whatever its nature, Julian took it seriously enough to send one of his top generals, Lupicinus, to take charge. Apparently Lupicinus was able to handle the difficulty, which it is reasonable to connect with early symptoms of the commingled unrest and sense of opportunity which five years later was to explode with a violence unknown in the island since the long-past days of Boudicca.

Julian's reign lasted only a little over two years, much of it spent in countering the arrogance of the Eastern bishops, before being brought to an abrupt end in battle with the Persians in 363 A.D. He was succeeded by one of his generals, Jovianus, who lasted only a little over eight months before dying of an over-full stomach and a charcoal brazier discharging carbon monoxide in a closed room. Jovianus was followed by another officer of Julian's, Valentinianus I, an able soldier and administrator who, if we are to believe Gibbon, became increasingly choleric of temper with time and the annoyances of power.

5

ONE PERSISTENT cause of the continuing success of Roman armies over the centuries against tribes violating the frontiers rested on the inability of the barbarian chieftains to unite on a major scale, or, temporarily united, to maintain unity of command and co-ordinated purpose through an extended period. The inevitable, always repeated, result was their piecemeal defeat by the disciplined, tactically co-ordinated Roman troops.

There were, of course, exceptions. Roman armies had been cut to pieces by Hannibal; by the mounted archers of Parthia at Carrhae in 53 B.C.; in the Teutoburg Forest by the Germans in 9 A.D.; and had suffered defeat under Domitian on the Danube and humiliation under Valerian at the hands of the Persians. But in a sense, even these exceptions proved the rule, for in each instance the opponents were led by astute and harsh disciplinarians, capable of holding their troops together in the execution of a tactical plan. In some four hundred years these Roman defeats were not many. Now in Britain once again the tradition of invincibility, for what it was worth, was about to be broken.

History has hidden any identification of the organizing and persuasive genius who about 365 started to talk the Picts of Scotland, the Scoti of Ireland, and the Saxons of Schleswig into a co-ordinated attack to be delivered simultaneously against the British provinces from the north, east, and west, in what Ammianus Marcellinus described as the *"barbarica conspiratio."*

It must have taken time to win agreement to the unheard-of enterprise. One may wonder what secret meetings in hill caverns, what stealthy landings of envoys on both coasts of Scotland, what endless oratory in Highland crofts, what hushed gatherings in the glens, what treaties sealed in mead and that insidious distilled Irish innovation *usquebaugh,* or "water-of-life," what subordinated jealousies, what mollified distrusts took place before arrangements were complete and, sometime in 367 A.D., put into action.

The result was disaster, overwhelming and nearly complete. In the north the Highland clans stormed the Wall, slaughtering its defenders and sweeping south along Roman roads marked by burning towns and farmsteads. Apparently the barbarica conspiratio had involved in its preparations some of the foederati of the Lowlands, for Ammianus Marcellinus talks of treachery among allied troops he names *arcani.* The word means "secret" and may apply to non-uniformed irregulars with spying functions much like the *frumentarii* of earlier times. If so, their false reports might well have misled the Wall commander into a specious security.

In any event, the Duke of Britain met the invaders with what troops he could gather around the nexus of the Sixth Legion. His forces were defeated with heavy casualties, and he himself was killed.

On the Saxon shore successive waves of ships landed contingent after contingent of yellow-haired warriors who stormed the great coastal forts, dumping the bodies of their victims over the walls and into the fortress wells, leaving grisly evidence of their savagery to be excavated in our own times. The Count of the Saxon Shore, like his colleague the Duke, paid with his life for his inability to stem the tide.

In the west the exultant Scoti landed along the Lancashire and

Cheshire coasts, burning and killing with that ecstatic joy in combat for its own sake so presumably a characteristic of the race.

On all three sides the triumphant barbarians closed in upon the provinces. For the first time in its history the Fosse Way behind the Trent-Severn line was crossed in force by enemies and the fairest, most settled, most cultivated portion of Britain, untouched by war or pillage for three centuries, was mercilessly looted and burned. At Eburacum the stately praetorium of the Sixth Legion, scene of the deaths of two Roman Emperors, was again wrecked, its contiguous vicus (or colonia) and the surrounding farmsteads given to the flames. The no less stately fortress of the Twentieth Legion at Deva, which had suffered capture but not too much destruction in the great raids of Allectus' day, met the same gruesome fate.

Through the roads and bypaths of the provinces the raiders roamed at will; seeking out rich and comfortable villas to destroy; cattle to kill and eat; men, women, and children to slay and leave for the wild forest creatures to consume. Only at walled and staunchly defended Londinium, Verulamium, Camulodunum, and a few other fortified towns were the invaders balked of their booty and held at bay. In the north the Wall forts and their vici were leveled, including the vicus of Borcovicum (Housesteads), which had curiously been by-passed in the disorder before the coming of Constantius. All, including the oft-shattered Corstopitum and the forts and towns south of the Wall, were heavily, many mortally damaged.

When word of the disaster reached Valentinian in Gaul he promptly sent one of his generals, Jovinus, to investigate and report —report presumably on what the situation required from the limited resources of the Praefecture to rectify. The news Jovinus brought back from a reconnaissance that could not have been without personal danger was dismal enough. The barbarians were roaming southward as far as the fields and towns of Kent, undeterred by any obstacles other than their own surfeit. Perhaps Jovinus was able to report on the fact that Londinium and a few other fortified cities were still holding out.

Valentinian reacted with vigor. At what cost to his pressing frontier problems on the continent can only be imagined, he dispatched another general, the already famous Comes Theodosius, with an army described in contemporary accounts as composed of Heruli, Batavii, Jovii, and Victores, to the rescue of the ravaged island provinces.

Landing at Rutupiae in Kent he had to fight his way to Londinium where he was greeted inside the walls with hysterical joy by townspeople and refugees from the countryside. Relieving the city from pressure, Theodosius moved out to track down and destroy the enemy.

Long before his arrival it is probable that the originally well coordinated and directed attack had broken down into the normal barbarian anarchy of small independent bands heavily burdened with plunder. Theodosius rapidly cleared the southern areas, then moved north and west, hunting down the erstwhile triumphant tribesmen.

In a few months he drove the battered remnants of the clans beyond the Wall. With the provinces temporarily restored, he crossed the Wall in force, proceeding at least as far as the abandoned Antonine Wall, carrying stern Roman vengeance to all within reach. Claudian, writing a generation later, implied that Theodosius reached the northern limit of Scotland and chased the Picts across Pentland Firth to hazardous refuge in the Orkneys. But Claudian was a poet, not above exaggerating distances and marches unknown to him save by hearsay.

Theodosius forced the submission of the Attacotti, a branch clan of the Caledonii, who sometime earlier had moved out of their Highland fastnesses and settled in the fertile region of the Lothians. In this area between the two walls, Theodosius organized a new province, the fifth in Britain, to serve as a cushion against new attacks and as a base of operations for campaigns to the north. In honor of the Emperor, he named it Valentia.† But instead of moving in Roman officials, he seems to have left its administration and responsibility for maintaining the peace in the hands of the paramount chieftain of the Attacotti. The result was the building of a loyalty to Rome in the Attacotti, destined to have important results in later generations.

With order restored, Theodosius set about the weary process of reconstruction. The Wall and the damaged fortresses behind it were rebuilt, but in a manner far inferior to normal Roman standards. The differences emphasize the shortages of means and of manpower under which the whole Empire of the West was suffering.

The vici which had grown up close to the fortresses of North Britain and the Wall had formerly housed the dependents of the

---

† After Valentinian I. For its possible connection with the later name of Wales, cf. page 246.

garrisons, as well as merchants and others whose livelihood rested on the expenditures of the troops and persons from the surrounding countryside. Quarters within the forts were designed exclusively for military personnel. But after 370 A.D., as Theodosius managed to get the forts re-established with strong but rough masonry, space inside was made available for women and children, traders and others, survivors of the Pictish whirlwind. The result, demonstrated by archeology, was a confused medley of patched-up living quarters appearing in what once had been headquarters and administrative buildings, in warehouses, and even in former stables. As Dr. Richmond put it, "A centurion of the old order would have blanched at the sight." ‡

Accompanying this change for the worse, in itself indicative of shrinking military manpower, increasing financial stringency affecting the Empire as a whole made regular, or even intermittent, payment of the troops in specie more and more difficult. The government therefore issued grants of land in the neighborhood of the fortresses as partial payment, adding when possible subsistence payments of staples. The soldiers were encouraged to farm these land grants in the hope that they would at least in part feed themselves and their dependents from the produce. A natural result was that less and less time was given to military duties. The frustration of commanders faced with the breakdown in training and discipline can be imagined. By degrees both *limitanei* (fortress personnel) and *comitenses* (field troops) became part-time soldiers, worth about as much for immediate combat commitment as their prototypes in our own day. We must, it seems, look on them as primarily caretaking troops, able to put up some defense and, in the case of the comitenses, patrol and render a modicum of assistance to the foederati beyond the Wall. But that given discipline, training, and some combat experience they would again turn into first-rate troops they were shortly to demonstrate.

Theodosius, before departing from Britain, seems to have paid equal attention to the eastern and western sea flanks by extending the system of coastal defense forts and signal stations on both coasts. In Northumberland, Durham, and Yorkshire the new installations must have received their supply and reinforcements by sea; for they were often located in remote districts far from roads or other land

‡ Richmond, *op. cit.*

connections with the frontier establishment. On the west coast, Theodosius rebuilt and regarrisoned the old fortress at Segontium (Caernarvon) on the Menai Strait between North Wales and Mona. This bastion provided an advanced base for the Irish Sea fleet primarily based on the expanded naval installations at Cardiff. It is an indication of the inexorable priorities facing Theodosius that this fortress far out on the western flank was re-established, while the immense and twice-destroyed home of the Twentieth Legion at Deva was abandoned from this time onward. But it is possible that a deciding factor in this decision was the silting up of the Dee River mouth, seriously impairing the value of the Deva fort as a base for sea patrols and making rehabilitation of the ruin a useless expense.

Perhaps to Theodosius' defense arrangements we can ascribe the transfer of Legio II Augusta from South Wales to Rutupiae in Kent, which is recorded in the *Notitia Dignitatum* as its location. However, we cannot be sure of the date of the transfer, which may have been made by the Roman general Stilicho at a later date.

In the midst of these energetic measures to defend the island, evidence of the unshaken determination of the Emperor to hold the British provinces, the surviving population of Roman Britons wrestled with its own problems of reconstruction. It was no easy task. Many of the smaller towns had been destroyed, never to be rebuilt. The wide-flung villa system had suffered heavily. Estate-owners with their workers and small farmers returning to their land found their homes and barns burned, their cattle killed or driven off, their tools stolen or destroyed, seed for planting difficult to obtain, their fields in weeds. In addition, although some halfhearted measures of relief appear to have been taken, the population as a whole was helplessly restricted by the economic policies of the time which had stiffened from Diocletian's original decrees into a vicious circle of bureaucratic regulation. Coupled with these initiative-destroying conditions, the expenses of a topheavy civil government and a costly military establishment could be met only by confiscatory taxation. The joint squeeze appears to have damaged seriously the normal potential for recovery inherent in the Roman British people.

Yet for all their hardships and anxieties, the island provinces were no worse off than the Western Empire as a whole, which for two hundred years had been the victim not only of repeated barbarian forays across the frontiers but also of brutally destructive civil wars and rebellions fomented by rival candidates for the imperial purple. In this last suicidal lunacy Britannia, as in the long-gone days of Albinus, was again to be enmeshed.

6

AMONG THE senior officers who had accompanied the Comes Theodosius to Britain was a fellow Spaniard, a certain Magnus Clemens Maximus. He was left in high military command in Britain on Theodosius' departure. Maximus, who afterward became the subject of much Welsh legend under the name of Maxim Wledig, and who appears in Rudyard Kipling's *Puck of Pook's Hill,* is connected with the rehabilitation of Segontium (Caernarvon)—which he may have supervised under Theodosius—and with its later abandonment. While in the neighborhood, in normal response to romance or to the need of companionship, he is supposed to have found a Celtic wife, daughter of a Welsh tribal chieftain.

There is no evidence that Magnus Maximus was any other than a loyal and trustworthy servant of the Empire until events caught up with him. The events followed the death of Valentinian I in 375 A.D. He was survived by his brother Valens, Augustus in the East and his son Gratianus, sixteen years of age, who succeeded Valentinian I in the West. A year later, for reasons lost to history, Gratianus caused the highly respected Comes Theodosius, the savior of Britain, to be beheaded, thus earning the distrust of the troops in Gaul and Britain. Then, in the disorders after the death of his uncle Valens, and while trying to suppress an uprising of Gothic settlers in 378, he elevated to be co-Augustus of the East the son of the murdered Theodosius, bearing the same name.

In 383 A.D. the troops in Britain denounced Gratianus and proclaimed their own commander, Magnus Maximus, Emperor, in spite of his protests (recorded by two historians and ridiculed by another).§ When news of the action reached the garrisons of Gaul and the Rhine frontier, they enthusiastically endorsed the selection, seized Gratianus, and slew him.

Maximus in Britain, either helplessly or hypocritically, bowed be-

§ Orosius and Sulpicius Severus versus Zosimus.

fore the demands of the troops, marshaled them for transshipment
to the continent, and there, joined by the forces of Gaul, put his fortune and his head at risk by challenging not only the twelve-year-old
Valentinian II in Rome, but also Theodosius I in the East, whose
father had done so much to advance Maximus' own career.

We need not follow the fortunes of Magnus Maximus on his continental foray to his defeat and death at the hands of Theodosius I
at Aquileia in 388, save perhaps to notice that his British troops,
trained and disciplined by the vicissitudes of war, gave a good account
of themselves. What was important for the future of Britain was
that his expedition was large, including not only some 30,000 troops
(of which 12,000 were from the Wall frontier garrisons of limitanei,
comitenses, and exploratores), but also, according to tradition, many
thousands of civilians, men, women, and children.

It is not clear to what extent this luckless expedition denuded
Britain of troops. It has been noted that the Wall garrison as a whole,
after the restoration of Constantius Chlorus, has been estimated at
25,000 men. But this full-strength complement was, during the years
of Constantine the Great's continental wars, regularly whittled away,
so that if Magnus Maximus took a further 12,000, the force remaining must have been weak indeed. On the other hand he seems not to
have drawn heavily on the naval strength or on the coastal defenses
under the Count of the Saxon Shore.

Whatever the ensuing weakness of the northern frontier, the
Picts, perhaps remembering the painful lesson taught them by the
Comes Theodosius, or more likely, restrained by the treaty-bound
Attacotti, gave no signs of aggression. The naval patrols on both
coasts, supplementing the land defenses, appear to have been adequate restraining influences on the Saxons and the Scoti from Ireland,
giving the hard-pressed population some years of peace.

In 395 A.D. Theodosius I, sole Emperor, died, rather uniquely for
one of his hazardous eminence, a natural death. His will split the
Empire again, bequeathing the East and West respectively to his two
sons, Arcadius and Honorius. At the time, Arcadius was about
eighteen and Honorius eleven years of age.

As guardian of the young Honorius, Theodosius I named in his
will Stilicho, his *Magister Militum,* or senior military commander.
The son of a Vandal who had entered the service of Rome and risen
to the rank of officer of auxiliaries, Stilicho proved himself a loyal,

trustworthy servant of his fledgling charge, and one of the truly great generals of antiquity.

Once the succession was settled and imperial affairs reasonably in order, Stilicho undertook a whirlwind campaign designed to relieve the Western frontiers once and for all of barbarian pressure. He moved swiftly, first into Gaul, and thence into Germany, driving back the Franks and other Germanic tribes in defeat and disorder. Adding diplomacy to his talents, Stilicho negotiated treaties with the defeated tribes, and arranged for their settlement in peace on vacant lands within the Empire's borders.

With the frontiers of Gaul and the Rhine temporarily quiet, it seems probable that Stilicho paid a quick visit to Britain. Either he, or a deputy carrying out his orders, again reorganized the island defenses and strengthened them in some degree. Offensive action seems to have been limited to naval expeditions directed against increasingly powerful sea forays originating in Ireland. The slim classical references to this campaign receive some endorsement in Irish legends centering about that boisterous hero, Niall of the Nine Hostages, *Ard-Righ* ("High King") of Eire, from 387 to 404 A.D., when he is vaguely reported to have met his death by drowning off the Isle of Wight. There is evidence that he was the most venturesome of the Irish chieftains who, taking to the sea in these and succeeding years, harried the west coast of Britain and planted colonies of their tribesmen in Galloway, north of the Wall, in Cumberland, Lancashire and thickly in North Wales.

Certainly there was some dealing with the Irish, for about this time cohorts of Scoti begin to appear in the Rhineland garrisons. It is unlikely these levies were forcibly recruited into the imperial service by landings in Ireland itself, but probable that they were drafts on the extensive colonies already established in Britain.

It may be from this time, and a consequence of Stilicho's conciliatory policy, that remains of the first Saxon settlements and cemeteries in Yorkshire can be dated—evidence of some attempt at amicable adjustment with newcomers who, however unwelcome, were more easily accommodated than exterminated. These early settlements followed one hundred years of sporadic raiding and pillage on the east coast, while presaging the interminable march of invasion and immigration which was to dominate the next four hundred years of British history.

Again there was peace in Britain and in the West. The energy and military talents of Stilicho had revitalized the tortured provinces while his statesmanship had converted ravaging invaders into peaceful settlers. Everywhere external enemies of Rome Eternal had been defeated or rendered harmless. The Army, showing astonishing vitality and discipline under a general of supreme ability, was once again, as in the days of old, proving its invincibility in the field.

So in fleeting hope passed the last years of the turbulent fourth century A.D. and the year 400 began, the 1,153rd since the founding of the City. Surely for the majority of its citizens what had endured so long, what had in every century of its existence surmounted mighty challenges, what generations had built into a Commonwealth of Man, would endure forever. Who living in that year could be brought to believe that for Rome, the giver of law, order, and peace to the western world, the transmitter of the supreme culture of Greece, the inheritor and guardian of civilization, an end could be set?

Yet in fact the sun that had so long burnished the far-flung eagles was already below the horizon and the long twilight fading rapidly toward the dark of interminable night.

7

AGAIN, as too often before, the accelerating collapse arose in internecine warfare.

In 403 A.D. Alaric the Goth, acting ostensibly as general for the young Emperor of the East, Arcadius, led his ferocious but disciplined tribesmen into Italy as far as Mediolanum (Milan). The ineffectual adolescent, Honorius, Emperor of the West, fled to the security of marsh-surrounded Ravenna, leaving the whole unpleasant problem to his Magister Militum, far north in Gaul.

Stilicho reacted with his customary energy and decision. Recognizing that however stark was the continuing pressure on the Rhine frontier, it still could not command equal priority with a direct threat to Italy, he did not hesitate to gather at once an army to move into Italy, levying heavily on the Rhine defenses and even ordering in from Britain one of the legions, hoary with tradition, stationed on the island since the days of Aulus Plautius, XX Valeria Victrix.

It must have been plain to Stilicho that these desperate measures to meet a threat to the homeland left Britain weakened and the Rhine frontier wide open; that beyond the latter new swarms of restless Franks, Visigoths, Burgundians, Vandals, and others were being piled up by irresistible population pressures in far-off Asia, spear-headed by a new entry on the European scene—an assemblage of bellicose nomads tracing their origin to distant Mongolia and called, for lack of a better translation of their name, *Hsiung-nu,* simply Huns.

But this risk had to be taken. With the army so hastily gathered, Stilicho crossed the Alps and in a series of brilliantly directed battles inflicted severe defeats on the forces of Alaric at Polentia near Turin, and again at Verona. Alaric, perhaps aware that time was on his side, discreetly withdrew his Goths into Illyria.

Before Stilicho could move to restore the Rhine and British garrisons a new trouble arose at home. In 406 A.D. a Scythian from north of the Black Sea, known to history as Radagaisus, obtained mastery over a mixed clutter of nomad tribes, crossed the Danube, moved down through Pannonia and with minor opposition poured his hordes into the Po Valley. Moving inexorably south and west he laid siege with his host, variously estimated at between 200,000 and 400,000 —which must have included a majority of useless camp followers, dependents, and hangers-on—to Florentia on the Arno—today, art-hallowed Florence.

Stilicho, to contest their passage, had but a small army of veterans, perhaps 30,000. Yet with consummate genius, fortified by guile, he maneuvered Radagaisus and his horde into the hills of Faesulae (Fiesole), where starvation brought the invaders quickly to terms. Stilicho accepted their surrender on the promise that he would spare their lives if they departed peaceably from Italy. He would have been insane to keep that promise, and his giving it can be justified, if justification in such an extremity is required, not alone by the military ethics of the day, but by the already demonstrated fact that Radagaisus was matched in military ineptitude only by his perfidy. Once the barbarians were in his hands, Stilicho had Radagaisus swiftly dispatched and his followers sold into slavery.

But the time required to deal with this threat to Italy cost Stilicho, and Rome, the Rhine frontier. There, in 406 and 407 A.D. the long border, maintained over so many centuries at so much cost in blood and treasure, simply and terribly collapsed. The Germanic tribes swept in mass across the Rhine at a dozen or more points, passed the empty fortresses which for so long had interdicted the greed of their forefathers, and spread in irresistible tide through Gaul.

Curiously, the extent of physical damage done, at least after the early exuberance, seems less than might have been expected. Many of the frontier cities, like Metz, are reported as totally destroyed, but the authorities whose accounts survive, of whom Orosius is typical, dilate on the atrocities visited on bishops, clergy, and virgins while remaining vague on more secular demolition. Colonia Augusta Treverorum, the stately headquarters city of the Praefectus Galliarum, was taken and looted, but the great headquarters building remained to fascinate a millennium and a half of tourists as the "Porta Nigra." Lutetia Parisiorum, the island in the Seine that had been the favorite residence of Julian, and was to become the soul, if not the conscience, of the French people, was similarly overrun and pillaged. The hordes swept on, undeterred by any organized resistance, their numbers and depth constantly increased by new migrations swarming in the rear of the already bewildered vanguard.

This whole affair has been described as an irresistible flood of barbarism breaking over civilization. This is true only to a certain extent. Long centuries of contact with Roman life across the controlled frontiers had in part justified Hadrian's hope—that the barbarians, by observing and benefiting from intercourse with the settled life within the frontier, would acquire some vestiges of civilization themselves. The intruders therefore were far from uncivilized and were driven at least as much by pressures behind as by promise before.

The picture evoked after hindsight and investigation have had their say may be likened, with obvious differences in both magnitude and conditions to the westward migrations in the United States—long lines of wagons, carrying families and driving livestock, seeking with determination unhindered by any ideas of property ownership a new life in better surroundings. If the original occupants of the land got in their way, so much the worse for them.

The one man who could perhaps have stemmed the tide, or at least controlled its flow, was not there. In the same year that saw the flood of Germanic settlers move south across Gaul, Stilicho fell before the court intrigues of one Olympias, possessing the credulous ear of the Emperor Honorius at Ravenna. Stilicho's death gave Alaric the Goth his opportunity.

In successive campaigns Alaric moved freely through Italy, avoiding only Ravenna, secure behind its guardian marshes, as far south as Rome itself. In 408 he besieged the Eternal City and allowed it to ransom itself with an outpouring of coffers filled with the accumulated wealth of ages.

His appetite whetted, he returned in 409. In 410 the City was taken and plundered—the first time a foreign enemy had been within its gates since Brennus and his Gauls, eight hundred years before. Reports of these cataclysmic events succeeded only in annoying Honorius, safe in Ravenna and wholly absorbed in the care and feeding of his prize poultry.

But the ignominious fate of Roma Eterna is beyond the scope of this tale of Britain. What matters is that the loss of imperial control of Gaul to the Germanic tribes effectively cut off, for at least a decade and perhaps longer, the governments of the British provinces from the seat of Empire.

8

WHEN THE fact of its dangerous isolation became understood in Britain, when the couriers with the official correspondence—the imperial rescripts, the querulous demands for overdue taxes, the civil and military promotion lists, the *mandata* on appealed legal matters, the authorizations and accompanying specie for pay of the Army and the bureaucracy—failed to arrive, there must have followed anxious consultations between the Vicarius and his senior military officers. It is not surprising that under the fateful circumstances dissension should break out and ambition discover opportunity.

In the autumn of 406 A.D., a certain Marcus, a soldier, was acclaimed Augustus by the garrisons still on the island. He was accepted by the civil authorities, surely under duress, only to be quickly murdered by dissidents. A citizen, perhaps a *curialis* of Londinium, Gratianus by name, essayed to replace him as Augustus. He succeeded, and earned the same fate within a few months. An elderly soldier, Constantius—later nicknamed "The Tyrant"—seized local power and went through the ceremonies of accepting the imperial designation "Augustus et Imperator." Either from hope or resignation, he was confirmed in the five provinces.

One might reasonably suppose that this Constantius, securely in control of an island realm that was to content many later kings, would have been satisfied to put his house in order, to attend to the island defenses, and from the gratitude of the population win an acceptance which, if the German cordon across Gaul were ever removed, would earn him the approbation of Honorius.

Instead, he and his son, Constans, formed another expeditionary force—evidence enough that the adventure of Magnus Maximus some twenty years earlier had not wholly stripped Britain of its military resources—and embarked for the continent, leaving behind an island to all practical purposes defenseless.

Even after making full allowance for ambition, the motivation for this decision remains mysterious. So far as Constantius could know, Gaul was still held by armed bands of Germans far beyond his ability to handle. In addition, if the imperial forces from Italy were able eventually to restore the situation in Gaul, his presence there could lead only to embarrassing and possibly lethal resentment. From the hindsight of fifteen centuries it seems a wholly lunatic venture.

Yet there may well have been factors mitigating the apparent recklessness. It seems likely that the overwhelmed Roman authorities in Gaul would have appealed for aid, not only to the central government but to their island neighbor. In addition, it appears that the power of the German thrust had lost its force, and that the invaders were so scattered in search of plunder and land on which to settle that they could offer no concentrated resistance to Constantius' British forces.

In any case, he is reported to have been hailed by the residual Romanized population as a deliverer, as he may in fact have been. Speedily he won enough control of the Gallic provinces to set up headquarters at Arles, and to be accepted as Augustus. His son, now glorying in the title of Caesar, with the help of rounded-up detachments of the Gallic army ironically named *Honorarii,* as quickly won over the allegiance of the Spanish provinces.

For a time things went well. Constantius, now master of Britain, Gaul, and Spain, was lucky enough several times to escape assassination by emmissaries of Honorius, which should have given him some appreciation of his standing at the Imperial Court. But the defeat, capture, and death of his son Constans, and the rebellion of his own general, Gerontius, reversed his fortunes. In 407 A.D. Constantius and his youthful second son, Julianus, were captured at Arles and put to death by orders from Honorius, who apparently could spare time from his poultry to exercise the less onerous of his imperial duties.

If the expedition from Britain had been aimed at seizing for Constantius the Tyrant the imperial throne, it was unsuccessful; if to rescue Gaul and restore the Western provinces to the Empire, it was unappreciated. The price was left, in the main, for Britain to pay.

The continuous, if individually minor, drafts on the British garrison by Constantine the Great and the losses suffered in the great barbarian assault of 367 A.D. could hardly have been made good by Theodosius, and the diminished residue was surely heavily levied upon by Magnus Maximus in his bid for empire. The inadequate remnant, again drafted for the continent by Constantius, may well have stripped Britain of its last able-bodied defenders.

Archeology confirms that the seventy-odd-mile stretch of Hadrian's Wall, with its supporting complex of hinterland forts, was now abandoned, the sentry walks empty, the forts and milecastles deserted, their gates either open or ready to swing wide at the first push, the contiguous villages that had once known the cheerful avarice of merchant and prostitute silent in the loneliness of emptied houses and shuttered shops.

Farther south the once magnificent and stately fortress at York, still bearing the scars of the destruction of 367 and the rough-and-ready restoration of Theodosius, presented its wind-whipped façades to solitude, within and without, a sort of evacuated Pentagon; its corridors and offices responding only to the scurrying of rats; its barracks, mess halls, hospital, and elaborate baths cold, desolate, forever forsaken.

The ominous course of events was not lost on the townsfolk and farmers, the inhabitants whose forefathers for sixteen generations had held themselves Romans. Archeologists tell us that many of the small towns not already depopulated were at this time evacuated, their people fleeing to the supposedly impregnable, larger walled cities. Yet this exodus could not have been total, and the picture develops of many once bustling towns now the abode of small groups with nowhere to flee, refugees in near-empty villages from which all communal life and organization had departed.

That there was a flight from the larger farming estates called villas seems probable. Yet it must have been far from universal, if simply because the island requirement for food, only to be met by retaining and nurturing the land, could not have permitted a total breakdown in agricultural activity. Within the generally foreboding situation some of the wealthier villa-owners perhaps moved their families and portable riches to the safety of walled towns, leaving their slaves and laborers, under a bailiff, to work the land.

Others buried their valuables, hoping to return. At Mildenhall in Suffolk the now anonymous owner of a magnificent silver dinner service,¶ either at this time or in the earlier crisis of 367, carefully buried it against recovery when the times should have turned for the better. It was dug up by accident in this century, mute evidence of the refinement, wealth, and comfort surrounding the daily life of a farming estate owner of Roman Britain.

Yet premonition of disaster does not invariably carry the means of coping with it. There was nothing, really, for most of the populace to do, save stay where they were, preoccupied with the problems of day-to-day existence. And the civil government had no other course than to continue to exercise what authority and perform what functions its curtailed means permitted.

In 410 A.D. some serious but unrecorded trouble caused the officials in charge to apply formally to Emperor Honorius for succor. That worthy in reply, perhaps remembering in pique the costly efforts required to overcome the challenge of Constantius the Tyrant, testily bade the islanders look to their own defense.

9

IT WOULD be interesting to know by what means, over what route through strife-torn Gaul, surmounting what vicissitudes and dangers, the imperial courier, bearing what amounted to relinquishment of

¶ Now on display at the British Museum.

central authority over the island provinces, passed to Britain.‖ We can believe that the purport of his message, when laid before the remaining provincial authorities, precipitated what today we would call a governmental crisis.

These anonymous functionaries and administrators, quite probably able, even courageous men trained in the long traditions of the Roman civil service, were ill-prepared for independence. Every time in the long past when the Province had been endangered, either by barbarian attacks or by the folly and ambition of its governors, the Imperial Government had gallantly, and often at great cost, come to its rescue.

Nero had sent reinforcements to replace the losses suffered in Boudicca's revolt; Vespasian had dispatched Legio II Adiutrix to support Cerealis; Agricola, subduing the north had received large reinforcements of auxiliaries; Hadrian had sent in Legio VI Victrix even at the cost of weakening the continental frontiers; Antoninus Pius had sent reinforcements from the Rhine frontier to Julius Verus to put down the Brigantian uprising of 155 A.D.; after Albinus embraced calamity, Severus, with new troops, had renewed the island defenses; Constantius Chlorus had made good the losses suffered in the usurpation of Carausius and Allectus; Theodosius and Stilicho had found time amidst pressing continental dangers to furnish protection and help from limited resources urgently needed elsewhere. No Roman Briton could reasonably complain that the Imperial Government, at any time of insular peril, had not acted with energy and generosity in the full discharge of its responsibilities. But now it was different.

Now Britain was on its own, ringed around by savage predators, ready and eager to strike its weakened corpus. To the civil officials of the British provinces, and to the few military commanders still present, all men accustomed by training and strict regulation to make no major policy decisions without guidance and prior approval from distant and omnipotent superiors; to the population itself; the truth, the dawning sense of isolation, must have been a shattering experience.

‖ Scholars formerly held that this year, 411 A.D., saw, with the dispatch of Honorius' letter, a complete and final break between Britain and the central government. This view is now disputed, and some indications, hardly deserving the name of evidence, tend to show that the contact and some form of control were renewed, for a time at least, around the third decade of the fifth century.

Yet for a while all was well. Desperation in a body politic often enough creates its own remedies. As in many later times, a mood of hardy indomitability seems to have seized the Roman Britons, causing them to react with unbreakable courage to their exposed and dangerous position.

Contrary to the reports of earlier historians, the breaking of the imperial umbilicus, if break it did, involved no wholesale exodus of "Romans" or even of whilom imperial officials. There was, of course, no place to go, no place to hide. Gaul was unsafe, Spain loaded with hazard, Ireland hostile, Germany and the Low Countries unthinkable, and Italy—Italy? Had not Rome itself, the Eternal City, already been taken and plundered?

Doubtless there was little thought given to the idea of flight. Instead, a powerful sentiment that was not yet British patriotism, or even nascent nationalism, played its part in keeping things going. The overwhelming majority of the population, including soldiers and officials, were Britons as well as Romans. This island was their home, the home many had never left even for short excursions. It was the abode of honored ancestors over long centuries of the Pax Romana with its ingrained respect for law, for order, for the majesty of the universal commonwealth of peoples that was the whole meaning of the word Rome. The lush green of British pastures, the brooding mystery of mountain and moor, even the predictable harshness of winter weather, were a sacred heritage, fiercely to be defended, arduously to be maintained.

The days were grim, the future, so far as it could be dimly discerned, appalling. The challenges remained, but now carrying seeds of moral regeneration to grow in time into a sturdy and enduring characteristic of the island folk.

For a while at least, the predatory ambitions of the Picts were restrained by the loyalty of the foederati kings beyond the empty Wall. But along the west coast, the sons of Niall of the Nine Hostages, under the new High King, Niall's nephew, Dashi, cheerfully pressed their forays and sent new immigrants to swell the colony settled in North Wales. There is much evidence that the Roman British authorities solved this problem by persuading King Cunneda of the Attacotti to move with his fighting men and families southwest across the Wall and into Wales, there to restrain and possibly induce to peaceful ways the truculent Irish colonists. Cunneda, it seems, accepted the invitation, moved his clan to Wales, performed with at least partial effectiveness his mission, and in the process perhaps brought with him the Roman name of his Lothian home—Valentia.

Superficially at least, there seems to have been for some time little change in Britain. In fact, to the bureaucrats in Rome, busily fussing about their assigned tasks, there was no change at all in the status of the British provinces. Under date of 428 A.D., some industrious compilers got out an official directory, called the *Notitia Dignitatum*. In it are listed the various high officials of Britain, along with a station list of troops.

However, the *Notitia* lists the garrisons of the Wall fortresses, implying them as still on duty, whereas archeological evidence makes clear that the Wall had been stripped of manpower much earlier. There are other discrepancies. In general, the *Notitia* reflects conditions and stations and offices as they were in Britain at about 375, before the continental adventures of Magnus Maximus and Constantius the Tyrant. Perhaps a reasonable explanation of the differences rests in the fact that information from Britain ceased to be sent to Rome with the insurrection of Magnus Maximus, that communication was never renewed, and that the compilers of the *Notitia* were forced to use the last detailed information available to them.

A more revealing glimpse of conditions in Britain after its relinquishment by Honorius rests in the report of a visit to the island in 429 A.D. by Germanus Autissiodorensis, Bishop of Auxerre in Gaul, and the mentor of the fugitive slave from Ireland who was to become Saint Patrick. His episcopal presence in Britain was connected with the virulence there of a theological aberration known to history as the heresy of Pelagius.

Little is known of the early life and antecedents of this disputatious evangelist. His contemporaries sometimes gave him the surname Brito. The name Pelagius, by which he has come down in history, might, in corrupt Greek, carry the meaning of "the man from across the wide sea." The two combine to suggest that he was born in Britain. If so, he was far from the last of the island breed to bring a vigorous mind and an individual point of view to theological subtleties.

Most of his writing and disputation took place between 410 and 417 A.D.; first in Rome; later in Africa, where he and Saint Augustine seem to have exchanged ideas amicably until the latter recoiled in pious horror before Pelagius' radical notions; and later still, in Palestine.

In that troubled century, when the Church fathers, with considerable acrimony and some interdiocesan bloodshed, were attempting to beat out an acceptable dogma, Pelagius was a lucid thorn in exegetic flesh. He argued against the doctrine of original sin, thought baptism useless, and held that if Man depended less on divine assistance, and more on his own efforts, life on this earth might improve.

Such brazen assertions of man's congenital innocence, such faith in the ability of the species to improve itself in the oft-demonstrated absence of divine concern met short shrift in that theocratic age.

Yet for a while—mute evidence that the Empire still contained a sizable number of independent minds—his ideas spread with surprising rapidity, creating first alarm, then consternation, and finally anger among the Church fathers.

An imperial edict issued in Constantinople in 418 A.D. anathematized these anticipations of Protestantism as dangerous heresy, inviting exile and confiscation of property on all who professed them. Since exile from the Empire involved the surrender of a parlous security for none at all, and as property was hard enough to hold onto under the best of conditions, it is not surprising that enthusiasm for Pelagius' doctrines waned.

But somehow they had found wide acceptance among the Christians of Britain. Perhaps the imperial edict never reached them, leaving them unaware of their intellectual arrogance. Or a case can be made for asserting these bold doctrines suited to the dangers of Britain, giving men encouragement to overcome by their own efforts disasters which higher powers, in spite of prayers and alms, had clearly failed to prevent. It was this painful situation the good Bishop of Auxerre was sent to correct.

The very fact of his presence in Britain is evidence that there was at least some communication and travel between the island and the continent, and some amelioration of conditions in Gaul enabling him to leave his diocese on such an errand.

In Verulamium, Germanus engaged in earnest theological discussion with the Christian congregation. Accompanying him, ready to advance any arguments Germanus in the heat of disputation might overlook, was his nephew, a lesser churchman, Lupus (the Wolf) Trecassinus, later known to the medieval faithful as Saint Loup of

Troyes. The congregation of Verulamium, influenced perhaps less by the arguments of Germanus than by the personal courage and leadership he showed in beating off a Saxon raid, appear to have been convinced of their errors and brought back into orthodoxy by him.

Reporting on the success of his mission, the Bishop added that he had found Britain peaceful, even wealthy. Food was abundant; flocks and herds prospering, money in adequate supply—a possible result of the populace having no longer to pay the imperial imposts —the civil government obeyed; the soldiers loyal; and most important, the Church, short of its passing involvement in the Pelagian heresy, small in numbers, but devout.

Twenty years later, about 450 A.D., the then aged Bishop paid another visit to the island, perhaps to observe for himself the results of his holy work. We have no report on this journey, possibly because whatever hopes he had entertained were rudely disabused.

10

In the years between, conditions in Britain had sadly deteriorated. The sea raids of the Saxons in particular, supplemented by those of their kinsmen, the Angles, and some ferocious barbarians called Jutes, steadily increased in tempo and savagery. More and more of the raiders came with families waiting aboard ship for a successful landing to pave the way for permanent settlement. One after another, often enough several at a time, the great coastal forts of Constantius Chlorus' construction were stormed, their remaining defenders slaughtered. The immigrants, following the bidding of their fierce sky-gods, cared less than nothing for the anger of the thickly populated Roman pantheon, or for the moral protests of the weak Christian church in Britain.

Slowly the raids and settlements increased in frequency to become an almost continuous immigration. Yet it was fiercely resisted by the Roman Britons, defending their homeland and their civilized heritage. The newcomers had to fight for every inch of ground they tried to hold, and were often enough defeated in battle to make the overseas venture a chancy business. But numbers and persistence told. The Roman Britons were gradually pushed back from the east coast along the stretch from Yorkshire around South Foreland to the Isle of Wight. But it was a slow, fighting retreat, not the genocide that Victorian writers have implied, leaving a vacuum into which the triumphant Saxons moved in racial purity.

What archeology proves beyond reasonable doubt is that the town life of Britain did for a while disappear wherever the Saxons gained mastery. Many small communities that had risen under Rome to a wholesome civic life and quiet prosperity were built on sites that are desolate today, as they have been since Saxon times. Rutupiae, the chief supply base and naval station of Roman Britain; Verulamium, the only city to attain the dignity of a municipium; Corstopitum, the supply and ordnance support center of the Wall; Calleva Atrebatum, once a major southwest road junction; Viroconium on the Severn; Magnis on the Welsh border; Venta Icenorum in Norfolk—these and a hundred other small towns and villages, which for three centuries had known a pulsing life, are today but mounds and mossy walls, often enough hidden deep beneath agricultural lands, attracting only antiquaries, archeologists, and the occasional bemused tourist.

Yet even within the growing Saxon Pale the destruction of towns and cities was not, indeed could not be, complete. Some cities and many towns survived. Londinium, Camulodunum, Aquae Sulis, Glevum, Deva, Durnovaria, Dubrae, Noviomagus, Isca Dumnoniorum, Ratae Coritanorum, Eburacum, Lindum, Venta Belgarum Luguvalium, Pons Aelius, Cataractonium, and many others are but examples of the continuity of history and of life; Roman towns and cities preserving through centuries of danger and chaos an identity continuing into our own times.

Doubtless among these and similar sites there were long periods, perhaps centuries, when the thread of community life was broken, later to be spun anew by others attracted perhaps by the supply of building materials ready at hand in the ruins of once solid Roman construction.

The Saxons and their kin were scarcely less obliteration-minded with the villas of the large farming estates spread through the southeastern countryside than they were about towns. Archeology has disclosed hundreds of ruins of once prosperous, even luxurious, country houses, laid waste in Saxon times and never thereafter restored.

It is idle to suggest that so destructive and protracted a process was not accompanied by heavy loss of life. But it seems inappropriate to imply the total extermination of those Roman Britons unable to flee before the advancing Saxons. In the midst of war and fury there is at least as much room for the play of human instincts as within the canons of a law-abiding society.

Women, expecting the worst, found it bearable, often enough pleasant; men, preserved from slaughter for serfdom, found mitigation of slavery in the attractions of the yellow-tressed Saxon girls, with freedom sometimes following an enforced union. Time assuaged all, and new mixed generations listened with equal boredom to tales of a father's triumph or a mother's reluctant submission. So, as the immigrations slowly advanced, were born in continuous inter-racial mixture the ancestors of the conglomerate island people, destined in future ages to assume on a wider stage the long-vacated responsibilities of the Pax Romana.

Slowly, as the Saxons, the Angles, and the Jutes advanced, the shrinking remnants of the Romanized government held authority only within the environs of Londinium and perhaps Eburacum, together with some of the western cantonal capitals. We do not know when even the forms and procedures of Roman administration disappeared, with the responsibility of maintaining resistance against the invaders devolving more and more on the foederati, the Celtic chieftians, partially Romanized, to whom the oncoming foe were no less a menace than Rome itself had been for their ancestors. Among these foederati, perhaps the most powerful was a vague figure, half tradition, half myth, Guertigerinus, transposed in later history into Vortigern.

Perhaps noting that when booty or territory was at stake the Saxon, Anglian, and Jutish pirates fought each other as cheerfully as they attacked Britons, Vortigern, by uncertain legend, appears to have negotiated with a Jutish chieftain named Hengist to bring his own following to Britain, and there, in return for land, employ his warriors in the defense of the island.

Hengist came, landed at Ebbsfleet on the Isle of Thanet, not far from the pillaged fort and supply base of Rutupiae and set up housekeeping, perhaps in the year 449 A.D. Although the year is in doubt, the legend persists, and the coming of Hengist is the date long accepted, in ignorance or disdain of what had gone before, as the beginning of English history.#

Perhaps because Hengist felt that Vortigern's death released him from the obligation of their agreement, it was not long before he became an expansionist and pillager on his own account. Yet the resistance offered by the Roman Britons was fierce and unrelenting. A full twenty-five years passed before Hengist and his "eorls" secured for themselves the ancient land of the Cantii, whose name they preserved in making it over into the Jutish Kingdom of Kent.

In the meantime the Scoti on the west and the Picts on the north were far from idle if we are to accept at face value an extract from Gildas, writing in mid–sixth century:

> No sooner have the Britons gone back to their land than the foul hosts of Picts and Scots land promptly from their coracles . . . they seize upon all the northern and outlying part of the country as far as to the Wall. Upon this Wall stands a timorous and unwarlike garrison. The wretched citizens are pulled down from the Wall and dashed to the ground by the hooked weapons of their naked foes . . . the citizens desert the high Wall and their towns and take to a flight more desperate than any before. Again the enemy pursue them and there is slaughter more cruel than ever. As lambs by butchers, so are our piteous citizens rent by their foes. . . .**

But the depredations of the Scoti and the Picts soon faded in importance as against the remorseless build-up of pressure from the east. Over the long years the Saxons, Angles, and Jutes established independent kingdoms in Northumberland, Yorkshire, East Anglia, Mercia, and along the Channel coast in Sussex, Hampshire, and Dorset. The Roman Britons were thrown back, often after long delays brought on by their continuing resistance, to find a harsh but defiant security in Cornwall, Wales, in the mountains of the Cheviots, the Cotswolds, and the Pennines, and in the Lake District of Cumberland and Westmoreland.

The struggle was inconceivably protracted. Not until 577 A.D. —one hundred and twenty-odd years after the landing of Hengist— did the Saxons, by defeating the Roman Britons at the battle of

Cf. note, p. 210.

** One wonders how Gildas, even immured in a monastery, found the peace among so much travail to write *De excidio Britanniae.*

Deorham, win through to the Bristol Channel, capturing the ancient Roman cities of Corinium Dobunorum (Cirincester), once the third city of the province, and the center over centuries of a thriving wool trade; and Glevum (Gloucester), site of Vespasian's camp in 43 A.D. and later a colonia of veterans. One may wonder at the reactions of the Saxon array, pausing in their advance at Aquae Sulis and pondering the purpose of the huge Roman bathing establishment.

Slowly, through the western areas still held, the use of the Latin tongue faded, but did not easily die. Gildas not only writes in Latin but indicates it was still widely read among at least those with some education. But the always vigorous substrata of Celtic dialects reasserted themselves in everyday speech, to continue down to our own day as living tongues in Wales and the Scots Highlands.

The process in the West was undoubtedly hastened by the superior ability of the Celtic villagers, never so Romanized as the townfolk, to withstand the hardships inseparable from a fighting retreat, and to accept a reversion to barbarism as the price of freedom. Under such conditions, persisting through generations, the cumbersome procedures of Roman bureaucracy became liabilities. Discarded one by one, they were soon forgotten. Along with their disappearance naturally went all but racial memory of the order, the rule of law, they had once maintained.

By 500 A.D. the Saxons and their kin, already looking askance at one another, held the coast and the countryside east of a line drawn from the Humber estuary to the Isle of Wight. Within this line the wanton destruction of what had been painstakingly built over four centuries was widespread.

Londinium, proud center of commerce and government, was reduced to a few miserable hovels backed against walls torn at but too sturdy to destroy. Camulodunum, Lindum, Durnovaria, Durovernum, and other towns shared the same violent fate before in more settled times people moved back into the foundations of ancient buildings from which future generations of archeologists would patiently reconstruct the homely details of everyday life under Rome. On these weary ruins the newcomers built again, to create medieval Colchester, Lincoln, Dorchester, and Canterbury.

As new hordes landed, the process was extended into York by the Saxons and into Northumberland by the Angles. Through all this tormented area were other towns, like Calleva Atrebatum (Silchester), largely abandoned before the Saxons could reach them, which had reverted back to nature, their buildings collapsed, their walls subsided, the growth of scrub and weed encroaching every year, to build a topsoil eventually concealing much of what had once been humble civic centers of participants in a world civilization.

The once magnificent Roman roads, a network comprising about six thousand miles, deprived of care and maintenance, cracked and buckled, then eroded under recurring rain and frost. Soon the long highways which for so many centuries had known the purposeful tread of the legions were but abandoned tracks connecting anonymous ruins, both silent evidence of wasted human effort. Yet so sturdy were the substructures that, when order came again to Britain, the Roman roads provided the foundations on which much of the new highway system was built.

One mighty, perhaps co-ordinated, effort was made, somewhere around the beginning of the sixth century, to throw back the tide of invasion and barbarism, to restore the traditions and order of Rome. It is associated in song and story, in legend and in prayer, with the name of Arthur and his Knights of the Round Table. Whoever this Roman Briton may have been, his shade can forever find immortality in the poetry woven about his exploits. He fought in all, Nennius tells us, twelve myth-misted battles, winning resounding victories. The twelfth and last, at never-located Mount Badon, so dismayed the Saxons that fifty years passed before the advance was resumed.

Even after the passing of Arthur, resistance was maintained, no longer by people we can call Roman Britons, but by Celtic Britons, whose Roman traditions and heritage had been largely lost in the bitterness and the hardships of the generations-long struggle. A British king still held Cumberland into the seventh century, which may be the reason why Nennius could refer to the extensive civil settlement which had grown up around the cavalry fort at Old Carlisle as "Guasmoric, near Carlisle, a city which in English is called Palmcastre," implying its continued existence into his day, and why the Roman walls of Carlisle itself were standing in all their massive dignity in Saint Cuthbert's time, toward the end of the seventh century.

The stubborn resistance of the Celtic Britons sometimes turned into offensive action. In 633 A.D. Cadwalla, the Saxon-hating Celtic king of North Wales, in temporary alliance with Penda of

Mercia, defeated and slew mighty Edwin, king of the Anglians of Northumberland, exhibiting the latter's severed head on the ramparts of an old Roman fortress at York. But in his triumph he essayed too much. Pursuing the fleeing remnants of Edwin's army north on Dere Street, he caught up with it, re-formed and turned at bay under Oswald, successor to Edwin, and was destroyed. The last major effort of Celtic Britain, short of the fastnesses of Wales and the Highlands, took place near the ruins of ancient Corstopitum, and the still standing, if badly scarred, Wall of Hadrian where Dere Street passed through.

During much of these later years of conflict the civilizing influence of Rome had returned to Britain, wrapped in the panoply and armed with the supernatural authority of the Christian Church. Its missionaries, assiduous in conversion, seem to have been less than successful in applying the ethics and moral teachings of Christ to the merciless struggles for power.

Through all this anarchy, chaos, and destruction the land remained, largely, a desolation. The plowlands, deserted or indifferently worked, shrank before the onward march of forest and thicket. The Saxons and other newcomers farmed the river valleys in desultory fashion, formed their various petty kingdoms, generated rivalries, and fought among themselves in the lack of indigenous victims.

But of Roman Britain, of its long-maintained and staunchly defended civilization, scarcely a trace remained, save in the ruins of once stately edifice and monument. Even these after a time stirred no memory or nostalgia, nor any emotion save superstitious awe.

XI

THE END OF ROMAN BRITAIN

. . . Mutato nomine de te,
Fabula narratur.
—HORACE, *Satires*

1

IT HAD BEEN A LONG ASSOCIATION BUT NOW IT was over.

Since Plautius and his legions had stormed ashore in Kent nearly six hundred years earlier, the southern half of Britain had followed the Roman road. It was a road which, if not always smooth, had never lacked signposts.

Now the road had crumbled, become a path, dark and twisting, leading no man knew whither. An age was ending, a society held eternal in collapse, its bewildered members unable to read, or reading accept, the handwriting on the wall.

During half a millennium an order imposed from without on southern Britain had found a nucleus of acceptance, a generated loyalty and pride to hold through peace and war, through revolt and invasion, through quiet days and long uneventful years.

With Roman order had come at first a kind of liberation, an increase in individual freedom and security of person, both deriving from the inhibitions visited on tribal anarchy and petty tyranny by the law and the legions of Rome.

With this imposed order, with this novel safety of person and property, had come a stable agriculture, a lucrative commerce, an unimagined ease of movement and social mobility, educational opportunity resulting in widespread literacy, an ecumenical language, a welcomed heritage of literature, art, and architecture, a sense of pride in being part of the broad stream of civilization.

From these foundations a society had grown, locally self-governing under the overriding precepts of the Ius Gentium protected by a strong central administration capable of maintaining order and holding safe the frontiers. Cities, towns and villages grew where none had been before, forests were cleared and marshes drained to make way for simple farmsteads, while the ever-growing network of Roman roads brought to all a sense of unity, of being one people, of sharing, for weal or woe, a common destiny.

This society was not Italian-Roman, nor Greco-Roman, nor even Gallic-Roman, but uniquely British-Roman. The Celtic islanders, tempered by Roman custom, restrained by Roman law, accepted the innovations while their basic characteristics invaded the amalgam, turning it into something neither contributor had been before.

Then, as the centuries passed, there was both continuity and the fusion of new strains. Beyond doubt, in 400 A.D. there were many respected and self-respecting Britons who could proudly trace their ancestry in unbroken generations to the legionaries who had landed with Plautius,* others who displayed among their *lares familiares* the death masks of forefathers, men of the Sixth Legion, who had first set foot on the island in the long-gone days of Hadrian. Still others knew, in pride or guarded reticence, of ancestors from the auxiliary units, soldiers garnered from distant province and border tribe, who, earning Roman citizenship, had married locally and settled, to make for themselves and their posterity a life in Britain. Gauls, Thracians, Spaniards, Levantines, Africans, Italians, Frisian Islanders, Hungarians, Moesians, Dalmatians, Illyrians—scarcely one of the many and diverse races that made up the Empire was not, as the years went on, to add its blood and strain to the island populace. And, of course, there were always the ubiquitous Greeks.†

These variant strains commingled with the indigenous Celtic race over many generations to produce the people who at the beginning of the fifth century A.D. called themselves Roman Britons. Few, even

---

* A more extensive pedigree, if no better, than that which titillates our Mayflower societies.

† E.g., the tombstone of Barates of Palmyra recovered at Corstopitum, and that of Regina, his wife, unearthed at Arbeia (South Shields).

of the prescient, could then have known that they were about to undergo another violent and ultimately dominant admixture.

2

IN SPITE of the volumes that have been written, seeking to discover or invent in the fall of Rome the causation of long-latent weaknesses, it seems fairly established that as of 406 A.D. the Empire of the West, although under heavy pressures at home and abroad, was still a going concern, still meeting and, as far as a contemporary could see, able to meet forever its imperial responsibilities. The fact seems to be that many elements, some inherent, others unnecessary, and the unfortunate chance of the moment combined to produce sudden and quite unpredictable disaster.

There was the traditionally slow means of communication, making too centralized control always tardy and sometimes impossible. There was the possible, but questioned, insidious loss of citizen manpower, which combined with the reluctance of landowners to release laborers for the Army, with expediency, and perhaps with notions of false economy to produce the barbarization, both in men and officers, of the imperial forces. Then there were the stifling controls imposed on the economic life of the Empire by a swollen and inept bureaucracy, which had the effect of curtailing production, and therefore tax revenues, even while the extravagance of court and government demanded increase.

Perhaps the most vitiating factor was the political failure to establish a constitutional process for an orderly succession to the throne, resulting in the dismally repetitive and always sanguinary struggles for power.

But with all these handicaps the Empire had survived since the days of Commodus. There was no reason to believe it could not continue. Something more, something unforeseen, was needed to bring down the lofty, if strained, but still majestic edifice. This something was provided by the unfortunate chance of the moment which found the Western army under Stilicho so occupied in Italy that there was no force available first to halt, and later eject, the German flood that in 406 A.D. swept over Gaul and even penetrated the Pyrenees into the long-undisturbed Spanish provinces. It was this disaster which had the immediate result of throwing Britain back on its own hopelessly inadequate, because so often hemorrhaged, defense resources precisely at the time when the Saxon tide was surging into torrent.

Gaul itself seems to have been partially restored to the Western Empire in the years following, generally by making a virtue of necessity and recognizing in some foederati relationship the German enclaves then settled through the countryside, in return for a *de iure* acceptance of the Emperor's suzerainty. The process seems to have been not too difficult, since the German newcomers, long resident on both sides of the Rhine, were far from barbarians. Knowledgeable of civilization's amenities, they were more anxious to share in than destroy its material base.

In any event, a sense of common interest seems to have developed between the new settlers and their neighbors, the Roman Gauls, persevering, and thereby setting an example, in their Roman ways. For in 450 A.D., when Attila and his horde of Huns invaded Gaul, Aëtius, the Roman general and three times consul, after years of negotiation and seeking accommodation with Attila, was forced to give battle. The various Germanic enclaves of new settlers joined the Roman Gauls in rallying to the eagles. From the joint levies Aëtius was able to fashion an army which, at Châlons-sur-Marne in the summer of 451, inflicted a decisive defeat on Attila, slaughtered many thousands of his predator Huns, and forced the remnant back across the Rhine in disorder.

It was a battle long considered one of the most decisive of the Western world, as it may well have been, for it saved Gaul for Roman civilization. The common dangers shared and overcome in the defeat of Attila encouraged the development between the German settlers and their Roman-Gallic neighbors of a live-and-let-live relationship which, if not amity, was at least a mutual tolerance involving some interdependence. Granted so much, the supranational role of sex played its part; the new generations accepted civilized customs, so that when Clovis the Frank was laying the foundations of medieval France, Roman law, tradition, outlook, and language persisted, naturally not without change and adjustment, but nevertheless as fundamental and ineradicable characteristics of the emerging nation.

3

UNDOUBTEDLY there was some restoration of communication and travel with Britain in these clouded decades. But the enfeebled Western Empire and the Gauls themselves, hard-pressed within and without, could ill afford, and never sent, the material assistance in the form of adequate military reinforcement that alone could have ameliorated matters in Britain.

Had the battle of Châlons turned out otherwise, it is possible subsequent events in Gaul might have more closely resembled the total collapse and practical obliteration of Roman civilization in Britain. For the Saxons, the Angles, and the Jutes, on the whole, were as savage and as insensitive to the blessings of civilization as were Attila and his murderous Huns. They sought in Britain not to share in a long-established and stable society but merely to seize new territory on which to establish their own familiar tribal arrangements. What they could not use, what they failed to appreciate, what they did not understand, that they would destroy.

The result for a period of some four hundred years, a passage of time nearly as long as that in which Britain had played its participating role in the Roman hegemony, was utter chaos, with savagery and terror the rule of life, destitution, hunger, cold and dirt its sorry lot. Through all those dismal centuries a Briton's life was no safer than his sword could command or his flight preserve. To plant a crop offered no temptation in the absence of any real assurance the sower would live to reap its increase. Patiently to nurture livestock was but to attract rapacity. Peddlers deserted the roads and merchants their shops to raider bands. Currency and credit disappeared, taking along with them that minimal exchange of goods and services essential to any life above that of brutes. With ample cause, men ceased to trust each other. The collapse of civilized life was complete.

Yet, as always, life went on. Within the anarchy, and the unremitting violence, requiring the span of generations to disclose promise, something else, and better, was happening. In many areas there was much vacant land, where the surviving and watchful Britons, perhaps fearsomely, welcomed Saxon aggregations seeking settlement rather than plunder, as reinforcement against more transitory marauders.

As the newcomers intermingled and interbred with the Roman Britons in these areas, some at least of the veneer of a remembered civilization leavened the mixture, producing a people predominantly Saxon yet different in curious ways from their Germanic brethren still living in barbarism across the North Sea. As the Saxon tide moved west, this process was continued over many generations.

Meanwhile for the more recalcitrant and unyielding Britons the moors and caves of Cornwall, the mountains of Wales, and the Highlands of Scotland remained never-invaded havens, predominantly Celtic in mores, tradition, and attitudes even to this day.

The newcomers fought among themselves, in diversion from the unprofitable task of exterminating Britons. Northumbria and Mercia, East Anglia and Kent, Wessex and Sussex each sought dominance in unending strife, each praying the aid, and invoking the protection of the Christian god whose missionaries, from Rome and Ireland, had, among other gifts, brought the Latin language and much of Roman tradition to their still truculent converts.

But of Roman civilization, as exemplified in the one-time imperial province of Britannia, scarcely a trace remained. Language, custom, arbitrary government, and rudimentary law were all those of the Saxon conquerors. Not until Aelfred of Wessex, in the closing years of the ninth century, rekindled a flame in Dane-harassed Britain might his countrymen of diverse origins dimly discern a coming order, an approaching rule of law, an end to purposeless anarchy.

Beyond this, no man could prophesy. There were the already mixed island people unaware of new and vigorous Norman infusion to come. The British destiny would depend on the labor, sacrifice, and courage with which the island folk met unending turmoil in ages yet ahead.

There was also the land, green and misty under summer sun, gray and forbidding under winter skies; land already ancient, concealing beneath field, mound, and forest the long-dead ashes, the ghostly ruins, and the unnumbered graves of Roman Britain.

BIBLIOGRAPHY

1
Classical Historians

Various classical authors are mentioned or quoted in the text; they are here identified. They exhibit widely varying degrees of reliability and bias.

Polybius A Greek historian (c. 202–120 B.C.) long resident in Rome, a friend of Scipio Africanus the Younger, the destroyer of Carthage, of which event Polybius was an eyewitness. A fulsome admirer of Roman imperialism, Polybius wrote his *Histories* in forty books, of which five survive, together with many fragments known to us through excerpts and quotations from later writers. He was a philosophic historian of considerable merit, constantly seeking cause and effect in the course of events.

Caesar, C. Julius The Roman politician, soldier, statesman, and dictator (100–44 B.C.). A man of transcendent abilities, he wrote two reports of his activities in surviving classics distinguished by their austere Latin prose: *De Bello Gallico*, describing his conquest of Gaul and his forays into Germany and Britain; and *De Bello Civile*, recording and justifying his struggle with Pompey for control of the Roman state.

Celsus, Aulus A Roman encyclopedist who wrote in the reign of Tiberius (14–38 A.D.). Of his work eight books on medicine survive; they exhibit a surprisingly advanced level of Roman surgical practice. He writes of tonsil removal techniques comparable to those in use today; of plastic operations on the face; of lichotomies; of the removal of goiters; and of operations for hernia and cataract. His work implies the general absence of anesthesia.

Tacitus, Publius Cornelius (55–117 A.D.). One of the greatest of Roman historians, famed for his concise Latin style. His *Annales* and *Histories*, major portions of which are lost, describe in terms of acidulous disapprobation the careers of the Caesars from Tiberius through Domitian. His *Germania* glorifies the freedoms of barbarism in terms foreshadowing Rousseau, while his short biography of his father-in-law, Agricola, displays as alive in that great proconsul all the Roman virtues he deplores elsewhere as having vanished. He thought, and wrote: "The chief duty of an historian was to judge the actions of men so that the good may meet with the reward due virtue, and the evil may be deterred by the condemnation of posterity." Whatever else may be said for this point of view, it clearly discourages objectivity.

Suetonius (Caius Suetonius Tranquillus) (c. 70–140 A.D.). A friend of the younger Pliny, and for a time one of the Emperor Hadrian's secretaries, until dismissed with others about 122 A.D. Most famous for his *De Vitae Caesarum,* the lives of the twelve Caesars from Julius through Domitian, characterized by gossipy anecdote, personalized scandal, unsupported libel, and scurrilous implication. He is a raconteur of palace misbehavior, and tells us little or nothing of the Roman world outside the court.

Appian (Appianos of Alexandria) (active around 160 A.D.). A Greek who practiced law in Rome, he wrote a history of Rome, in Greek, in twenty-four books, of which eleven survive intact, as do fragments of others. He seems to have drawn largely on the works of earlier writers and is ignorant of western geography.

Strabo The famous Greek geographer and traveler (64 B.C.–19 A.D.) wrote in Greek his *Geographica,* which, save for one gap, has survived. He also wrote *Historical Studies* in forty-three books, following Polybius in describing Roman history to the establishment of the Empire. This work is lost.

Fronto, Cornelius (fl. 140–160 A.D.). Known as "The Orator," a native of Cirta in Numidia, he was tutor to Marcus Verus (later the Emperor Marcus Aurelius) in the reigns of Hadrian and of Antoninus Pius. Of his *De Bello Parthico* but a fragment survives.

Dion Cassius (c. 150–235 A.D.). A Roman senator, born in Nicea in Bithynia, he wrote in Greek a history of Rome in eighty volumes, of which twenty-six survive. Dion Cassius is our sole source for the Claudian invasion of Britain.

Herodianus (c. 180–245 A.D.). Wrote in Greek a history of Rome from the death of Marcus Aurelius to the accession of Gordian III (235 A.D.). Herodian is reported as poorly thought of by the historical school of Alexandria, although later writers praise him. He seems to have been generally reliable, although accused by contemporaries of bias in favor of Pertinax.

Vopiscus, Flavius (fl. 250–300 A.D.). One of the six authors of the *Historiae Augustae,* a compilation of biographies of the Emperors from Hadrian to Numerian, covering the period 117–284 A.D. Vopiscus is supposed himself to have written the later biographies, from that of Aurelian through Carinus. Generally unreliable.

Spartianus, Delius Another of the authors of the *Augustan Histories,* about whom little is known; even his name is uncertain. He wrote, probably, the biographies of Hadrian and his successors through Caracalla.

Eusebius (c. 265–340 A.D.). Bishop of Caesarea in Palestine, held to be extremely erudite by contemporaries, he wrote a chronicle in Greek that is the source of much of our knowledge of the years immediately preceding 325 A.D. Also wrote *Historia Ecclesiastica,* a church history to 314 A.D.; a biography of Constantine the Great; a *Demonstratio Evangelica;* and other works. Reasonably reliable where not immersed in pro-Christian polemic.

Eutropius (fl. 320–380 A.D.). He held a secretarial post under Constantine the Great, and wrote in Latin a history of Rome in ten books—from the founding of the city through the accession of Valens, to whom his work was dedicated. There were other writings, now lost.

Vegetius (Flavius Vegetius Renatus). He wrote *De Rei Militarii* during reign of Valentinian II (371–392 A.D.), to whom the work was dedicated. A classical work on Roman military doctrine, much revered in medieval times, it was a plea for a return to the standards of training, discipline, leadership, and organization of the old Roman Army.

Ammianus Marcellinus (c. 330–390 A.D.). Born in Antioch in Syria, he wrote a history of Rome in thirty-one books, of which volumes 14 through 31 have survived. He wrote in Latin, in a clumsy style marred by Hellenisms, but in general strove to be both truthful and accurate. He appears to have been one historian who actually served in war (under Julian against the Persians), obviously knew his subject when he dealt with campaigning, and rounded out his account of the times with such diverse matters as Egyptian monuments and hieroglyphics, army artillery weapons, and other side issues. On balance, he is by far the most trustworthy of the latter-day historians.

Claudius Claudianus A Greek, brought up in Alexandria, he went to Rome about 395 A.D. He has been described as the last of the Latin poets, writing hexameters of vigor and power in which he praised the young emperor Honorius and his general Stilicho, while excoriating the villains surrounding and advising Honorius' elder brother, Arcadius, Emperor of the East. His work displays a genuine love and admiration of imperial institutions and achievements.

Sulpicius Severus He was born about 363 A.D. in Aquitania, the southwest province of Gaul bordering on the Pyrenees. He was the author of several books of letters and a *Sacred History* abounding in errors of fact and chronology. Generally unreliable.

Orosius (fl. c. 450 A.D.). Bishop of Tarragona in Spain, he was a friend of St. Augustine, with whom he maintained a correspondence. Apparently at the latter's urging, Orosius wrote a history of the world to

417 A.D., containing much legend, tradition, and special pleading for a Christian interpretation of events.

Zosimus (fl. c. 450 A.D.). He wrote in Greek a history of the Empire, from Augustus to 425 A.D., in six books, all of which survive. He seems to have relied heavily on earlier writers, sometimes to the extent of copying whole chapters. An obdurate pagan, he was uncomplimentary to the Christian Emperors and paid little attention to attaining an accurate chronology.

2

Classical Sources for the Geography of Roman Britain

Ptolemy's Geography (*Geographia Claudii Ptolemaei*) was published in Alexandria betwen 125 and 150 A.D. The author is chiefly famous for his work on astronomy—called after an Arabic transliteration, *The Almagest*—which governed astronomical thought until upset by Copernicus. His *Geographia* covers the then known world in terms of latitudes and longitudes of places, starting with a zero meridian through the Canary Islands. Some of the extant texts have maps attached which may or may not be contemporary with the author. The map of Britain appearing in Book II of the *Geographia* suffers from distortion and the general ignorance in that era of the island land mass. His data for Londinium, for example, are in error, placing the city about 2 degrees too far east and 2.5 degrees too far north.

The Antonine Itinerary (*Itinerarium Provinciarum Antonini Augusti*) is a book of road routes throughout the Empire, giving distances in miles between places named. It probably dates from the time of Caracalla, with later corrections and additions. The British section gives the main routes up and down and across the island to the forward forts of Hadrian's Wall. The distances given are generally closely approximate to fact. An example is Route VII of the *Itinerary*, from Noviomagus Regnensium (Chichester) to London, as follows:

		Correct Roman miles
Item, a Regno Londinio mpm *	xcvi	112
Clausentum (Bitterne)	xx	29
Venta Belgarum (Winchester)	x	11
Calleva Atrebatum (Silchester)	xxii	24
Pontibus (Staines)	xxii	27
Londinio (London)	xxii	21

* "mpm" *milia plus minus*. The Roman mile, or *mille passuum*, was 1000 Roman paces of 5 Roman feet each. Various estimates place its length at between 4842 and 4854 English feet, or about 92 per cent of an English statute mile.

The Notitia Dignitatum (*Notitia Dignitatum tam Civilium quam Militarium in Partibus Orientis, in Partibus Occidentis*) is a station list of installations and assignments of civil and military officials throughout the Empire, published about 428 A.D. The British section is compiled from data collected at least a half-century earlier. The list is a primary source of much information on the frontier forts and on the coastal defenses under the command of the Comes Littoris Saxonici.

The Peutinger Table (*Tabula Peutingeriana*) is a distorted strip map twenty-one feet long and one foot wide, dating from about the time of the *Antonine Itinerary,* giving places and distances throughout the Empire. Part of the map is missing, including all but the southeast of Britain.

The Ravenna Cosmography (*Ravennatis Anonymi Cosmographia*) is a list of countries, provinces, cities, and rivers of the known world. Although dating from the eighth century, all data included appear to be of Roman origin. No distances are given.

3
Pre-Roman Britain

Lionel Casson, *The Ancient Mariners.* New York, Macmillan, 1959.

M. P. Charlesworth, *Trade Routes and Commerce of the Roman Empire.* Cambridge, Cambridge University Press, 1926.

V. Gordon Childs, *Prehistoric Communities of the British Isles.* London, Chambers, 1940.

J. G. D. Clark, *Prehistoric England.* London, Batsford, 1940.

C. F. C. Hawkes, *Prehistoric Foundations of Europe.* London, Methuen, 1940.

J. Hawkes, *Early Britain.* London, Collins, 1946.

Paul Herrmann, *Conquest by Man.* New York, Harper, 1954.

T. Rice Holmes, *Ancient Britain and the Invasions of Caesar.* Oxford, Oxford University Press, 1907.

E. T. Leeds, *Celtic Ornament.* Oxford, Clarendon Press, 1933.

4
Rome, Republic and Empire

The literature on Rome is encyclopedic. I have tried to list here only those works generally accessible to American readers interested in the over-all background.

R. H. Barrow, *The Romans.* London, Pelican Books, 1949.

W. Buckland, *Text Book of Roman Law.* Cambridge, Cambridge University Press, 1921.

J. B. Bury, *History of the Later Roman Empire.* 2 vols. New York, Dover, 1957.

J. Declarieul, *Rome the Lawgiver.* New York, Knopf, 1926.

S. Dill, *Roman Society from Nero to Marcus Aurelius.* London, Macmillan, 1911.

Will Durant, *Caesar and Christ (The Story of Civilization,* Vol. III). New York, Simon and Schuster, 1944.

Edward Gibbon, *The Decline and Fall of the Roman Empire.* 3 vols. New York, Modern Library, n.d.

————, the same, abridged by D. M. Low. New York, Harcourt, Brace, 1960.

Edith Hamilton, *The Roman Way.* New York, Norton, 1944.

R. M. Haywood, *The Myth of Rome's Fall.* New York, Crowell, 1958.

Theodor Mommsen, *History of Rome.* New York, Meridian Books, 1958.

H. M. D. Parker, *The Roman Legions.* Cambridge, Heffer, 1958.

M. Rostovtzeff, *Social and Economic History of the Roman Empire.* Oxford, Clarendon Press, 1926.

J. C. Stobart. *The Grandeur That Was Rome,* 3rd edn. London, Sidgwick and Jackson, 1951.

Graham Webster, "The Roman Army" (pamphlet). Chester, Grosvenor Museum, 1956.

Mortimer Wheeler, *Rome Beyond the Imperial Frontiers.* London, Penguin, 1955.

5

Roman Britain

*E. Birley, *Researches on Hadrian's Wall.* Kendal, Titus Wilson, 1961.

* ————, *Roman Britain and the Roman Army,* 2nd ed. Kendal, Titus Wilson, 1961.

G. C. Boon, *Roman Silchester.* London, Max Parrish, 1957.

J. C. Bruce, *Handbook to the Roman Wall,* 11th ed. Newcastle-on-Tyne, Andrew Reid, 1957. Edited by Prof. I. A. Richmond.

A. R. Burn, *Agricola and Roman Britain.* New York, Macmillan, 1954.

M. P. Charlesworth, *The Lost Provinces, or The Worth of Roman Britain.* Cardiff, University of Wales Press, 1949.

Winston S. Churchill, *The Birth of Britain (History of the English-speaking People,* Vol. I). New York, Dodd, Mead, 1956.

R. G. Collingwood, *The Archeology of Roman Britain.* London, Methuen, 1930.

————, *Roman Britain.* Oxford, Clarendon Press, 1923.

———— and J. M. Myres, *Roman Britain and the English Settlements,* 4th ed. Oxford, Clarendon Press, 1956.

*Leonard Cottrell, *Seeing Roman Britain*. London, Evans, 1956.

F. Haverfield, *The Roman Occupation of Britain,* rev. George MacDonald. Oxford, Clarendon Press, 1924.

George MacDonald, *The Roman Wall in Scotland,* 2nd ed. Oxford, Clarendon Press, 1934.

S. N. Miller, *Severus in Britain* (*Cambridge Ancient History,* Vol. XII).

V. E. Nash-Williams, *The Roman Frontier in Wales.* Cardiff, University of Wales Press, 1954.

I. A. Richmond, *Roman Britain*. London, Pelican Books, 1955.

R. E. M. Wheeler, *London in Roman Times*. (London Museum Catalogue #3.). London, 1930.

* Titles marked with an asterisk are of special and up-to-date interest. Cottrell's *Seeing Roman Britain* is an invaluable guide to extant evidences of the Roman period.

6
Periodicals

The following scholarly journals, not easily accessible to the American reader, teem with studies of special facets of Roman-British archeology and history. Those quoted or referred to in the text are marked with an asterisk.

Antiquity. London. A quarterly giving a general view of archeological progress.

Archeological Journal. Published by the Society of Antiquaries, London.

Archeologia. London.

Carnuntina. A Continental archeological journal, centered on researches at Carnuntum, the Roman fortress and settlement on the Danube east of Vienna. It carries contributions on general Roman frontier problems, and published Professor E. Birley's discussion of Hadrian's frontier policy in its issue of 1956.

Journal of Roman Studies. London. Covers yearly advances in archeology and history.

Proceedings of the British Academy. London.

Proceedings of the Society of Antiquaries of Scotland, Edinburgh.

Archeologia Aeliana. Published by the Society of Antiquaries of Newcastle-on-Tyne; largely devoted to the archeology of the Hadrianic Wall complex.

Transactions of the Cumberland and Westmoreland Society of Antiquaries.

*Transactions, Durham and Northumberland.

*Transactions, Dumfrieshire and Galloway.

Other county and regional antiquarian societies through England and Scotland occasionally publish new reports.

7
Official Publications

The Ministry of Works publishes guide pamphlets, written by distinguished archeologists, on most of the British Roman sites it maintains as national monuments. These are obtainable from Her Majesty's Stationery Office, York House, Kingsway, London, WC2. Those referred to or quoted in the text are:

Sir Mortimer Wheeler, "Maiden Castle, Dorset";
K. M. Kenyon, "Viroconium, Roman City."
E. Birley, "Corbridge, Roman Station."

8
Map

The Ordnance Survey Map of Roman Britain (third edition 1956), published by the Ordnance Survey, Chessington, Surrey, is indispensable for place names, road net, location of finds and villas, and other data.

INDEX

Generic terms occurring with great frequency—e.g. Rome, Romans, Britain, Britons—are not indexed. "Caesar" and "Augustus," titles of later emperors, are indexed only for the original bearers.